For Gillian.

With love – loads

KONSEP LAGENDA SDN BHD
Kuala Lumpur 59100
MALAYSIA
TEL: 283 5240 FAX: 292 1348

ISBN 983 9778 33 8

First published September 1995

Cover Design: L. Too
Type set by Konsep Lagenda Sdn Bhd

Printed by
Ritz Print Sdn Bhd

WATER FENG SHUI FOR WEALTH

AN ADVANCED MANUAL ON WATER FENG SHUI
BASED ON THE WATER DRAGON CLASSIC

LILLIAN TOO

BEST SELLING AUTHOR OF THE FENG SHUI SERIES

Other books by the author:
Feng Shui
Applied Pa Kua Lo Shu Feng Shui
Practical Applications of Feng Shui
Chinese Numerology in Feng Shui
The Chinese Dragon
Strategies for Career Success
Creative Visualization
Making your First Million
Tap the Power Inside You
Explore the Frontiers of your Mind

Audio Cassettes by the author:
Creative Visualization
Developing Success habits
Positive Affirmations
Making your First Million

Lillian Too's latest and most exciting new addition to her phenomenally successful FENG SHUI series of books

---

WATER FENG SHUI FOR WEALTH

---

offers an exciting and advanced compass school formula
that reveals the secrets behind
the creation of the auspicious water dragon.
Written in her inimitable, down to earth style,
this book explains ....

♣ how water flows in the garden can be arranged to attract and capture the vital dragon's cosmic breathe thereby attracting abundant good fortune and enormous prosperity to residents.

♦ how door orientations can be altered to capture auspicious chi from rivers and streams which flow past buildings or homes bringing great wealth to residents.

♥ how water symbols like ponds and waterfalls, fountains and wells may be built to simulate the wealth bringing qualities of natural bodies of water

♠ and how to avoid, diffuse and disperse bad chi created by water flowing in inauspicious directions, or collecting in places that clash with elements that cause misfortune and remorse ...

This book is an advanced text on one branch of Compass School feng shui.

This book is dedicated to
Jennifer Too

WHAT OTHERS SAY ...

*"Lillian Too a corporate high flyer until she called it quits five years ago, has found a fulfilling career in writing. The author of eight best sellers talks about her passion for the ancient Chinese belief of **feng shui** ...... "*

The SUN megazine 25 Nov 1994

*"Too, an ardent believer in **feng shui** lists three types of luck - heaven luck (what God gives you); earth luck (feng shui) and luck which man himself has the power to create .... there was no doubt her audience that day was not only captivated by Too's fluency, wit and humour, but also by her candour and down to earth attitude ... "*

New Straits Times 6 April 1995

*"Lillian Too might be better known to some as the first woman in Asia to head a bank, ... she attributes much of her success to the "science" of **feng shui**. Fully illustrated, her feng shui books plot the development of this ancient practice and offer concise explanations, hints and suggestions for readers to look at their own living and work space. The author's ... clearly written and fascinating books ... are sure to make all who read them look at feng shui with more seriousness and respect"*

Karen Smith in B International, Hong Kong. Sept. 1993

*Highly readable and well illustrated, this book (Applied Pa Kua Lo Shu Feng Shui) will delight you, whether you are a believer or a non believer of **feng shui**"*

Her World August 1993

*Lillian Too's practical, handbook style introduction to **feng shui** gives a simple yet comprehensive overview ... the book is at its best describing diagnosis of problems and offering remedies to improve the feng shui of affected dwellings. "*

The Star newspaper 17 Feb. 1993

"Lillian Too believes in the balance and harmony of feng shui ... which she says has been good for her and her family. The lady is something of a legend in Malaysian corporate circles ... and very motivated in her writing ... "

Malaysian Business Nov. 16 1993

*" Having gained esteem and experience in the corporate world quite inaccessible to the ordinary person, she has now turned her hand to writing, and the art of **feng shui** is right up her street.... "*

Corporate World Nov. 1993

WATER FENG SHUI

SECRET FORMULAS OF THE WATER DRAGON CLASSIC

CONTENTS

WATER FENG SHUI

CONTENTS

OPENING NOTES

This book on Water Feng Shui came about by chance and without planning. I had actually decided not to write any more books on the subject - I had felt that the four which preceded this one contained enough information for the amateur practitioner to gain sufficient insights into this wonderful science, and in the process would have started to appreciate the multiple dimensions of its underlying philosophy and its ancient wisdom.

I also felt that going too deep into the subject, particularly when it involved difficult and complex compass school formulas could defeat my original purpose for writing these books. I feared that in offering something too technical, boredom could overtake the reader and cause a turning away from, rather than a move towards greater interest and exploration of the subject.

When I published my first book, all I wanted was to increase public awareness of feng shui. I set out to persuade my readers that living as we do in this part of the world, where knowledge of feng shui is still available from practicing masters and original texts, it would be a waste not to investigate feng shui.

I wanted to convince people that feng shui was more than just village superstition; that the philosophy behind its practice was both noble and beautiful, deserving of further study and serious attention - to live in harmony with nature and with the physical landscapes of the earth. To become aware of subtle invisible energy lines in the environment - in short to apply this ancient practice in a modern context, and in the process enjoy its benefits as well ! And who knows - even to grow rich and become prosperous !

In the last two years, interest in feng shui has certainly increased - indeed, I was surprised to discover that there are over fifty feng shui consultants in Malaysia alone - and all doing a brisk business. I was therefore convinced that four books on the subject were quite sufficient - seeing I have neither the intention nor the inclination to become a feng shui consultant.

But events seem to overtake me. Over the Lunar New Year, as is the custom with us during this festive season, I visited my Malaysian feng shui *si fu* - Master Yap Cheng Hai - who is also a very dear friend.

Quite casually and without any previously planned intention of doing so, I found myself asking him, " *whatever happened to your water dragon formula ... I remember you used it quite a lot in those early days during the Seventies when you were doing the feng shui for all those up and coming business people... "*.

Cheng Hai was only too pleased to tell me that those very people whose feng shui he had vastly improved by using the water formula had ***fart thart*** (*become rich*) beyond even his wildest dreams ! Some of them have indeed become household names in the world of finance and big business. Some have gone on to become successful political figures. Yet more have built successful businesses but stayed very low profile.

But **all of them** had become rich and wealthy.

"So shall we write a book about water feng shui", I asked laughingly, excited at the prospect of compiling such a valuable formula for posterity. It seems that the role of preserving all these feng shui formulas in a form easily understood by the average person has fallen on my shoulders !

I only half expected Mr Yap to agree - he is after all a most busy man; and having already given us two outstanding formulas on feng shui, it would be stretching my friendship with him just a bit much if I took yet a third formula from him especially one which so directly addresses the subject of wealth and prosperity. I knew that no matter how difficult the formula was, I would not be able to resist the opportunity of turning it into my fifth book on feng shui science.

It took Mr. Yap a while before consenting to the release of the Water Dragon formula to the general public. But when he informed me of his willingness to do so, I could not wait to begin ! This book is the result.

This book deals with a very specialized branch of feng shui.

The formulas and tables contained herein are extracted from the handwritten notebooks of one of the most prominent feng shui Masters from Taiwan. Master Chan Chuan Huay was widely respected by many of Taiwan's great industrialists of a previous era - his clients, according to Master Yap Cheng Hai, *included the sugar king, the plastics king, the cement king, many of the most successful tycoons* of this rich country.

Mr. Yap spent five years understudying Master Chan, during which time he came upon these notebooks, and also became one of Master Chan's best students . When it came time to leave Taiwan, Cheng Hai humbly requested to copy the old Master's notes. To his great surprise, the old Master shook his head. That will not be necessary, he told Cheng Hai, and proceeded to pass them over as a parting gift. When he returned to Malaysia, Master Yap Cheng Hai immediately incorporated his new knowledge on water into his practice - and soon became known among feng circles in Malaysia and Singapore as something of an expert on water.

That was well over twenty years ago, and since then, he has witnessed the formula create one multi millionaire after another ! The old Taiwan Master's Water Dragon notes, and Master Yap's advice have indeed made countless families enormously wealthy !

I therefore wish to acknowledge Master Yap Cheng Hai's generosity in sharing his notes with us. Perhaps I should explain. In the Chinese scheme of things, old formulas that represent a special skill, or a closely guarded secret are seldom parted with so easily. Most times, these secrets referred to as special *kung fu* are passed on only from Master to Disciple. And even when the disciples are taught, the Master almost always holds back some key ingredient, reserving this only for his best and brightest student - someone deemed worthy of taking over the Master's mantle when the latter departs this world.

It is important I share my sentiments with you, the reader - and to tell you that in passing the knowledge to me, Master Yap was not only generous with the time he spent with me, but also with the genuine details he gave me. There was never any question of holding back. It was always - *how can we make it easier for the reader to understand - to practice*. And where he was unable to satisfy my probing, in every instance he would go to great lengths to refer to his other texts, and check with various other sources, before coming back with an answer that would satisfy me. So that, as with the writing of my second book, I have truly enjoyed collaborating on this one so much !

Mr. Yap Cheng Hai also possesses six extremely valuable but different feng shui *Luo pans*, i.e. the feng shui compass used by feng shui practitioners - and each of these *luo pans* contain the secrets of six different masters.

Much of the notes on water flows would have been unintelligible without the explanations contained in each of these compasses.

With the notes and the compasses, Mr. Yap Cheng Hai was able to help me structure the methodology in a simple and easy-to-understand manner. To simplify the practice further, we have also devised reference diagrams that make it easy for the layman to easily investigate what is or is not suitable for his particular circumstance.

This book therefore explains how to use the method for arranging the direction of water flows, and for tapping the most auspicious directions for entrances and exits of water.

The method also describes where it will be auspicious to place a fish pond, a waterfall, a fountain or even just a well. It offers recommendations on where water should collect and settle; where the garden should stay dry, how the water should move, how it should curve and meander ...

The symbolism used refers to the creation of an auspicious *water dragon* within your compound or garden - one that is placed in such a way that it attracts abundant and great wealth for everyone living in the house.

This book is thus more advanced and complex than the simple guidelines associated with the practice of landscape school of feng shui. This book is about attracting money feng shui luck. Water represents money. Water signifies the flow of wealth. Water is the ultimate money symbol.

When you build a *water dragon* in your garden it is meant exclusively for attracting money luck. But in so doing, you will also be activating other auspicious indications of feng shui.

Good feng shui rarely brings just wealth alone. When the alignments of energy lines are conducive to auspicious feng shui, other benefits also accrue. Thus while an auspicious Water Dragon will definitely bring great wealth when aligned correctly, it will also bring long life and filial children.

At this point, readers are reminded that in the general practice of feng shui, the old masters list eight major life situations which collectively represent good feng shui, with money being merely one of the eight.

These aspirations of mankind are represented on the feng shui compass by each of the four primary and four secondary directions, so that the sector symbolized by the relevant direction was deemed to represent the particular aspiration desired. This is summarized as follows:

1. getting rich and wealthy (south- east)
2. having children (sons) who are filial and successful (west)
3. enjoying a good and happy marriage (south-west)
4. advancing to great heights in one's career (north)
5. getting help from rich & powerful people (north-west)
6. experiencing good health and family relationships (east)
7. achieving recognition, respectability a great name (south)
8. enjoying success in learning and attaining academic honors (north-east)

According to certain Schools of feng shui, each of the aspirations listed above can in fact be *activated* according to certain guidelines, thereby enhancing the chances of achieving any particular chosen aspiration. Thus if you wish to become rich, you should *activate* the wealth corner i.e. the south-east corner.

When you do this in addition to building a water dragon it does not necessarily mean you have increased or expanded your wealth creation potential. Good feng shui is good feng shui, no matter which method you successfully use. One method does not give you insurance for some other method. But my advice is - sure, go for it ! Practice all the methods !

In this connection however, where you find yourself being forced to choose between, say, tapping the big water represented by a stream near your house, but it means having to alter your door direction such that it is facing one of your inauspicious directions - the advice has always been - GO FOR THE WATER ! In other words, water overtakes quite a lot of other considerations, especially if money is what you want !

Water feng shui is not difficult to practice because of the way the formula works. Indeed, the story behind the Water Dragon formula is that when it was first practiced by one of China's most famous feng shui masters - Master Yang Chiew Ping (of the Tang Dynasty), the formula was said to have been devised to assist the poorer classes. Thus its application does not require massive renovations or changes.

It should not surprise anyone however that different masters do possess different methods. Nor should it surprise anyone that feng shui has many variations. Thus when you decide to apply a particular recommendation, or if you decide to construct a *water dragon* in your garden, make sure you take a common sense approach.

First, do not make mistakes in your compass readings or measurements.
Next, be as simple as possible in the implementation of recommended directions. No need to build a *dragon* that is too long !
Third, try to select an auspicious day to start construction work. The Tung Shu does offer auspicious and inauspicious days for construction.
Fourth, calculate the numerology aspects of any changes you make to the drains and water flows i.e. whether it is auspicious or inauspicious to undertake construction work at certain corners of the garden during the year in question. (Check my fourth book *Chinese Numerology in Feng Shui* for this).
Fifth, implement recommendations correctly i.e. close up drains that flow in the wrong direction, and place grills over drains that need to be exposed.

Much of feng shui has to do with correct and accurate application. If you engage a feng shui consultant to help you design your water dragon, request that he supervises the contractor doing the work. If this is not possible, make sure **you** understand the reasons for the change, and know the exact dimensions and configurations of the change - then supervise thoroughly.

When I built my *water dragon*, I went to great pains to ensure no mistakes were made. Barely a week after I had built my *dragon*, I signed an extremely lucrative deal which brought the money flowing in ... it was a great feeling. When I lived in Hong Kong, I had a *natural water dragon* in the hills that undulated towards the sea ... just below my apartment. The "stream" flowed in a most auspicious direction for everyone occupying that particular apartment block (Carolina Gardens in Coombe Road on the Peak), and I know for a fact that everyone living there has prospered and continues to prosper. I am thus convinced of the potency of water in bringing auspicious money luck. If this is what you are looking for, investigate your water flows carefully, then make the changes necessary ! Build your water dragon !

Good luck, and may you definitely prosper !

Lillian Too
Kuala Lumpur, August 1995

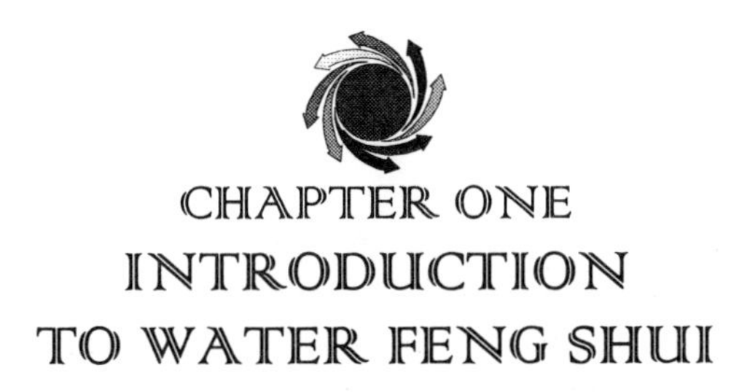

CHAPTER ONE
INTRODUCTION TO WATER FENG SHUI

Good King We^n visits the sage
beside the river Wei,
The time of great good fortune
and much benefit has come;
The hard times are over
And every plan succeeds;

A fortunate time begins.

"Water flows on uninterruptedly
And reaches its goal
The image of ***Abysmal*** *repeated*
The superior man walks in lasting virtue
And carries on the business of teaching.
If you are sincere, you have success
And whatever you do succeeds.
Remorse vanishes "
from the **I Ching**, on the Trigram Kan

CHAPTER ONE

The harmonious flow of water creates wonderful and auspicious feng shui energies that bring opportunities for business growth. When oriented correctly, water and all the various manifestations of water that are within view of the main door or entrance of a building attracts great good fortune to the home.

This is because the flow of water is believed to mirror the flow of the invisible *chi* currents that swirl around the earth; and according to ancient texts on the subject, depending on whether the flow - its direction and orientation is auspicious or not to a particular home or building, the *chi* created can either be *sheng chi* - which brings great good fortune in the form of wealth and prosperity; or *shar chi* which brings great misfortune manifested in loss of money and money making opportunities!

In the text on water feng shui, the promise of great good fortune caused by getting the water alignments and orientations correct is colourfully described as

> *the dry tree is blossoming once more*
> *its branches and leaves get reborn*
> *misfortune easily turns to good fortune*
> *there is much cause for celebration* !

In the same way, the text also warns against incorrect flows of water caused by poor or inauspicious alignment. Amongst the dire warnings given:

> *dense clouds fill the sky but no rain comes*
> *you see the flower but it is in the mirror - it is not real*
> *you have many ideas in your mind ... but nothing works*
> *even good plans cannot be successful.*

The old texts on feng shui suggests that water exerts significant influence on one's money luck. Water can bring prosperity or it can cause you to lose everything. If you are engaged in commerce, and you need just that extra edge to get your business successfully off the ground and flying, you might want to seriously consider designing the flow of water that passes in front of your main door according to feng shui principles.

The element of water in feng shui

Water is one of the five elements that feature significantly in the analysis and interpretation of feng shui. The other four elements are **fire, wood, earth** and **metal.** Understanding this principle of the five elements is vital to the practice of feng shui - and also in the practice of other branches of Chinese divinitive sciences.

This is because the objects and structures that make up the landscapes of the world are deemed to fall within one of these categories.

Analysis is then based on how these elements relate to each other. There is a productive and a destructive cycle in the relationship of these five elements to each other. This is summarised in the diagrams illustrated here.

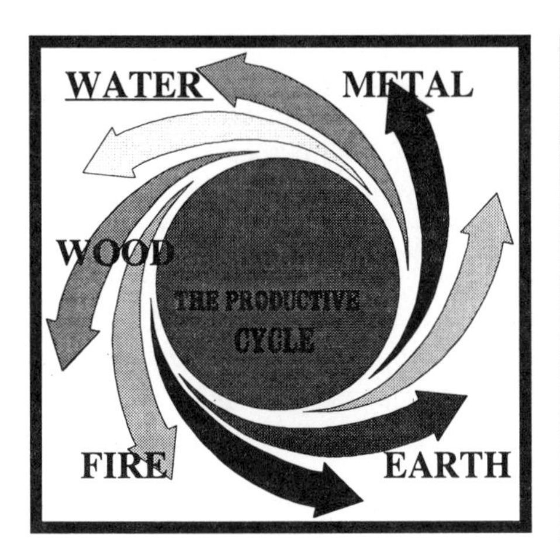

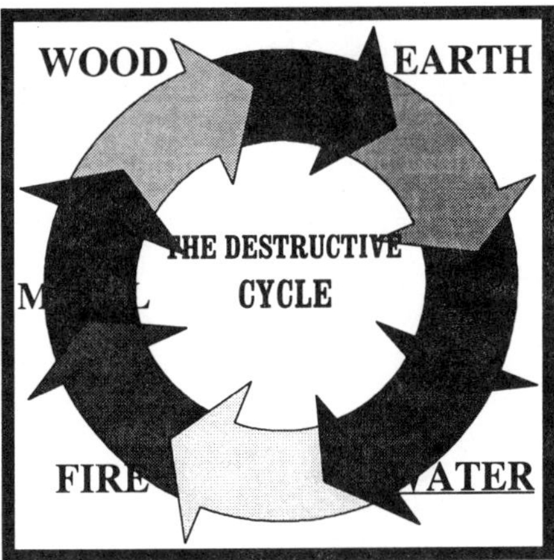

From the illustrations above, observe the relationship of Water to each of the other elements. You will note that all four of the other elements have a relationship with water.

Thus looking at the Productive Cycle, observe:
that **water** is produced by **metal,** thus exhausting it
and in turn produces **wood** and is exhausted by it

And looking at the Destructive Cycle, observe also:
that **water is** destroyed by **earth**
and in turn destroys **fire**

The relationships between the elements become extremely crucial when practicing feng shui because every direction of the compass is represented by one of these five elements; this means that in every house, every building and every room, there will be one or more corners or sectors which will be representative of one of these elements.

This is because the old Pa Kua which has eight sides - each representing one of the eight compass directions - also has corresponding elements assigned to each of the sectors.

Thus, water for example is represented by the sector or compass direction NORTH in the version of the Pa Kua which arranges the Trigrams according to the later heaven arrangement.

NOTE: In all my books I use this arrangement for analysis because the later heaven arrangement is the one to use when investigating the feng shui of ***yang*** dwellings, ie houses of the living. The early heaven arrangement is used when investigating the feng shui of *yin* dwellings ie dwellings of the departed. For our purposes therefore, we shall always refer to the Pa Kua that is relevant for ***yang*** dwellings.)

The elements and matching compass directions are shown in the diagram.

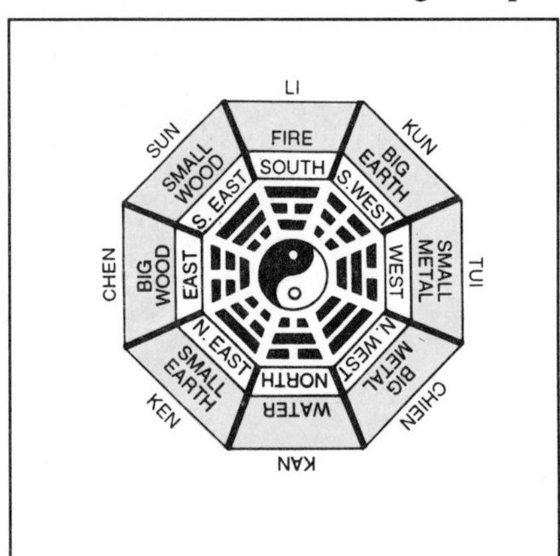

In water feng shui, as in general feng shui, there are two main schools of practice - the landscape school which requires an assessment of the physical characteristics of eg a river - its shape, its width, the quality of its water, its depth, the speed of its flow, the colour of its water, its freshness and so forth. And also the compass school, which makes use of the feng shui *luo-pan* to investigate auspicious and inauspicious directions according to set formulae that have to do with understanding the multiple relationships between the sectors of the Pa Kua and the numbers of the Lo Shu square. The formulae however merely offers the recommended directions and orientations. The next step involves investigating the physical landscape to determine the physical characteristics of the recommended orientations, because physical landscapes cannot be totally ignored.

Next, it is necessary to superimpose onto the analysis, the effect of the water being placed in recommended sectors, i.e. based on the latter's element representations. This is where the element relationships become important.

Put another way, when you start to investigate the way your water should flow, you need to also check the compatibility of the elements of the corner where your water flows out e.g. if according to the formula, it is auspicious for your water to flow out of your house in a north westerly direction, then you should also know that the northwest is represented by the element *metal*. You know that *metal produces water* - a compatible relationship, in fact quite an auspicious relationship. Thus, allowing the flow of water to leave from the northwest sector of your garden should not cause problems. This is because while following one formula, you are not simultaneously creating a *clash* between the elements.

Element relationship is a very vital and important component of feng shui practice - irrespective of the school of feng shui you follow. Feng Shui consultants who demonstrate a lack of deep knowledge of the element relationships do not truly understand feng shui and I can safely say that their knowledge can be considered to be relatively superficial. Every single feng shui master I have met who has come to me highly recommended has been a genuine expert on this subject - their knowledge of element relationships is so deep that sometimes I have been quite stumped at the way they peel away layers and layers of meanings by considering yet other factors. The process makes the analysis even more complex.

This is because the elements themselves have a *size* and *time* dimension to them. Thus you would have seen that East represents big wood while Southeast represents small wood. Also, while Southwest is big earth, the Northeast is small earth. And finally, while Northwest is big metal, West is small metal. Also every day of the year, every month, and every year has a representative element. These often exert some small effect on overall feng shui. It is because of this that you experience *good days* and *bad days*.

According to master practitioners, element analysis cannot merely be taken at its most superficial levels. It is necessary to note whether big wood is meeting up with big metal or small metal - since the outcome of the meeting will not be the same.
They say, for example that while metal is said to destroy wood, it is only big metal that destroys wood.

Small metal (as represented by tools like saws and choppers and blades) in actual fact transforms wood into chairs and tables - thereby enhancing its value - so that small metal can be interpreted as being good for wood - big or small.

The same sort of analysis can be used for the two elements *fire* and *water*. While water is said to destroy fire, and therefore the two should theoretically not mix, it can also be argued that fire causes water to be changed to steam - a source of power. Fire can thus be interpreted as being good for water.

Each of these two elements, *fire* and *water* are represented only by one direction each - the North for water and the South for fire. Thus if your water leaves or exits your house in the north sector, theoretically it should be an auspicious indication. Water here strengthens water !

If it leaves in the south sector - the sector of fire, the elements would seem, (theoretically at least), to clash.

In such a situation, where the dilemma of having to choose between following the formula or following element analysis, it is necessary to look deeper. Since *water* can overcome *fire*, allowing the water to flow out in the south cannot do much harm, and could in fact do much good. This is indeed the case because usually the water that flows out of most homes can be deemed to be small water (drains, streams) which, when combined with *fire* creates steam - an indication of power being produced !

The influence of yin and yang

An additional complication arises from the influence of *yin* and *yang*. This is represented by the symbol shown here and in effect refers to the complementarity of opposites. Yin and yang balance reflects the state of the Universe as seen through the Chinese perspective. According to them, the five elements actually represent the heavenly stems of which there are ten. Thus each of the five elements has a *yin* or a *yang* characteristic. It therefore follows that there is *yin* water and *yang* water, and it is necessary to investigate whether the water that flows past one's home or building is *yin water* or *yang water* !

Yin water can be identified as water that is murky, dark and deep. It is also slow moving. *Yang water* is clear and clean but it moves fast. The most ideal form of water is that which combines both *yin and yang*. Thus clean and clear water that moves slowly is an example of well balanced water.

When you start to use the formula to re arrange the water flows around your home, the most common structure you will be working on will be your **drains.** Unless you are very rich and have a very large piece of land and you can actually create a small meandering stream in your garden, the drains around your home are the most practical structures to work with !

Please remember therefore to factor in the *yin and yang* balance. Keep your water flows moving along gently - nether too fast nor too slow. Make certain your drains are clean, and that they do not get clogged up or blocked by old leaves. And most definitely do not allow water to get stagnant in any portion of your drains since this creates too much *yin* energy which can even turn pernicious and harmful. If there is a stench, the water has definitely become stale and a source of bad *chi.* Do remember that when there is too much *yin* energy, it denotes sickness, ill health and sometimes even death.

Natural water

Natural water is part of landscape feng shui and represents the *shui* (水) part of feng shui. In the landscapes and terrain of the Earth, natural water occurs everywhere - as the seas and the oceans; as rivers and streams; and as lakes and waterfalls. These bodies of water occur in thousands of different shapes and sizes, nestled in all kinds of terrain. Water feng shui which taps into the auspicious *chi* of these natural waters, requires the size, shape and surrounding attributes of the water to be carefully investigated so that the wealth bringing *chi* of the water flowing by is effectively directed to flow into the home. This is an advanced practice of feng shui, and it needs to combine compass school calculations with the layout of the land to come up with the necessary recommendations.

The idea of tapping into the natural waters of the earth is based on the assumption that water symbolizes wealth and prosperity. That it is possible to do so is based on the efficacy of the *water dragon compass school formula* which suggests that auspicious or inauspicious luck from water depends on:

the way it flows pass
the main front door,
and the way it enters and leaves the compound
which makes up part of the home.

To succeed in activating the good luck *chi* of natural water bodies and waterways, it is necessary to study ***the formula*** contained in the **water dragon classic,** and then to understand, ie think through, the way the formula can be applied to your home or building.

The presence of ***natural water*** is considered auspicious because it is regarded (from a feng shui viewpoint) as being vastly superior to ***artificially created water***. Indeed, in the water dragon classic, the applications of the water flow formula implicitly suggests that all of the water refered to is natural water rather than artificial water.

Thus in the classic, the instructions given *require the house to be changed* or altered in order to suit the water flowing past. As such, in the old days, front doors had to be oriented in such a way that the flow of water would be auspicious; and the house itself built in such a way that the water leaving the compound is viewed as flowing in an auspicious orientation.

The tapping of the good luck *chi* of natural water was a very important and vital aspect of advanced feng shui practice. Most of the family homes of the old business families of Taiwan, I am told, have auspicious water orientations which follow the precepts of the water dragon formula.

If there is a view of attractive, clean and nicely flowing water from your home, you would be well advised to study the formula carefully to see how you can best tap the good luck *chi* of the water flowing past. In fact, knowing the formula and being aware of the water flow method of feng shui becomes extremely important if you live in a home or an apartment block that is located near or adjacent to a **river** flowing by; or if you live by the **sea** or near coastal areas. Or near a **mining pool** or a peaceful **lake**.

These are bodies of natural water which can and should be activated to bring or divert good luck *chi* towards your home. Those fortunate enough to do so should, since the water luck that is activated will be *as big as* the river that flows by, or as the lake that sits in full view of the house.

Thus if you live near a big river (assuming it is relatively clean, and is flowing slowly past) the money potential which can be activated and diverted into your house will be enormous !

Having said that, however, I am assured by my feng shui *si fus*, that in their experience, often, even tiny little streams have proven extremely potent in attracting plenty of money luck when their orientation of flow is deemed to be auspicious vis-à-vis the main door !

At the same time, I am also told that sometimes, **living too near the sea** can cause there to be too much water, so that instead of bringing good luck, the sea can be the cause of too much water - hence creating *shar chi* for the house. This happens when the waves on that particular beach are too big and appear too threatening, and the house is exposed to imbalances caused by the lack of other elements like trees and sheltering structures.

Also when the waves are big this suggests too much wind. When there is too much wind and too much water, the energies created are fierce and destructive - the feng shui is not considered auspicious. One should therefore not site one's home at or near such locations.

NOTE: When investigating water it is always important not to forget other aspects of basic feng shui. The importance of harmony and equilibrium should feature in the analyses; the complimentarity of *yin* structures must be balanced with *yang* structures; and congenial interactions with the other four of the five elements (**fire, earth, wood and metal**) must never be ignored.

Generally therefore, a view of natural water flowing by is regarded as auspicious - but the water must be clean and unpolluted. It should not be flowing too fast, because fast flowing water are purveyors of bad *chi*. Nor should it appear dead and un-moving.
Stagnant water is far worse than having no water at all.

Artificially created water

But what if you lived, as so many do in today's urbanized world, in a home where there is absolutely no view of water at all ? What if the nearest river is miles away, and the nearest lake or pond is completely out of sight from where you live ? Does this mean it is not possible for you to use the water flow formula and activate prosperity luck ?

The answer is that where natural water is missing, it is **possible to simulate nature by creating artificial water** - hence swimming pools of all shapes and sizes, decorative ponds filled with water lilies, canals of whatever width, waterfalls of any dimension, and fountains in any shape - all man made manifestations of water - are perfectly capable of creating auspicious energy flows. The answer therefore is YES, it is totally possible to build and create artificial water dragons, which will work just as efficiently as purveyors of excellent and auspicious *chi* flows !

Indeed, it was in the early years of this century that practicing feng shui Masters of Taiwan began using the water dragon formula in a way which left the building itself intact, and instead concentrated on building or designing artificial waterways, ponds and waterfalls in the compounds of homes which would harmonise with the home itself.

They thus used the water dragon formula from a different perspective, so that instead of only investigating the orientation of the house and its main door, they also examined the direction and orientation of water flows around the house. At first, much of these solutions were in the nature of experiments to test the effectiveness of the formula.

But as results proved amazingly workable, the practice of the formula, as it is used today by those in the know, focuses more on the building and construction of artificial bodies of water and waterways than on re-orientating the main door of the house. The end result is the same, of course - to harmonize and balance the *chi* of the door with that of the water; only the method used is dissimilar.

Applying the water dragon formula this way is much easier. This is because in the context of most domestic households, the formula is actually best applied to the flow of water in the humble **drain**, a structure most people take for granted. According to experts on the water dragon formula, when the household drain is designed to simulate an auspicious flow of water, it transforms into a *water dragon*, capable of bringing much prosperity and wealth luck to all the residents living within the household irrespective of whether they are related or not. Thus even maids and gardeners living in the home will benefit from the water dragon's benevolence.

When applying the formula therefore, it would do well for readers to think in terms of **checking the flow of the drains around their homes**. This should be the first thing to be investigated before considering waterfalls and decorative ponds. The latter structures can definitely be included into the overall design of your garden's landscape, but it is vital to get the direction of water flow correct before thinking of other things.

The formula will reveal all the excellent and auspicious orientations for the flow of water. These calculations are based on the exact location and orientation of your main door. This is because the luck of the waterflow vis-à-vis any house or building is directly influenced by the orientation of the main door. The waterflow of the drain is also affected by the orientation of the entire house within the compound. The formula also reveals orientations and water flows to strenuously avoid.

To design artificial water structures that create good feng shui therefore, it is advisable to closely follow the water formula. This is especially applicable for those who wish to have swimming pools in their homes. Swimming pools can be either auspicious or extremely in-auspicious depending on their location and orientation vis-à-vis the main door. Its feng shui attributes are also affected by its shape, its size and its depth. It is wise to be careful when building a swimming pool in your compound.

WATER IN LANDSCAPE FENG SHUI

The best types of water are slow moving and clean. Rivers that meander gently past, in full view of one's main door are said to be excellent. From a landscape feng shui perspective, this means the river flows gently past one's home in the lower land below, like in an armchair formation - ***the green dragon white tiger formation*** - this kind of configuration is believed to bring enormous good fortune, and prosperity is supposed to come to the family for not one, but for several generations. This is illustrated in the diagram here which also shows the flow of the auspicious water.

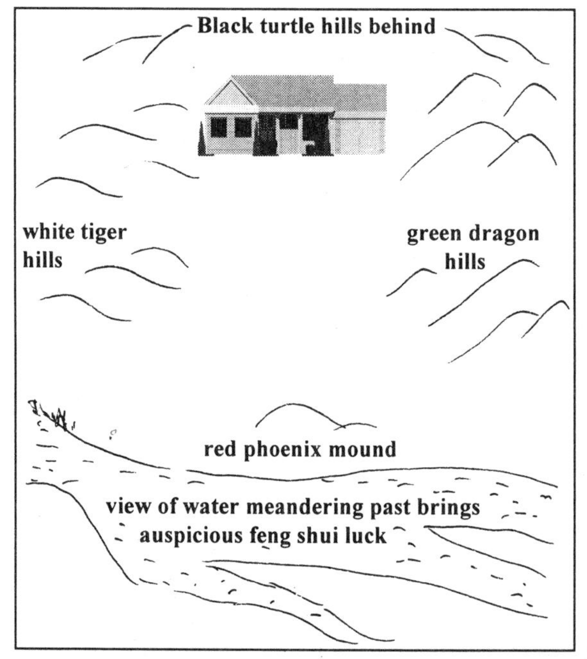

Rivers that flow past one's home should never be straight, or worse, seem aimed at one's building, since they then become transformed into dangerous poison arrows. The feng shui interpretation of rivers in general are based on guidelines of the landscape school. These guidelines are based on the symbolisms associated with the five elements, as well as on the four celestial animals - the dragon, the tiger, the turtle and the phoenix. These river characteristics and their feng shui attributes are illustrated on this and the following pages. In applying these guidelines, please remember that these guidelines are part of landscape school feng shui and are NOT part of the water dragon formula. Nevertheless, when applying either system, it is useful to take cognisance of the guidelines (rules) of both systems.

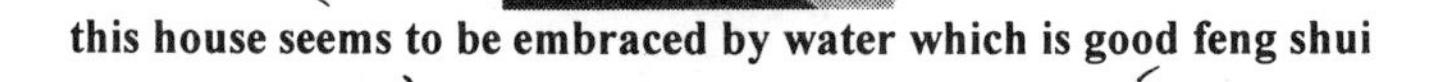

this house seems to be embraced by water which is good feng shui

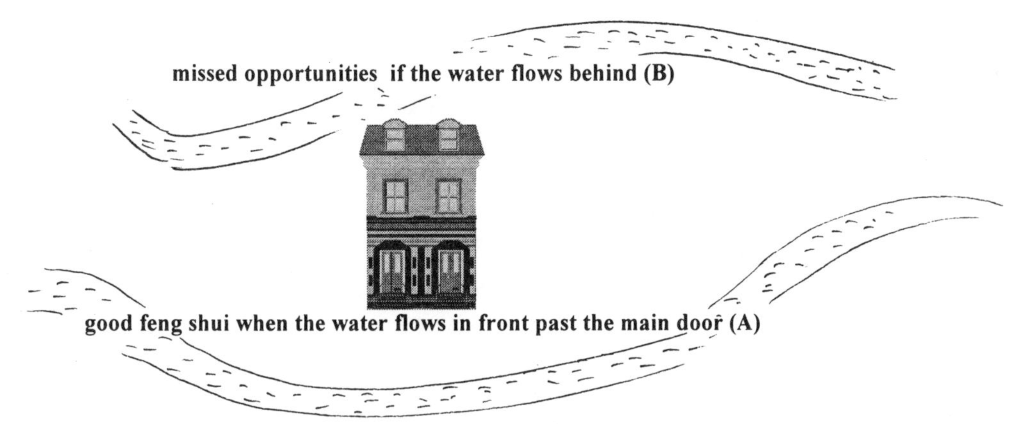

Landscape feng shui suggests that while it is auspicious to have a river or waterway nearby, to benefit from the river, it is important that the river flows past the main door. Otherwise, while opportunities for advancement and success may be plentiful, it is difficult for household residents to take advantage of these opprtunities. Thus when a river flows behind a building, the connotations are not so auspicious.

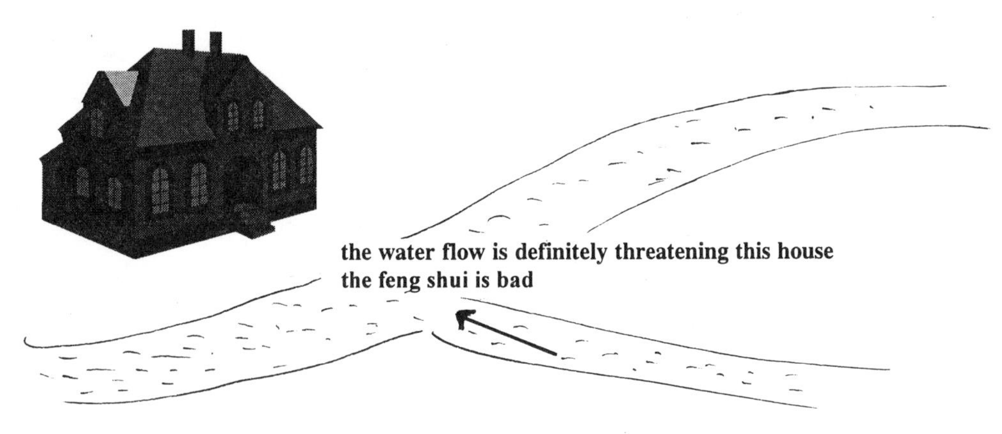

When a river appears to flow directly towards the main door of a house, the consensus is that it is not a good sign, and when it is also straight as well, according to landscape guidelines, the river has become a poison arrow and is a purveyor of bad chi, killing chi. It is a situation that does not suggest good feng shui. Further examples of bad feng shui vis-à-vis rivers, are indicated in the sketches here where the black squares/triangles represent buildings.

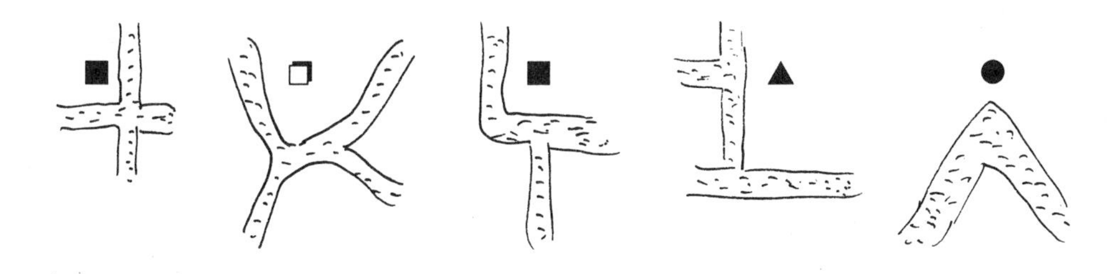

Reproductions of Landscape renditions of excellent natural water flows from the WATER DRAGON CLASSIC

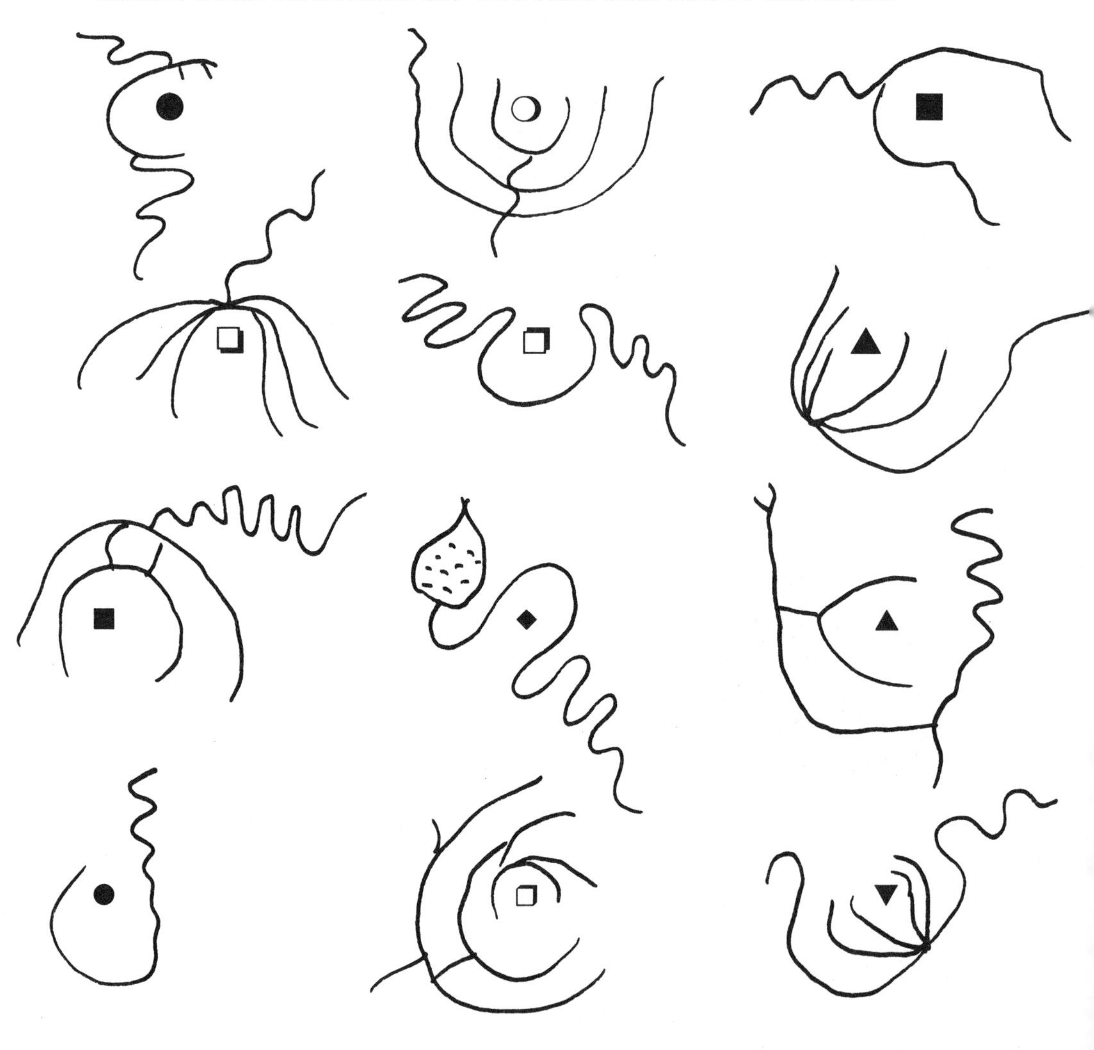

The above are water type locations which are indicative of prosperity, wealth, fame and posterity. I saw water arrangements like some of the above when I flew into Kuching earlier this year.
The rivers of Sarawak appear to have the potential of being extremely auspicious. They curve and wind, meandering gently along. Residents of Kuching should try to tap into their feng shui potential.

WATER IN PA KUA LO SHU FENG SHU

The application of the water element in the Compass formulas which deal with auspicious directions of individuals are based on its relationship with the other four elements i.e. wood, fire, earth and metal. Water is represented by the direction North, and it is in this symbolic relationship that water becomes significant in the practice.

In Pa Kua Lo Shu feng shui, individuals can determine whether they are East or West group people, and which are their four good and four inauspicious directions. There are many different ways to use these directions, and one of these ways is to apply one's most auspicious directions for the positioning and orientation of the main door. ❀

This is a very powerful method of feng shui, and readers are bound to become confused when confronted with the very real possibility that while following the precepts of one formula, they may not be able to follow the guidelines of another formula. It is thus quite possible that while your front door may be facing a direction that spells auspicious good fortune for you according to the Pa Kua Lo Shu method, it may not be very conducive to good water dragon feng shui.

Usually, it is possible to accommodate the guidelines of both schools. Indeed all it takes is a bit of creative and serious thinking. This is because both methods offer alternatives or options. There is normally more than one good direction or orientation and when it is not possible (for whatever reason) to tap one direction, there is always a second, and sometimes a third or even a fourth arrangement that is also auspicious, although of course it may not be as excellent as the first orientation recommended.

In situations when the recommendations clash, my feng shui *si fu* (master) suggests that if it is money that you want, you would do well **to tap the water !** This is because, he says, a house with good water feng shui benefits every person living in that house irrespective of their date of birth. When the orientation of the front door is made to suit certain individuals, it benefits only that person. Water feng shui is thus more meaningful for everyone.

❀ **NOTE**: The many practical applications of Pa Kua Lo Shu Feng Shui, as well as the formula itself have been comprehensively covered in the author's second book on feng shui entitled **Applied PaKua LoShu Feng Shui**. The book is available at all leading book shops in Malaysia, Singapore and Hong Kong.

Feng shui is a complex science and to the amateur practitioner, some of the recommendations and logic presented by different schools or systems may appear contradictory. Sometimes it can even be physically impossible to implement what is recommended e.g. according to the water dragon formula, my Uncle's water should be flowing right to left past his front door.

Unfortunately, this meant that the water would have to flow uphill, since his land slopes downwards from left to right. My Uncle was most skeptical. He was convinced it was an impossible recommendation to follow, and many of you readers might well agree with him.

He forgot that I have a most intelligent feng shui *si fu* who is both creative and clever. To those of you equally clever readers of mine, the solution must be quite obvious. Yes, that's right ... build the drain to let it slope from right to left and voila ! Play with the depth of the drain so that despite the natural slope of the land, the water can be made to flow in the correct direction !

Well then what about the public drain outside ? I mean my Uncle lives in one of those areas in Kuala Lumpur which require huge monsoon drains to cart away the rain water during the rainy season. Indeed, he has this huge, enormous drain just outside his house which flows from left to right - potentially a very dangerous orientation according to the formula. What can be done ? It is obviously impossible to change the drain outside. Even if BandarRaya were willing to oblige there is no way they can help ! Once again, my feng shui *si fu* solved the dilemma by recommending that a high wall be built to demarcate the inside and the outside of the house. By doing that, the outside drain no longer posed a threat !!

Oftentimes therefore, when confronted with practical problems or when faced with contrary or opposing recommendations, the way to proceed is to apply one's common sense. Feng shui is a very logical science. Everything recommended is based on the fundamental laws of the Chinese divinitive sciences. And **all** compass school formulas have their roots in the 8 sided Pa Kua with its arrangement of the eight trigrams, as well as the Lo Shu magic square. Understand these basics, and it should not be difficult to overcome problems of interpretation in your practice of feng shui.

An added bonus is that over time, and with practice, you will know enough feng shui so that it would be impossible for consultants pull the wool over your eyes - you will be able to judge his depth of knowledge quite easily.

WATER IN NUMEROLOGY FENG SHUI

We have seen that in addition to the spatial aspects of feng shui, there is also a time dimension to feng shui. This was dealt with in great detail in the author's fourth book **Chinese Numerology in Feng Shui**, which offers a comprehensive outline of *fey sin feng shui* - or flying star feng shui, a system which uses a formula to calculate the luck of rooms, houses, and buildings during different periods of time.

These time periods may be the twenty year cyclical period, the year under review or even the month or day. Because the calculation can be quite laborious, most feng shui consultants do not bother to calculate time dimension feng shui for their clients on a monthly basis. Generally they are satisfied with merely the twenty year period calculation.

Thus we are presently going through the period of 7 and this period will last until the year 2003. The formula will thus enable anyone to calculate the attributes - good and bad, auspicious and inauspicious based on numbers and meanings of numbers - of each of the rooms and corners of a house. Most important will be the calculation of the numbers that affect the luck of the main door.

In *fey sin feng shui*, there are two secondary stars which feature prominently in the analysis - these are the ***siang sin star*** also referred to as the water star and the ***chor sin star*** which is also called the mountain star.

Where water comes into the picture is the way these secondary stars move because depending on whether the numbers are auspicious or inauspicious, the presence of water can be good or bad.

The siang sin star:

This literally means the direction star i.e. the direction one faces. In the north the siang sin star faces north and in the south it faces south. Depending on how it flies around the Lo Shu grid, the siang sin star of each of the eight corners of any house (based on the eight directions) can either be auspicious or inauspicious depending on the number that it carries. ❁

Note:❁ Please refer to the author's book ***Chinese Numerology in Feng Shui*** which explains the Numerology formulas and how the stars fly around the Lo Shu grid. The lucky and unlucky numbers are also explained in the book.

According to the texts on *fey sin feng shui*, a siang sin star which carries an auspicious number should face some form of water for it to be effectively activated. Water is supposed to enhance the good effects of a lucky siang sin star.

Example: If the main door of your house faces north and is located in the north sector, and the siang sin star in that sector carries an auspicious number (e.g. the number 7 which means current prosperity), then if your front door also faces a body of water (e.g. a pool, an ornamental pond) it will be most auspicious.

When applying the water dragon formula to your house and its compound, it is useful to calculate the siang sin star numeral for the front door's sector of your house. This will give you additional information on what is required.

In addition it is also necessary to examine the *element* represented by the direction of your front door. And to see how it relates to water in the cycle of relationships, since you will be applying the water formula. In our example, because the direction of the main door is north which symbolizes water, the presence of water here is doubly auspicious.

Should the element represented by the main door's sector be an element that is destroyed by water (i.e. fire) or an element that destroys water (i.e. wood), it will be necessary to be more careful. Thus for sectors in the south (fire) or in the east and southeast (wood), the presence of water anywhere near the door may clash with the element of that sector. It would thus make sense to site any water flow (drain) further away from the front door.

It should be getting clearer now how the practice of one formula or system can be used to complement another. When it comes to *fey sin feng shui*, most feng shui masters in Hong Kong almost always strongly recommend that whatever feng shui inspired change is being effected, the time aspects of the change should not be ignored.

Indeed, in Hong Kong the feng shui consultants there do a roaring business each year just before New year because that is when many business people would request for their annual update of the flying stars for each month of the coming New year. They believe that this will then give them fair warning as to what will be their good months and what will be their bad months.

The chor sin star
This is the *sitting star*. Thus in the north, the chor sin sits in the north and faces south. In the east it sits in the east facing west. The chor sin is sometimes referred to as the mountain star because it requires something solid and large to sit on. The auspicious chor sin star is activated by the presence of something solid in its sector like a wall or a large rock.

The chor sin star should never be placed near water since this signifies the *mountain falling into the water* - a most inauspicious indication. If the number of the chor sin is a lucky number, this falling into water will mean a loss of money or opportunity. However if the number of the chor sin star is unlucky then falling into the water will dissolve the bad luck caused by the unlucky number of the chor sin star.

By calculating the movement of the siang sin and the chor sin stars, it will be possible to know exactly when these stars are auspicious and when they are inauspicious. This is indicated by their numbers, which change as they fly around the Lo Shu grid. By thus knowing, it will be much easier to ensure that the water can be arranged to complement the movement of the siang sin and chor sin stars.

It should perhaps be stressed that for the amateur practitioner, it may not be necessary to use all the different methods of the different schools. For the most part each of the systems have their respective strong points and most can usually stand alone on their own.

For those who wish to have a comprehensive view of the interlinks between the different systems however, this adjunct to chapter One should hopefully provide the linkage.

The element of Water is a very important element and when used correctly can be extremely potent in attracting auspicious good fortune. For businesses, the water symbol can be used to great effect if other relationships and symbols are correct.

A good friend of mine for example is born of the water element. He wanted to open a Chinese restaurant in London. His well meaning friends however tried to dissuade him. They told him that the restaurant business in London was already overcrowded; that it was too competitive, that it was a bad time seeing that the UK was going through a recession then.

They also told him (amateur feng shui experts them !!) that the restaurant business was signified by the element fire (to denote cooking) and that since he was a water person, that therefore the business was not suitable for him.

But Danny is nothing if not determined. He proceeded to rent space in London's Queensway district. Then he arranged to decorate his restaurant in black lacquer to signify water. More, he painted the well known Chinese water **wave** motif on all the walls. The effect was quite stunning, but more important was his willingness to go all the way with the use of water symbols to strengthen his chances of success.

Since his opening three years ago, Danny's restaurant has been full every day, morning and evening, and during weekends, especially on Sundays at lunchtime, it is virtually impossible to get a table unless one is prepared to stand in line from an absurdly early time !

Danny's water feng shui was based on his conviction that anyone born in water year will definitely do well in the restaurant business because small fire is good for water - it turns water into steam, representing power and energy. It is thus good feng shui.

In the practice of the ancient science of feng shui - as you start to delve deep into the water dragon formula, do make sure you temper your analysis with inputs from the feng shui fundamentals, and do apply the formula with a huge dose of common sense as well.

CHAPTER TWO
USING WATER FENG SHUI TO CREATE WEALTH LUCK

Good fortune comes like the sunrise
Everything improves when the sunlight shines;
The old well has been dry for a long time
Suddenly, fresh water bubbles forth, That is when good fortune
follows misfortune.

"*The wind drives over the water*
The image of ***dispersion***
Dispersion leads in turn to accumulation
Something ordinary men do not think of ;
The superior man contemplates his mansion
It furthers him to cross the great water
And to persevere "
from the **I Ching**, on the TrigramHuan

CHAPTER TWO

The Water Dragon formula contained in this book is a Compass based formula which offers recommendations in terms of compass directions of flow as well as angles of flow. In following the recommendations, due credence must also be given to the effect and influence of the five element relationships as well as to topographical considerations which have to do with landscape characteristics. Thus the levels of the land, the surrounding hills and buildings also exert their effect on the water feng shui one endeavours to create, and thus cannot be ignored.

The water formula offers specific directions of water flow, particularly the exit flow, and in some cases the recommendation for one direction is more complex than for another direction. The starting point is to first investigate which exit directions are deemed auspicious for your particular house or building, and then to go on from there to decide which specific direction is deemed the most suitable in your specific case.

Another approach is to investigate whether the existing flow of water may be creating bad vibrations and inauspicious influences on the feng shui of your house. If so, it may then be necessary to investigate alternative changes which can be made to the flow of water, in order to improve your feng shui.

Every house and building has its own characteristics, and even when the direction of the main door of two houses may be the same, each may require the application of a different direction of exit flow due to differences in terrain or in the layout of the house. Sometimes there are also other related recommendations pertaining to entrance flows of water as well as how the water should flow pass the main door. Thus, in applying the formula, it is necessary to be careful. A thorough understanding of the fundamentals of the formula and its application is thus useful before examining the formula itself.

THE FUNDAMENTALS OF THE WATER FORMULA

As this is a Compass based formula, practitioners are advised to invest in a good compass. Try to use one which has the exact degrees of compass directions. Any Western compass is suitable, and although the Chinese system places SOUTH at the top, this does not change the direction. Use any compass to determine the **actual** direction and go on from there.

If you do not have the degrees on compass directions indicated in your compass, use a simple protractor - the types used by school children for their mathematics - to determine the exact angle recommended. You will find when you refer to the next chapter which contains the formula, that all the recommendations are expressed as *bearing so many degrees from North*; these express the angle of the direction and it is vital to get this angle correct, otherwise you might inadvertently touch another direction thereby creating inauspicious instead of auspicious effects.

The suitable and unsuitable directions of water flow are based on the direction your main door faces. This means you must determine the exact direction of your main door, and it would be better if, when determining this, you try to express it in terms of also *bearing how many degrees from North*. **Take this reading from inside the house looking out.** By being this exact, you will be able to determine the relevant subsector of direction according to the Chinese **luo pan**. In Compass school feng shui, each of the eight cardinal and secondary directions are further divided into three subsector directions, making altogether 24 possible directions. Since the formula divides all houses/buildings into twelve categories, and since these categories are based on the subsector direction of their respective main door, it is necessary to get this preliminary part of the investigation right before proceeding to the next part.

When determining this direction, you may have difficulty deciding which door of your house is deemed to be the main door. According to feng shui definitions, the **main door** is the mouth *(kou)* of the house. This is where the residents move in and out of the house, and by extension this is also where the *chi* - good and bad enter into the house. If you have more than one main door, it is a good idea to decide categorically which you consider is your main door, and then make your analysis from there. Once you decide which is your main door, it is also a good idea to use it as often as possible and to construct it to look like a main door.

It is pertinent to remind readers that according to feng shui, the main door should be solid. Glass doors, especially see-through glass doors do not make auspicious main doors. Also main doors should open *out* onto some open space in the garden, and open *in* to some open space. It should therefore not be cramped and tight either inside or outside. Also do be reminded how important the main door is to feng shui. It must not be hit by poison arrows either from the inside or outside.

Protect your main door as best you can. Make sure it does not get hit or injured by inauspicious, hostile or threatening objects. If it is, even if it is facing your best direction, and there is the most auspicious water flow moving pass it, you cannot enjoy good feng shui.

Poison arrows exert very deadly and inauspicious influence. So do make certain you have taken this aspect of the practice into account before proceeding to construct a water dragon. Or looked at from another viewpoint; if you decide to change your main door to suit your directions and to tap outside water, make certain that in so doing you do not make your main door vulnerable to hidden arrows. Be very observant of your surroundings.✪

When applying Compass based formulas, I have often been asked whether the directions recommended apply equally to countries in the North and South hemispheres of the globe.
This question arises because it is widely accepted that to the Chinese, South represents fire because it is the direction of the equator - the source of warmth for those living in the Northern hemisphere; and that North represents the source of cold. If this is the case, then surely it can be argued that for those living in the southern hemisphere, the directions recommended should be *flipped around* i.e. that north becomes south, and east becomes west and so forth.

I have discussed this at some length with several experts and in particular with Master Yap Cheng Hai. They generally, and he in particular has indicated quite categorically that in respect of the water formula, it makes no difference whether your house or building is in the north or south hemisphere - indeed, that the directions recommended apply equally to **both** hemispheres.

For those of us who live in Malaysia, Singapore or Hong Kong there is of course no problem since being in the same North hemisphere as China, we can take the recommendations at their face value. But for those living in places like Australia and New Zealand, practitioners might want to bear this in mind as something worth while observing.

✪ For those of you who may wish to refer to a more comprehensive treatment of main doors and poison arrows in feng shui, I recommend you read my first book **Feng Shui** (purple cover) or my third book **Practical Applications of Feng Shui** (yellow cover).

Another significant fundamental of the water formula is the careful observance of the water flow as it passes in front of the main door, i.e. **whether it is moving left to right or right to left.** This direction of flow is taken from inside the house looking out, and is a very essential part of the formula. It is determined entirely by the direction of the main door.

It becomes especially important to get this flow correct when we are dealing with the auspicious directions of flow. If this component of the formula is not correctly applied, the probability of good feng shui is considerably reduced. Getting this flow correct may not always be the easiest thing to do, especially if the terrain of the land or its level is inappropriate. Or when there are big rivers and big monsoon drains in front of your house moving in the opposite direction. If this is the case with your house you need to investigate ways to get round the problem. At this stage, it is important to alert you to take levels of your gardens and grounds before you proceed.

PRACTICAL TIPS ON USING THE FORMULA

Undertake analysis on paper first: The best approach is to start by analyzing your existing *water* feng shui on paper before proceeding to draw out the plan for construction or change. Play with two or three alternatives, and consider whether you need to, or even want to build a water dragon. Sometimes it is sufficient to adopt the simplest approach and merely take care of your exit direction and the flow of water across the main door. Indeed, in all the twelve categories of houses listed under the formula, there are at least two excellent directions of exit flows that hold out the promise of excellent prosperity prospects.

The analysis can start with a fixed direction of the main door. For example you may already have designed your main door to face a direction that is auspicious for you under the Pa Kua Lo Shu method. If this is the case, then all you need to do is to determine your House category and from there proceed to find out what kind of water flow and exit direction will bring you even greater feng shui luck. This is the most simple way of applying the formula.

Analysis can also be based on existing water flows: It is also possible that you may not wish to alter your existing water flow because it makes conventional good sense for your drains to be located in a certain way.

If this is the case, then the advice is for you to go through all the auspicious directions of the twelve categories of houses. From the information then extracted, you can investigate the various alternative door directions that may be more suitable and auspicious for your existing drain or water flow. This same approach to the practice is also suitable for those of you who wish to align your main door direction to *tap* into the good feng shui of natural rivers or streams that are within view of your house.

Wells: Another practical suggestion to the implementation of water feng shui is that you should make sure as much of the water of your house as possible flows out through the designated auspicious direction. This is not always possible but with a little bit of creativity it is possible. Usually the best way to do this is to have all the water meet at some kind of collection point where you then design and construct a round or oval shaped well. Then let the water exit from the well in the desired direction. This is illustrated in the sketch here.

***Wells** are extremely useful components of water feng shui. Shown here is an example of how it can be used to collect all the water of the house before it exits the compound.*

*The water flows past the **main door** at the right hand side of this sketch in a right to left direction, and flows out of the house in the right hand bottom corner, where a **well** (marked ✪) catches the water that flows from the back.*

No directions have been indicated but in practice, you will need to work out your auspicious direction of flow before building the exit drain.

Do not forget to let the drain flow past the front main door. It is also advisable to make the well a good balanced size - neither too big nor too small. Feng Shui Masters always advice the use of auspicious dimensions, and shapes and sizes that spell good luck are round or oval with a diameter of either **32 inches or/by 35 inches** or perhaps smaller at **25 inches or/by 18 inches**. These are auspicious dimensions according to the feng shui ruler.

Note angles of water flow all round the house: When designing the drains to simulate the water dragon, it is advisable to take note of the angles of turns. Most drains are designed to turn in a sharp 90° fashion. Usually it is preferable if the drains turn in a more rounded fashion, so that no sharp angles get created.

Watch out for large boulders used in landscaping: If you use boulders and rocks to improve the aesthetics of your garden, make sure that these rocks do not resemble hostile creatures like rats or fierce looking cats. According to Chinese feng shui texts, hostile looking boulders can sometimes symbolize and create harmful chi when located in specific corners of the garden. Best to do away with anything that is too large.

Use concrete slabs to cover drains flowing in the wrong direction: Where it is too expensive to make too many changes to drains already built, it is possible to make these drains *disappear* by covering them with concrete slabs. By shutting them off from view, it is deemed that they no longer exist. Thus in homes which have underground drains, these are deemed to be non existent. Similiarly, it is also possible to use grilled metal covers on drains which are deemed to be auspicious. As long as they can be seen, covering them with grills allow for safety measures without compromising their feng shui aspects. The wells that you construct can also be similiarly covered with custom made metal grills. This is usually advisable especially if you have young children around the house.

Build a wall to block off outside drains: if there are outside drains that happen to flow in the wrong direction and are thus deemed inauspicious for your House category (remember this depends on your door direction), you can build a wall which effectively demarcates or blocks off a view of the offending drain. If a wall is too expensive, grow a thick hedge which can act as a symbolic divider. This is not necessary if the outside drain is flowing in a favourable direction.

Keep your drains always flowing with water: This is advisable if you seriously wish to tap into the good luck of your water flow. Do not allow your drains to completely dry up as this indicates a weakening of the good luck *sheng chi*. At the same time, it is also advisable to keep the drains clean. Do not let water stagnate in either the drains or the well (if you build one) since, apart from harbouring mosquitoes, stagnant water also creates inauspicious *shar char*.

BIG WATER & SMALL WATER

In using the formula to create wealth luck, you can and should differentiate between big water and small water. **Big water** refers to *rivers*, the *sea*, *lakes, mining pools* as well as large man made *canals*. As the name suggests, big water is usually bigger in size than the house or building itself and normally refers to natural bodies of water in the environment.

According to all the ancient texts on feng shui, water flowing past any ***yang*** building almost always bring wealth to the residents. This is because there is no necessity to consider entrance and exit directions unless the river or stream is flowing through your estate, in which case it is necessary to analyze the flow of the river in greater depth. When you have a view of water therefore, the consensus is that it is usually an auspicious indication.

Small water refers to usually to man made simulations of natural water. *Drains* and small man made landscape *streams* are considered to be small water, as are small garden *fish ponds* or *lotus ponds*. As the name implies, small water is smaller than the house or building.

When assessing the feng shui characteristics of water the general rules always apply i.e. the water should meander, it should flow slowly rather than too fast, it should be clean rather than polluted and it should never dry up.

In terms of their effect on the feng shui of a house or building, big water is generally considered to bring big wealth when aligned in an auspicious orientation to a house. Having said that however, the proper orientation of small water can also be equally potent and as powerful in attracting tangible good fortune.

ACTIVATING BIG WATER

The most important guidelines to follow in the activating of big water are **(i)** ensuring that the orientation of the main door is in an auspicious relationship to the direction of flow of the big water, and **(ii)** ensuring that the element relationships are compatible in that the water is located in a direction which represents a compatible element to where your main door is located.

Whether the big water is flowing from left to right or right to left is vital, and this depends on the Category of house it is, which in turn depends on the direction the main door faces. If it is not flowing in the correct direction, then it is advisable to adjust the direction of the main door.

This is because it is not always possible to live beside an auspicious natural big water. Residents in urban areas for example are hardly likely to be able to tap into a natural waterway unless the city has been built around a large lake or has a river flowing through it. It is therefore, always advisable for residents to tap the good fortune *chi* created by any big water around !

This is especially applicable to houses or buildings located near rivers. Having said that, it is equally vital that **the river must pass in front of the main door and not the back door**. Otherwise residents merely see opportunities but are unable to take advantage of them. When living near a river or other big water therefore, do make sure that you *face* the water.

Good feng shui is indicated when nearby river flows past the ***front*** *of the house as shown here.*

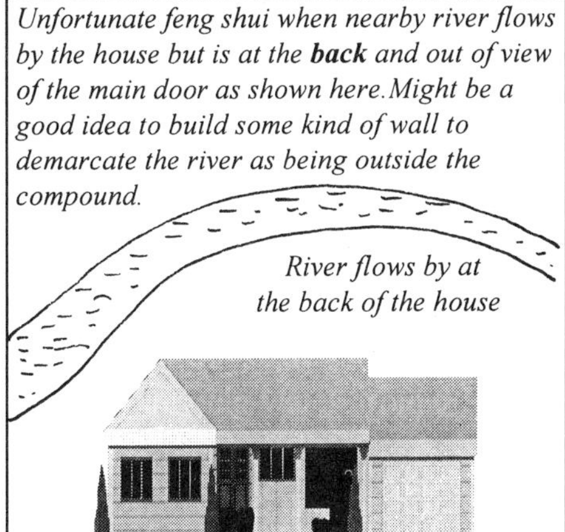

Unfortunate feng shui when nearby river flows by the house but is at the ***back*** *and out of view of the main door as shown here. Might be a good idea to build some kind of wall to demarcate the river as being outside the compound.*

If, for some reason you are unable to re orientate your main door such that the beautiful river near your house can be made to create auspicious *chi* for you, or you simply are unable to let your main door ***face*** the river, then it could be advisable to simply demarcate the river outside your house by building a wall to symbolically block out the view of the river.

While a view of the river is important, the direction of its flow is even more significant. Thus the successful tapping of a river's auspicious influences depends on whether it is flowing pass the house in the correct direction. This is part of the water formula, and for ease of reference for those of you living near rivers (or other waterways) wishing to implement this recommendation, the relevant water flow for each of the twenty four possible directions of your main door orientations are given in the sketches on the following page.

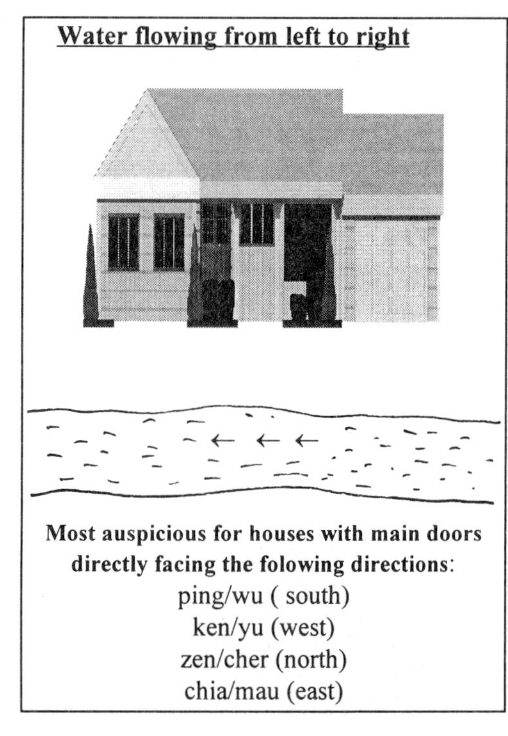

✣ The directions given in these two diagrams for water flows in front of the main door are based on the water dragon formula. These are deemed to be the most auspicious directions of water flow for each of the main door categories listed. Readers will note that for doors facing directly the four cardinal directions, auspicious water must flow from left to right.

If you live near the sea, it is better to be residing in a condominium than a bungalow house since this balances out the effect of the huge water symbolized by the sea. A condominium is part of a bigger building. Usually, living near the sea can cause there to be *too much water*, thereby leading to some imbalance. However, if the house is not too isolated, and specific measures are taken to balance with other elements that diffuse the effect of a preponderance of water, then the sea brings auspicious good luck.

It is also useful to investigate the size of the waves that habitually wash up on the particular beach that fronts your house. When there is too much wind and houses get subjected to frequent storms, the effect is not considered auspicious unless some kind of protection can be symbolically constructed.

ACTIVATING SMALL WATER

Small water generally refers to man made or artificial water structures which add so much to a modern garden. The best way to activate small water for feng shui purposes is by aligning these man made structures according to the water dragon formula, with the drain requiring the most careful attention. The exact flow of drains and their directions is dealt with in comprehensive detail in the next chapter. However it is also possible to introduce other man made structures into your garden if you so wish, and if you have sufficient space to do so. Dealt with here are three examples of artificially created water structures which not only have the potential of improving your feng shui, but they also add considerable beauty to a well planned garden.

Waterfalls. Probably one of the most popular man made simulations of small water that can be particularly effective in creating a great deal of auspicious *sheng chi* is to have a small artificial **waterfall** in your garden and in front of your main door . Ideally, the waterfall should be located in either the *North* corner of the garden, or in the *East* or *Southeast*. These are compatible sectors in terms of element relationships.

According to feng shui guidelines, a beautiful waterfall in full view of the main door brings opportunities for business and career expansion as well as much auspicious money luck. When building a waterfall, like the one shown here, let its size be balanced with the size of your house. A waterfall that is too large will overshadow the house, creating too much chi energy. Also, in using rocks and boulders for decoration, make certain they do not resemble anything hostile or threatening that could create shar chi, thereby hurting the front door.

And finally do not place the waterfall directly in front of, or facing the main door. This could have the effect of blocking favourable *chi* that may be flowing into the house. Waterfalls are best located towards the left hand side of the main door (ie inside looking out).

Readers of my first book on feng shui will recall I included an illustration of a waterfall with a suitably encouraging caption. I presented the book to two personal friends of mine, who decided, for a laugh, to invest in a small waterfall fronting their main door.

Michael built a petite waterfall in the front corner of his Damansara bungalow while Mr. G, a friend from varsity days erected a magnificent new waterfall in the far corner of his new mansion in Bukit Tunku. *Both saw tangible results within six months of building the waterfall.*

Michael received a job offer he simply couldn't turn down and is now successfully running one of Malaysia's largest and most dynamic private Colleges, and is a founder director of the fast growing Asian Strategy and Leadership Institute. More significantly he is now living in a bigger mansion in Country Heights. Meanwhile Mr. G, already a wealthy man, was granted the fabulous opportunity to build and develop Malaysia's newest WestPort project.

Fountains

Another very popular and equally effective structure which can be installed in the garden to enhance your feng shui is to have a water fountain. These come in various designs, with the water bubbbling forth in several different ways. Any design that suits your personal fancy can be quite effective. The best and most effective place to locate a fountain is to have in the front garden in full view of your main door. However, do make sure you have enough space before installing a fountain. To get the maximum benefits out of a water fountain, it is best to have some empty space in front of the door - at least twenty feet or more. This enhances the feng shui of the house considerably.

Fountains are best located in a sector of your compound which is symbolized by the water element (*i.e. the north*) or the wood element (*i.e. the east or southeast*) as these are compatible sectors.
For those who of you who may be especially fond of fountains, you can also install miniature fountains not unlike the one shown on the previous page - in either your home or office.

My good friends at Prudential Asia in Hong Kong wisely installed just such a fountain in their office premises at Alexandra House, from the day they began operations in 1987 and they have never looked back since. Prudential Asia is probably one of the most successful non-bank funded investment bankers and asset managers.

As with waterfalls, it is clever to introduce a sense of balance when creating a fountain. Do not let it be so large as to totally dominate the garden ... otherwise it will overwhelm you with too much energy, and this does more harm than good. In feng shui, keeping a sense of balance is a fundamental aspect of the practice.

A fishpond

This too is a great favourite with garden enthusiasts. In Malaysia, the keeping of beautiful *koi* or Japanese carp is a popular hobby and it makes sense to use the fishpond as a feng shui tool. In fact a fish pond is probably one of the most effective ways of creating favourable and auspicious *sheng chi*.

The introduction of fish is also very propitious since fish is generally regarded as one of the symbols of wealth and good fortune. The Chinese often refer to it when speaking about growth and expansion.

Fishponds need not be elaborate or too large. However they should be located in the north, east or southeast sectors of the garden. It is also pertinent to remind housewives that ponds and especially fishponds must never be located on the right hand side of the main door (inside looking out). This is because although they may be auspicious and bring wealth, they also bring additional wives and/or concubines.

This is an elaborate fish pond. Very auspicious.

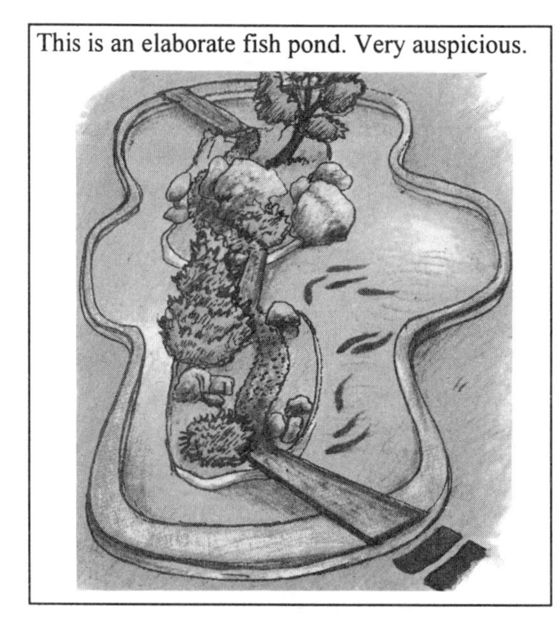

Feng shui masters warn that when a pond is located on the right hand side of the main door, the men of the family tend to stray or have a wandering eye, and even worse even leave the wife altogether. So do be careful ladies. You do not want a successful husband and then lose him to someone else !

The ponds illustrated on this page are just two suggestions of the shapes you can have for your fishponds. As shown, it is also possible to combine other auspicious symbols like waterfalls and fountains. The diagram on the left here shows a fishpond with the figure eight, which according to the Chinese is a very auspicious number. Both of the ponds shown here are suitable for keeping colourful Japanese carp. Please note that ponds should be deep enough and water kept moving.

A NOTE ON FISH It might interest readers to know that the Chinese of Hong Kong and Malaysia are extremely fond of the beautiful *Arowana*, which is generally referred to as **the feng shui fish**. This is a freshwater tropical fish found in the fast moving rivers of Pahang in West Malaysia, in the upper reaches of the rivers of Borneo and also in Indonesia.

They are extremely expensive and when fully grown can sometimes fetch several thousand dollars - especially if their scales have noticeably transformed from the original silver colour into either gold or pinkish red. It is believed that when this happens, it is a clear indication that the millions are coming !! Arowanas grow fast especially when fed on a diet of live goldfish. Usually one large aquarium should contain only one fish. When kept in a pond they should not be kept in pairs and instead, there should be either one, three, five or seven of them together - all odd numbers.
The picture shown on this page is a very good drawing of the **arowana.**

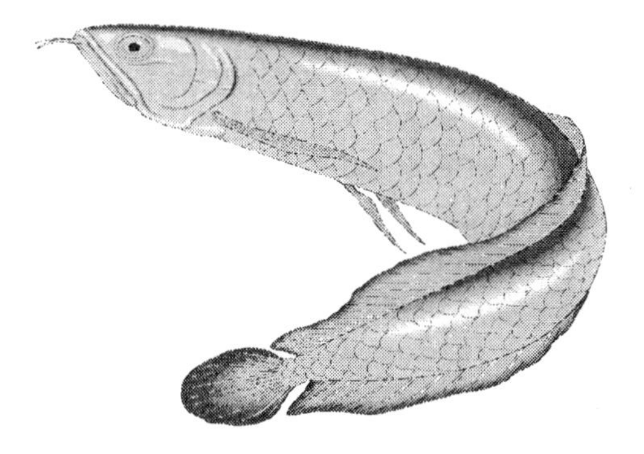

Other favourites for feng shui purpose is the goldfish, which the feng shui experts advise me should be kept in numbers of nine with eight red/gold ones and a single black fish. Keeping goldfish and arowana. are supposed to be extremely good feng shui for retail businesses especially the restaurants business.
Readers may also wish to know that should any of the fish die, it is no cause for alarm - since it is strongly believed that when this happens, they have merely succeeded in warding off some serious bad luck for the resident. Such bad luck may refer to a small burglary, being the victim of petty theft or some minor accident. Strange as this may seem, when I fell off my horse and had a serious concussion some four years ago, that same day four of my most beautiful Japanese carp died for no reason at all. I concluded that they must have taken the rap for me that day !
Otherwise I might have been more seriously injured.

Swimming Pools

The general feeling about swimming pools in the home is negative. Most feng shui experts do not really recommend the building of swimming pools in the home unless the house is enormous, with sprawling grounds and looks more like a country club, than your modest average size bungalow. This is because swimming polls tend for the most part to overwhelm the house. They are large parcels of water which create imbalance and when located in the wrong sector of the garden resulting in incompatibility of the elements, they end up causing more misfortune than good fortune. Secondly swimming pools tend also to be rectangular in shape and this could inadvertently create pernicious *shar chi* caused by its sharp angle corners. If directed at a door, this too could create misfortune.

If you are one of those who really value having a pool around, my suggestion is that you keep it a relatively modest size, and also that you have it *round, oval* or *kidney* shape. If the shape of the pool seems to wrap around the house, it could be quite auspicious since this simulates an auspicious configuration of water. If you feel having a pool that is too small defeats the purpose of having one, then I suggest you do away with the idea altogether. Go to your favourite club if you want a swim !

My feng shui *si fu* in Malaysia - Mr. Yap Cheng Hai - has often regaled me with stories of how great fortunes and great political names of a past era fell because of their inauspicious swimming pools. My strong recommendation is therefore to forget about swimming pools as I had to do !

The beautiful gold fish is extremely popular with small businessmen in Hong Kong - indeed it would be a rare establishment indeed that did not have an aquarium filled with ***nine*** *of these creatures. Gold fish of this type however are best kept indoors.*

GETTING THE LOCATION CORRECT

While it is easy enough to gain a knowledge of the auspicious symbols of water, it is really something else when it comes to actually installing one in the home. Usually this causes some problems because practice is always more tricky than theoretical knowledge.

The best and easiest way of locating the structures in the correct corner of the garden is to make an effort to demarcate the garden into nine sectors - like the Lo Shu square which has nine square grids. Next get a compass and mark out the various compass sectors. Thirdly, match the element of each sector and then refer to the section on element compatibility.

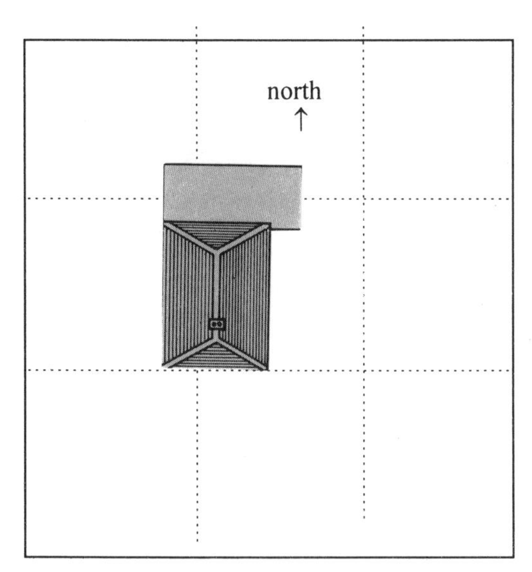

In theory this sounds easy, and it is if your land were perfectly square or even just regular in shape, as in the example shown in the sketch here. Then it involves merely a simple superimposing of the grid onto a drawing of the land. It of course involves measuring the garden, using a tape and markers. In the sketch you can see that the dotted lines enable you to establish the boundaries of the various sectors. Then it becomes easy to decide on the best location for your water structures.

When confronted with irregular shaped land the exercise does tend to get a bit tricky. In such situations, it often becomes necessary to be a little creative depending on the nature of the irregularity of the land. For instance if the land is **L shaped** or **U shaped**, the consensus is that you can assume that certain corners are deemed to be missing. If these happen to be your auspicious corners, then tough ! You will have to live with one less favourable corner. This is why feng shui experts always recommend regular shaped plots of land when asked to give advice to potential house or land buyers.

When the land is triangular in shape, or is too long at one end or it tapers to a narrow back, then the use of the Lo Shu type grid is not possible.

This means that certain key compass directions may be deemed to be in small supply, and you will just have to make do with what little of any direction there is. Look at the example reproduced here where the land is long and tapered. It should be obvious that certain sectors are in lesser supply than others. Also because of the main door facing towards the north, pond1's location while it may be acceptable for the door is located in the Northwest sector which represents metal. Thus in terms of element compatibility, it is not as acceptable as pond 2.

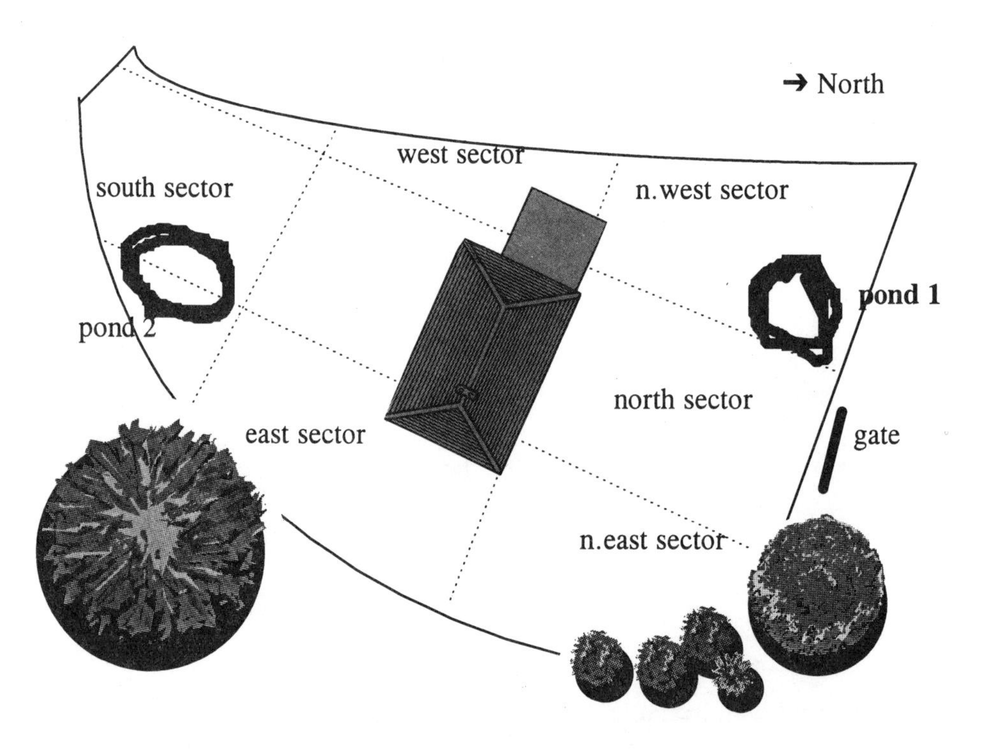

From the sketch above it is also easy to see how an attempt has been made to superimpose the nine sectors of the Lo Shu square even though the shape of the land is irregular. This exercise assists in the practice by making it easier to demarcate the various compass sectors.

If you decide to construct any of the water structures mentioned in this chapter, it is a good idea for you to make some accurate measurements of your garden or surrounding land so that the compass sectors get demarcated efficiently. This helps you to get the sector correct.

Here's another example to make the location of water structures clearer. This time the illustration has been made three dimensional to make it easier for the reader to visualise the location of a pond in an excellent sector i.e. the south east sector, a sector which not only symbolizes money and wealth but is also symbolic of wood, an element that is most compatible with water.

This is because water is deemed to make wood grow, and thus having a pond placed in a location as indicated in the sketch would be good feng shui. Also, from the main door looking out the pond is on the left hand side of the door and gate and is thus also excellent for the women of the household. Altogether then an excellent location for a water structure.

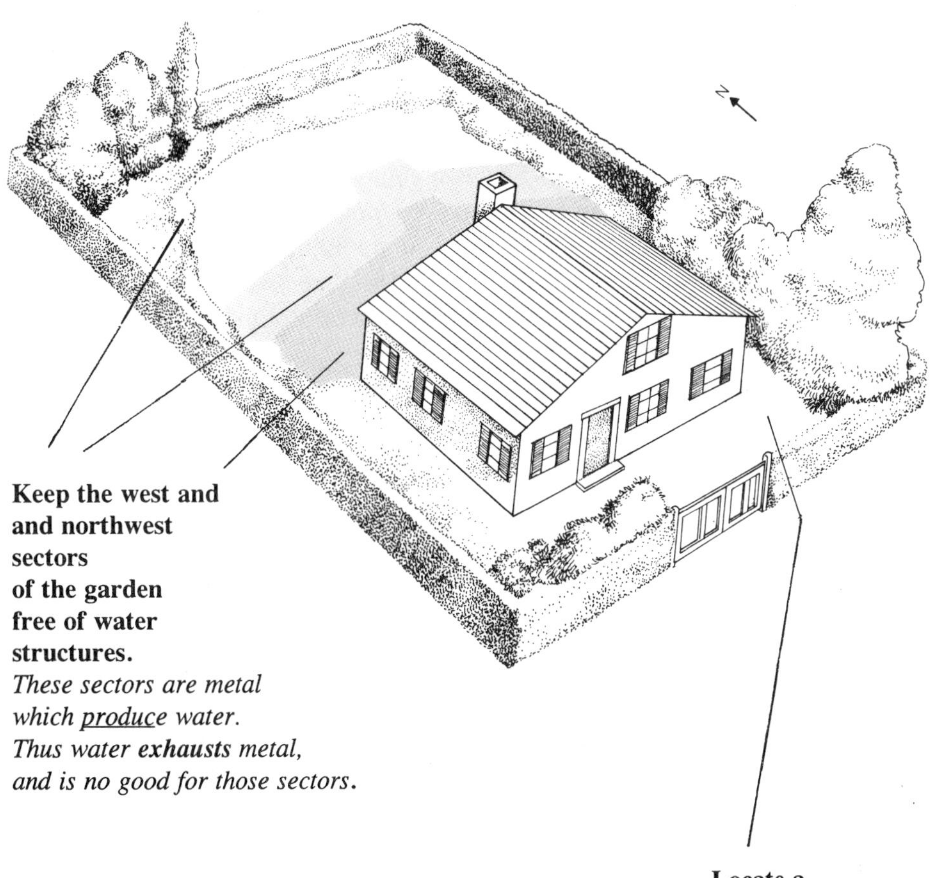

ACTIVATING THE DRAINS OF A HOUSEHOLD

No water feng shui can be complete if the **drains** of a household or building are not taken into consideration. I am referring only to exposed drains, where the flow of water can be seen. Anything that is covered from view can safely be factored out of the equation since these are regarded as being non existent.

While drains may seem rather insignificant, their influence over the intangible forces which create good or bad feng shui can sometimes be very spectacular. Auspicious drain flows are so effective and so subtle in attracting good feng shui luck that anyone interested in the practice of feng shui for wealth and money, should definitely focus on them as part of the practice. The formula for doing this correctly is explained in Chapter Three. Match your door direction to each of the categories of doors listed, and then see which are the best configurations and directions for your house.

Where necessary, make suitable corrections if you discover that your existing drain flows are inauspicious. Often, the effect of unfortunate feng shui may not be felt during the early years or when your *heaven luck* (according to your astrological readings) indicate you are going through a good period. But when all other indications turn sour and you are living through a bad period, inauspicious water feng shui cause the bad luck to be seriously compounded. This is what happened to several high profile successful men who seemingly lost everything all at once !

Bad water feng shui is therefore not always immediately noticeable. On the other hand if your water feng shui (and other feng shui configurations) are auspicious then even when you are living through a bad patch, you will come out relatively unscathed. Any loss you suffer will be minimized - what the experts refer to as *overcoming a bad period.* Those in business will somehow pull through, while those in the professions will escape getting entangled in serious difficulty.

PUBLIC DRAINS

When investigating the potential for activating good water feng shui for your house, it is also necessary to determine how the public drains outside your house are located vis-à-vis your land.

Domestic drains in modern houses are normally designed to flow round a house before exiting onto a public drain outside. These public drains may be located either in front, at the back or even by the side of your house or land.

Their orientation and direction of flow also affects your feng shui. Sometimes their location can also create difficulties for you in that you may not be able to let your drains flow out in the direction that you wish because the public drain is *inconveniently* located.

Look at the example shown here.
The public drain is located by the South side of the house. The formula recommends that the water should exit via the North/Northeast for residents to tap the best direction of exit flow. But this is difficult, thereby forcing the residents to use other less auspicious directions of exit flow.

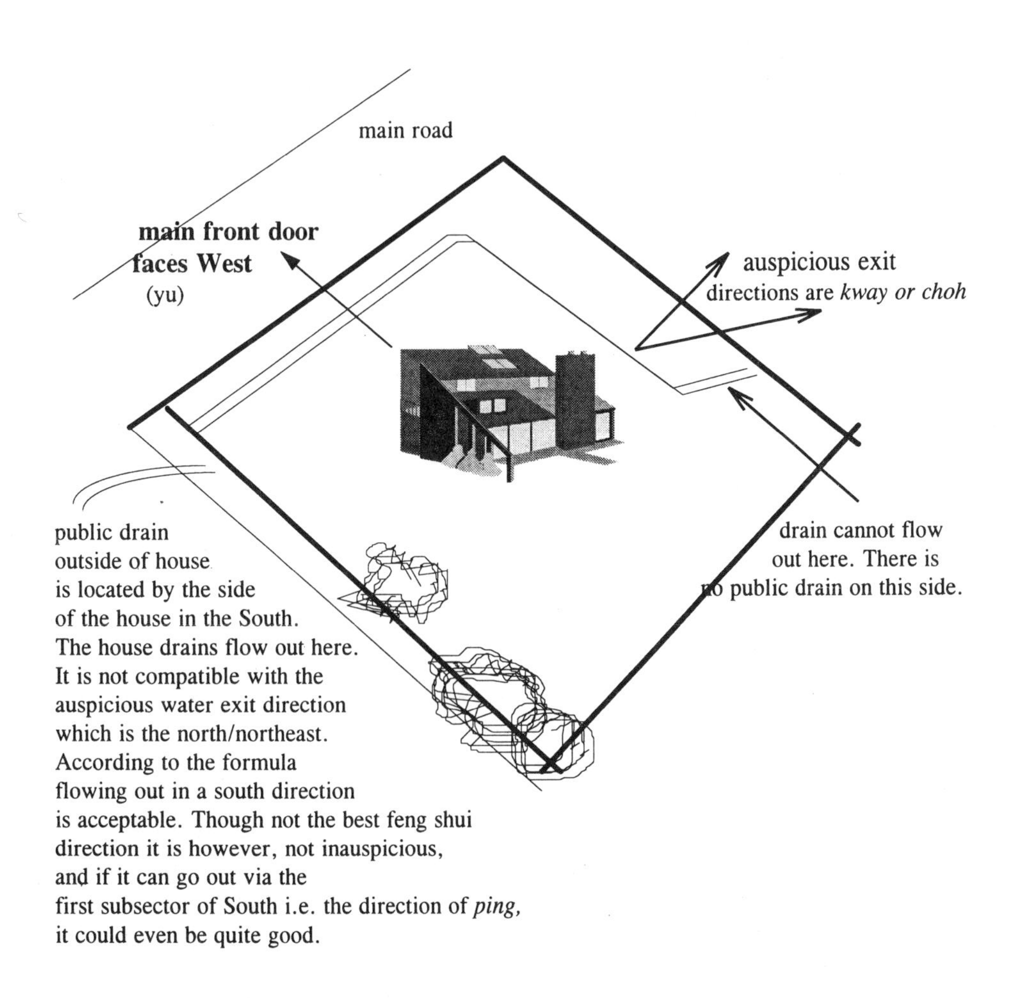

The previous example alerts you to the practical aspect of the formula before you start to examine the formula itself. It highlights a bungalow house, and the problem of implementation there can also be useful when considering large multi level buildings. **The example shown on this page puts the spotlight on link houses.**

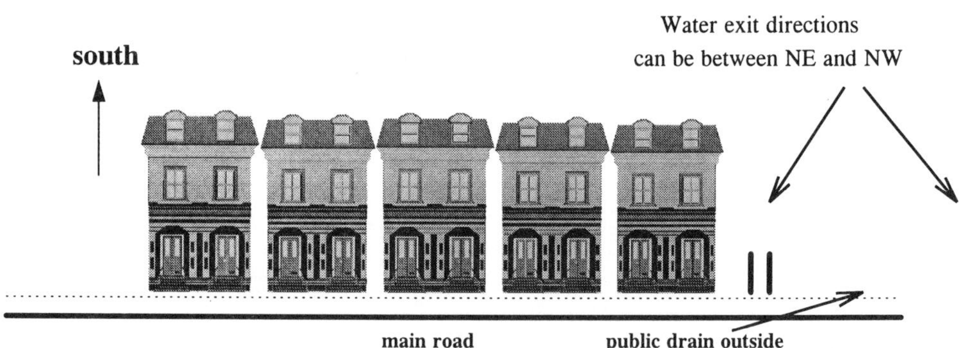

With link houses, the exit direction of drains is often constrained by the location of the public drain outside. As shown above, the houses in the centre probably cannot even have drains as there are probably no gardens. If there is a small plot of garden in front of the houses (as is the case with modern link houses built in industrial estates), and there is enough land to construct a proper exit drain, residents can select exit directions that are auspicious. In the example above house drains can exit in any direction between northeast and northwest.

Please remember that irrespective of the **length** of the exit drain, as long as the direction is clearly discernible, the orientation will be deemed correct.. There is however insufficient land to construct a water dragon. Owners of link houses are recommended to try and take advantage of auspicious directions that do not require what is referred to as the *hundred steps turnaround*. As the phrase implies, orientations requiring that condition can only be adopted when you have at least a hundred feet of land in your garden. Lest the reader feel disappointed at this, I hasten to add that the water formula's recommendations on the most auspicious orientation and direction i.e. given as **the first exit direction** in each of the twelve categories of doors does not necessarily require the construction of a water dragon. Linkhouse owners should try to tap their **first** direction instead of trying to build a water dragon which requires more stringent and difficult requirements.

CHAPTER THREE
THE WATER DRAGON FORMULA

The thirsty dragon gets water
Good fortune has come
Happiness is reflected on his face.
Every plan goes according to desire;
Here after …
good fortune follows automatically.

"*The lake has risen up to heaven*
The image of ***break through***
Thus the superior man
Dispenses riches downward
And refrains from resting on his virtue"
from the **I Ching**, on the Trigram Kuai

CHAPTER THREE

Before proceeding to the detailed references on favourable and unfavourable orientations of water flow contained in this chapter, it is advisable to first get very familiar with the *luo pan*, or feng shui geomancer's compass. The *luo pan* featured here is a very simplified version of this compass but it is an adequate tool for practicing water feng shui according to the formula given. In this context please be aware that not all feng shui Masters use exactly the same type of *luo pan*, although normally the first few inner circles may contain the same information.

Usually, by the time they attain *si-fu* status i.e. regard themselves as genuine Masters, they usually have either their own version of the *luo pan*, or have one that had been given to them by their Master, from whom they originally learnt the science. Sometimes, when they themselves become so advanced in their knowledge they may have one that is custom made according to their own codes and meanings, culled from years of practice.

Mr. Yap Cheng Hai, who actively practices the water dragon feng shui, as well as three other methods based on other formulas, uses six different compasses - some large and some smaller ones. He refers to them to counter-check on directions whenever he encounters difficulty in using one or two of the formulas. This is because, in the practice of feng shui, it is not always possible to follow any single formula to the exclusion of others.

The amateur practitioner should thus make it a point to also check other dimensions of feng shui science, especially in using the formulas pertaining to their own personal auspicious directions, as well as make the calculations relating to the intangible forces caused by time considerations. These two formulas have already been dealt with in two of my earlier books. Landscape considerations i.e. the topography of the physical terrain should also not be ignored.

For beginner practitioners, it is NOT necessary to purchase a *luo pan*. To start with, they are quite expensive. But more to the point, it is unlikely the beginner practitioner can really understand the deeper meanings indicated by single word descriptions in most of the compasses.

Far better to use the version given in this chapter as it is contains only the salient references required and is thus a simplified version.

In the *luo pan* reproduced on this page, the important rings to take note of are the two outer rings, which show the three subsectors of each of the eight compass directions. From the compass you will see that there are exactly 24 such sub sectors (3 subsectors X 8 directions = 24). These 24 subsectors indicate the exact location of main doors for investigating water feng shui.

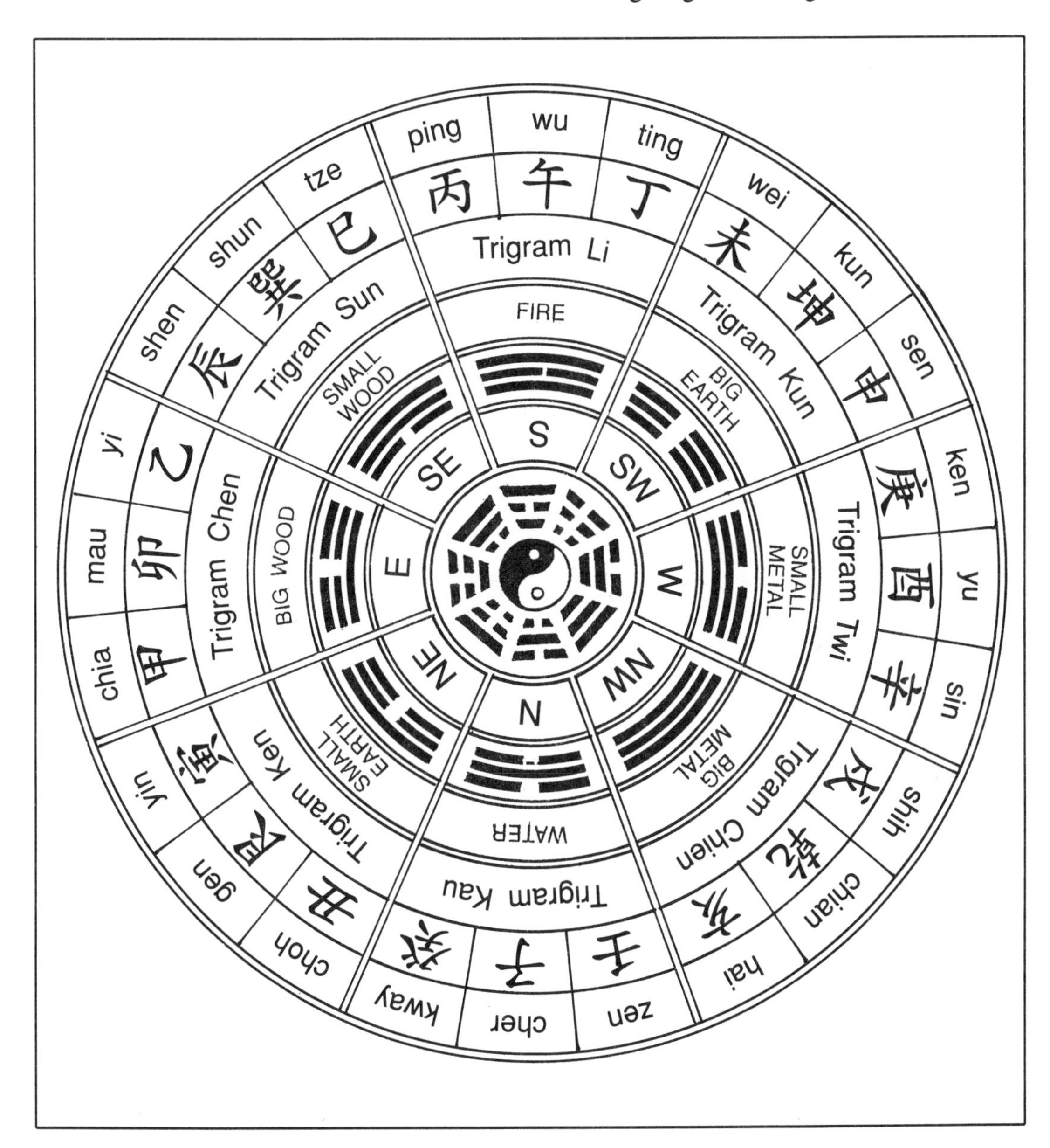

THE WATER FORMULA LUO PAN

Thus:
Note that for the direction South, the three sub sectors are *ping, wu and ting*. When investigating the favourable water flows of your building or house, the first thing you must do is to find out in which sub sector, your main door is located. This is the first step in finding out how the water should flow around, and in view of the main door.

The three sub sectors for the direction North are *zen, cher and kway*.
The three sub sectors for the direction East are *chia, mau and yi*.
The three sub sectors for the direction West are *ken, yu and sin*.

The three sub sectors for the direction South East are *shen, shun and tze*.
The three sub sectors for the direction South West are *wei, kun and sen*.
The three sub sectors for the direction North East are *choh, gen and yin*.
The three sub sectors for the direction North West are *shih, chian and hai*.

When you try to locate the exact sub-sector where your main door is located, first use a normal compass to find out the direction the door is facing. The direction is taken from inside the house looking out. Normally from a *luo pan* one will be able to see immediately which sub-sector the door is located at, but for the amateur practitioner, the best and most scientific way is to use the western method of computation, which is to measure the exact degrees, bearing north, the door's direction is facing. This way, there will be little or no room for error.

If you know that the entire circle equals 360 degrees, and you know that this is divided into 24 sub-sectors in all, then each segment or sub-sector will be equivalent to 15 degrees. From this, we can calculate the exact measurement of each of the sub-sectors.

If the exact bearing NORTH is 0/360 degrees, then the subsector named *kway* in the North segment (for example), will be bearing 7.5 degrees to 22.5 degrees **from** the direction North. This reference of the exact angle in terms of degrees bearing from the direction North is an accurate way of taking measurements of orientations.

To make it simple for quick references to be made, the exact measurements of the sub-sectors have been calculated and is summarised in the illustration on the following page.

Angles of the four cardinal directions:
North: 0/360 degrees; South: 180 degrees;
East: 90 degrees; West: 270 degrees;

The angles of the 24 sub sectors are indicated in the sketch below:
In the Northeast: *choh* is bearing 22.5 -37.5 degrees from North, *gen* is bearing 37.5 to 52.5 degrees from north, and *yin* is bearing 52.5 to 67.5 degrees from north. Thereafter, circling round, and knowing that each sub sector has a reading of 15 degrees, it is possible to then calculate the exact degree of any of the relevant angles. This precise measurement of the angle is absolutely vital in the practice of water feng shui, not only in getting the door location correct, but later also when building the physical structures of the drain or other water structure.

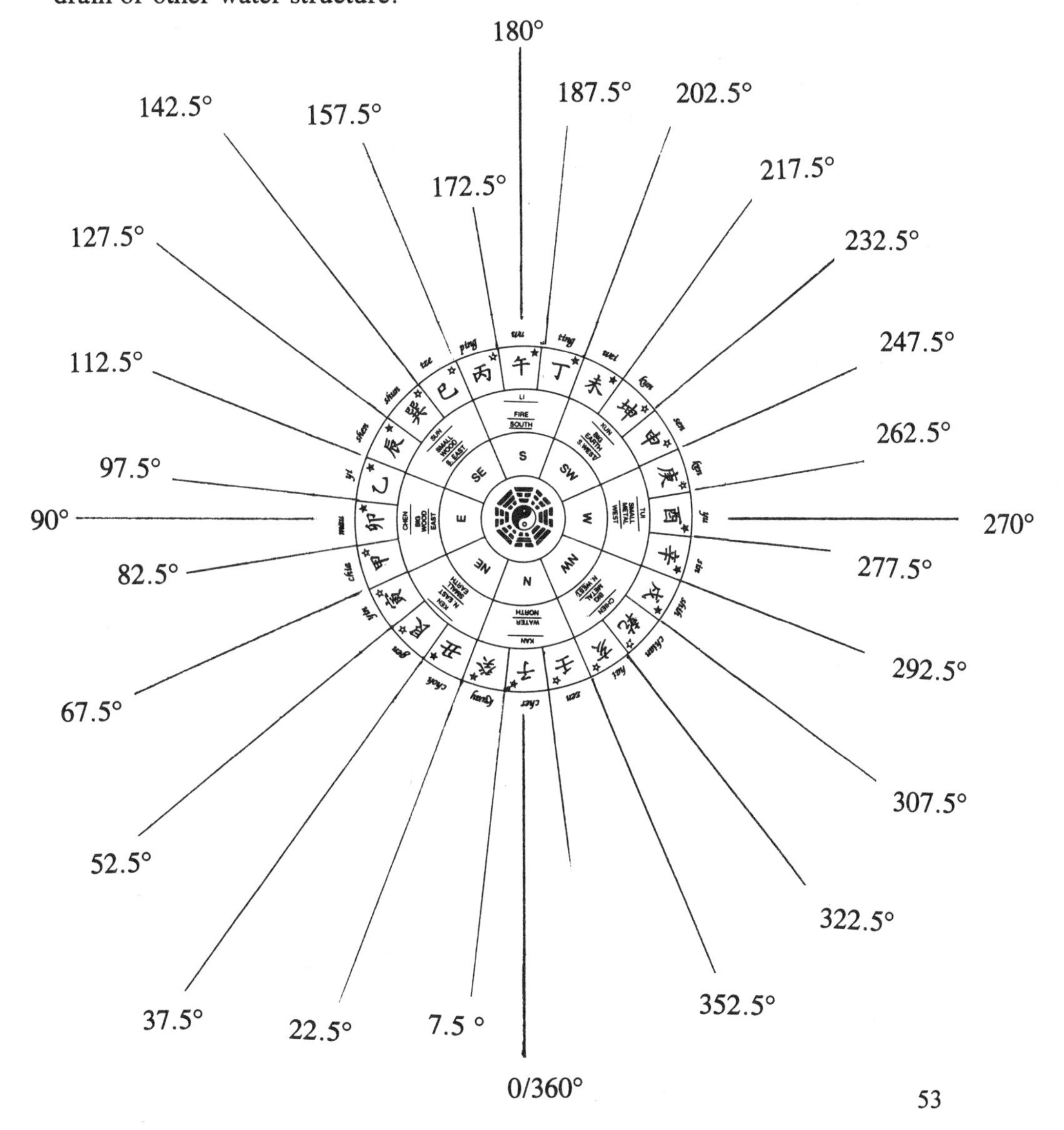

Angles of Water Flow

After you have understood how you can measure the angle of the main door by using any of the western style compasses that are freely available, you can also use the same method to draw out the angle of water flows. This is the most vital part of the actual construction of structures to conform to feng shui recommendations.It is also important to be familiar with the symbolic relationship of the different types of water angles to each of the five elements. This allows you to make sure that the shapes of the angles of water flows in each part of your garden will not clash with the element of that particular sector. The sketches on this page show the different types of water flows. Their suitability for each of the sectors of your garden is also indicated.

WOOD water (suitable for East, Southeast, and South)
METAL/GOLD water (suitable for the West, Northwest, and North)
FIRE water (suitable for the South, Southwest and Northeast)
EARTH water (suitable for Southwest, Northeast, West and Northwest)
WATER water(suitable for the North, east and Southeast)

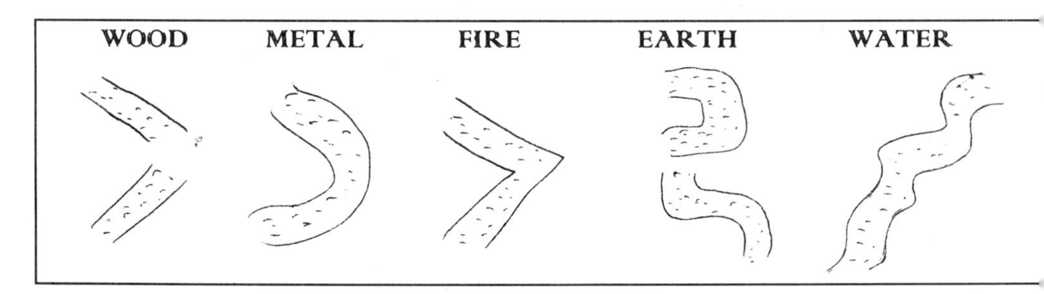

Entrances and Exits of Water

When you start referring to the formula, make note of any special instructions that applies to your situation regarding to the entrance and exit of water in your garden. The entrance of water is NOT as crucial as the exit.. Usually the manual stays silent on entrances except for certain categories of doors. On water exits however, the instructions are usually very explicit and it is really important to get the angle of the water flow correct. Try to be accurate in your measurement of the angle(s) recommended as being auspicious for your situation. There may also be instances when you will find it physically impossible to let the water flow out at the angle recommended. If you encounter such a situation, try to use alternative angles given

TWELVE CATEGORIES OF DOOR DIRECTIONS

According to this method of feng shui, there are twelve categories of door directions. Thus each category is made up of two subsectors. These twelve categories are indicated as follows:

Category One:

Main door faces *ping* or *wu* ie generally in the South direction.

Category Two:

Main door faces *ting* or *wei* ie generally in the South or Southwest direction.

Category Three:

Main door faces *kun* or *sen* ie generally in the Southwest direction.

Category Four:

Main door faces *ken* or *yu* ie generally in the West direction.

Category Five:

Main door faces *sin* or *shih* ie generally in the West and Northwest direction.

Category Six:

Main door faces *chian* or *hai* ie generally in the Northwest direction.

Category Seven:

Main door faces *zen* or *cher* ie generally in the North direction.

Category Eight:

Main door faces *kway* or *choh* ie generally in the North or NEeast direction.

Category Nine:

Main door faces *gen* or yin ie generally in the Northeast direction.

Category Ten:

Main door faces *chia* or mau ie generally in the East direction

Category Eleven:

Main door faces *yi* or *shen* ie generally in the East or Southeast direction.

Category Twelve:

Main door faces *shun* or *tze* ie generally in the Southeast direction.

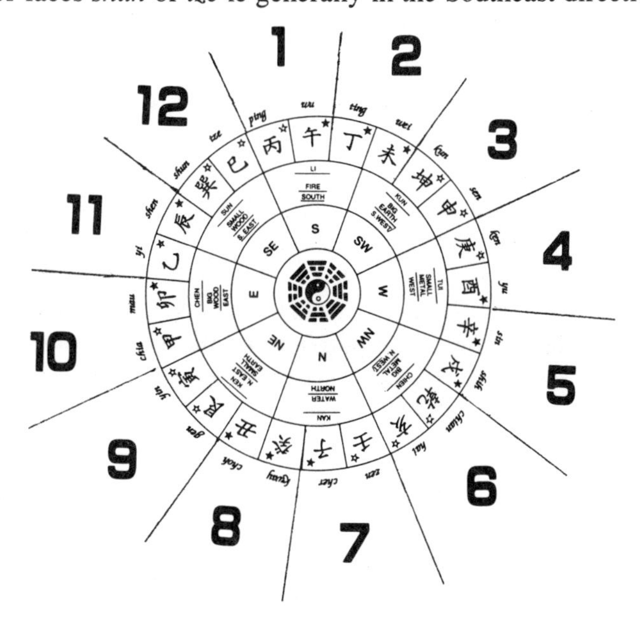

Twelve Water Flows for each Category

There are twelve different ways the water flow of any house or building can be designed, just as there are twelve different angles or orientations for the water to **exit** the compound. In the following pages, each of the twelve categories of doors will be treated separately so that the twelve possible water flows in each category of door will be dealt with.

To use the formula, first measure the exact location of your main door to determine which category your house belongs to. Then refer to the section of the text which deals with your door category. From there you will be able to devise a suitable plan for the most auspicious water flow for your house or building. Before you start to construct or change your drains please note **especially** the following:

- the entrance direction of your water (if any)
- the exit direction of your water. (Vitally important)
- whether a well is required before water exits from the house
- the direction of flow in front of your house (if left to right or right to left)
- suggestions regarding contours and levels(if any)
- suggestions for water loops (if any)

When applying the directions given to your particular situation, it is important to investigate the existing flow of your drains, and whether there are any existing pools, ponds or fountains, since these water structures must be factored into the whole picture. When you have many drains all flowing different directions, it is necessary to devise ways for the water to first collect in a well of some kind before letting it flow out of the house compound. If there are any natural streams or public drains just outside your house or building, and within sight of your main door, you have to determine whether they can be incorporated into your water dragon plan, and if so how you can do so using the directions given. If they happen to be flowing in the wrong direction, it is necessary to build either a fence, or plant some bushes or a hedge to block out the sight of water. By demarcating unsuitable water flows out of sight of the main door you would have diffused or reduced the bad effects of a wrong direction flow.

The application of the water dragon formula can have many different permutations and interpretations, and often times the easiest way to go about it is to keep the design of the drains or artificial streams as simple as possible.

CATEGORY ONE:
Door faces *ping* or *wu* (generally South)

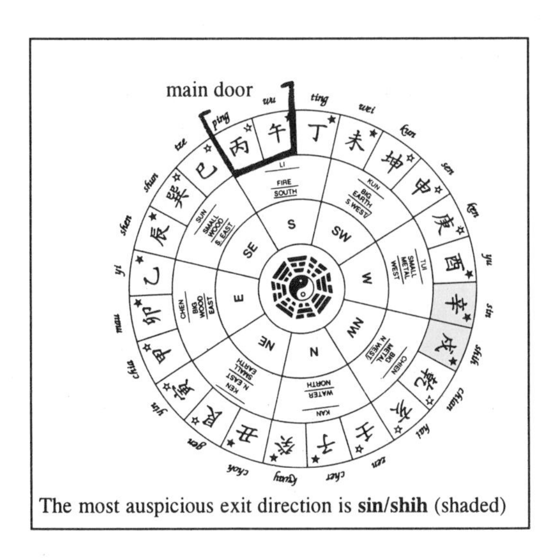

The most auspicious exit direction is **sin/shih** (shaded)

Direction of water flow in front, past the main door of the house or the building must flow from **left to right**, the direction taken from **inside** the house. For this category of door direction there are three very good exit directions. If possible try and tap the first direction indicated as this is the best; and if this is not possible then try to tap the second or third alternative. Most of the other water exit directions spell some misfortune or other and it is wise to make some effort to correct this if your existing water flow is inauspicious in this way.

The first exit direction:

This is the best, most auspicious exit direction for your water. This has your drain flowing out of your compound in either a *sin* or a *shih* direction i.e. in a direction bearing between **277.5° to 307.5° from North**. If you can follow this exit direction you will enjoy three combinations of luck.

Precious jewels will flow to the residents, and the master of the house will wear a jade belt around the waist. He could even be elevated to the ranks of nobility and enjoy widespread recognition. Prosperity will be exceptional and there will be a great abundance of money and wealth luck. In addition this house will have many descendants who will be loyal and who will bring recognition and honour to the family name. All the sons and daughters will be intelligent, and the direction is equally good for both the men and women of the household. Every type of luck will flow into the house.

If this water direction also meets up with good landscape feng shui, i.e. with the green dragon white tiger formation like in an armchair formation, and with the turtle hills protecting behind, residents in this household will enjoy the kind of wealth that can easily compare with the richest man in Chinese history ! If you are able to tap this direction, make the water flow big and abundant, as big as the size of your house can take in terms of balance. And if the water is a natural river passing your house, and it flows away from the house in a *sin* or a *shih* direction, truly, your good fortune knows no bounds ! This excellent water exit direction has been shaded in the diagram.

The second exit direction:
This has the water flowing out of the compound in a *ting* or *wei* direction. Although second best, it is still an excellent direction to tap in case you are unable to use the best direction. Build your drain such that it flows out of the compound in a generally South/Southwest direction, bearing between **187.5° to 217.5°** from North on the compass. Do be very exact when you build your drain. This is shown on the sketch here where the *ting* & *wei* directions have been shaded. If you succeed in tapping this exit direction for your water flow, you will definitely become rich, and it is also likely that the man of the house will attain a very high position of power in Government. Residents of such a household can enjoy a long life and there will be many descendants. Money and wealth luck abound.

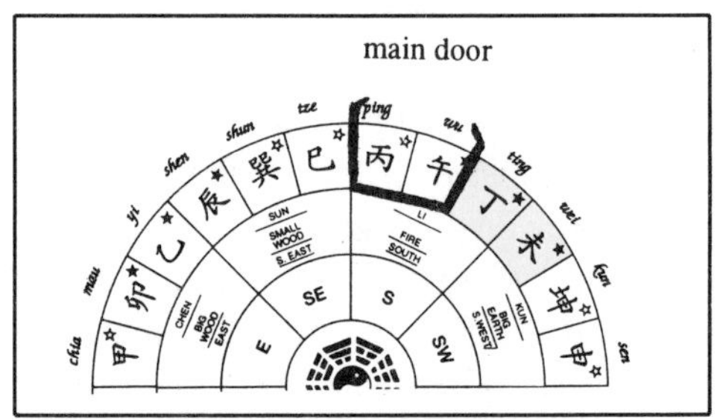

The third exit direction:
Here the water must flow from **right to left**, and it flows out of the house compound in a *chia* direction i.e. bearing between **67.5° and 82.5° from North**. This direction is as good as the second direction as there will also be plenty of wealth luck. A high position in Govt. is indicated for the master of the household. There is a great deal of money luck.
However this is a very difficult direction to tap. This is because the water MUST NOT go into either the *mau* or the *yin* direction (the two directions that lie next to the auspicious *chia* direction. It is therefore necessary to be very careful. Otherwise all the women in the household will become wanton and encounter extreme misfortune - and may even die ! The two directions *yin* and *mau* represent the two pillars of extreme danger for the women of the household.

The fourth exit direction:

This is when the water flows out of the house compound in a *shun* or *tze* direction. This is an inauspicious direction as it is believed to indicate a meeting with the death path. This direction can cause the death or maiming of the best son in the household. Business will go haywire, and could even collapse. There is loss of money and assets indicated, and even the health of the residents will not be good. Illnesses involving the coughing out of blood and soft legs (paralysis) are indicated. If water flows out in this direction (generally Southeast between 127.5° to 157.5° from North, no matter which direction the water flows i.e. left to right or vice versa, misfortune is definitely indicated. If your drain is flowing out of your house in this direction you are strongly urged to do something about it. Otherwise your troubles will continue to pile up.

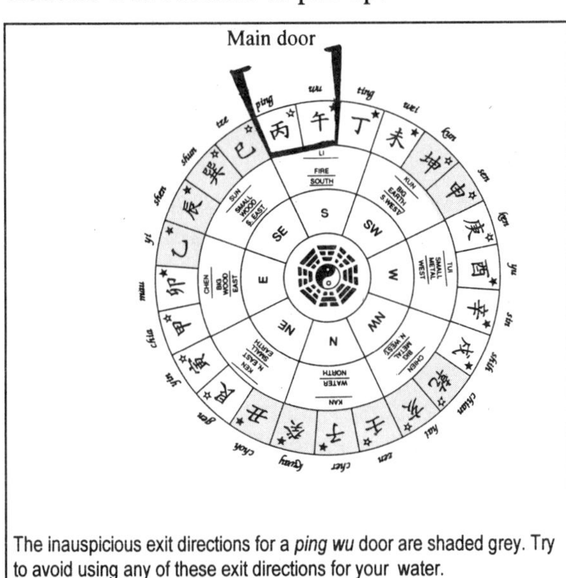

The inauspicious exit directions for a *ping wu* door are shaded grey. Try to avoid using any of these exit directions for your water.

The fifth exit direction:

This is the *yi shen* direction, and irrespective of the left to right or right to left flow, if your water exits in this direction, you will lose your property and other assets. This is a direction that spells disaster, and the youngest son is especially vulnerable. The young women in the family will also be hurt, and could suffer from extreme illnesses. This is an unfortunate direction.

The sixth exit direction:

This is when the water flows out in the *kway choh* direction. Again this is an inauspicious direction indicating a loss of money; and grave misfortune coming to the children. Prospects for improvement look dim, and it is far better to change your drains if they are presently leaving the house this way.

The seventh exit direction:

This is *zen cher* direction - once more a most inauspicious indication. Miscarriages, the loss of money and a very bad ending - all indicated. There will be total loss, and even if you succeed in living a long life, you will get poorer as you grow older. This is a most inauspicious direction.

The eighth exit direction:
This is when water flows out in the *chien hai* (northwest) direction. Again it is inauspicious, and should the household have sons, they will lose them; And if they live a long life, in later years they will experience poverty. Far better to avoid this direction.

The ninth exit direction:
This is when the water exits in **ken yu** (west) direction. The reading for this direction is that it is moderately OK. The household will have a shortage of sons; and will suffer some losses, especially of assets and properties; but there may some benefits in the beginning. The third child will get hurt. Generally, this direction says that if there are sons, then there will not be money; and if there is money there will not be sons. This means that a rich family having this sort of water exit direction will have no luck with descendants. This is because most of the sons, even though moderately successful will die young.

The tenth exit direction:
Again not a very auspicious direction. This is when the water flows out in the *kun sen* direction(southwest). Widow-hood is indicated for such a household. The men in the family will have short lives. There will be miscarriages and a lot of poor health is indicated - vomiting blood; coughing sickness and other forms of illness associated with lung disease. Definitely no money luck here.

The eleventh exit direction:
This is a moderately good direction, and occurs when the water exits in the *gen yin* direction (northeast).There could be some money but it is not very much. This direction is not auspicious for all young children in general and for the first born child in particular.

The twelfth exit direction:
This is a moderately good direction, and water flows out in a *ping* direction. Money luck is indicated and residents can get rich. A lot of children is also possible, but not all will turn out well.
The luck of this direction is also not very stable. This direction is also dangerous. In exiting, the water must not touch *wu,* (lying just next to *ping*), because if it does, it will cause a total loss of money; and grave misfortune will overtake the family. So do be very careful if your drain is exiting in a generally south direction i.e. the same direction as your main door. It is suggested that if you have a choice this direction is best avoided.

CATEGORY TWO

Door faces *ting* or wei direction (South/Southwest)

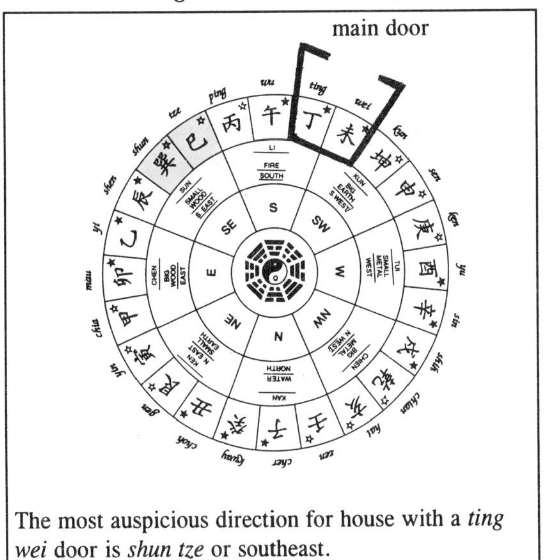

The most auspicious direction for house with a *ting wei* door is *shun tze* or southeast.

In a category two house, the direction of water flow in front of the main door should move from **right to left** for it to be auspicious, and once again, readers are reminded that this is taken from inside the house. In this category there are three excellent exit directions, and two moderately good ones. Obviously everyone would wish to tap the first direction which is the most auspicious, but if this is somehow not possible either because of the type of house you are living in, or because the main public drain outside your house makes it impossible then try to tap either of the other two good directions. At any rate, you must make strenuous efforts to correct drains that flow out in an inauspicious manner as the bad luck caused can be quite severe.

The first exit direction:

The best and most auspicious direction for the water to exit from a house with a *ting wei* main door is *shun* or *tze* i.e. in a direction bearing **127.5° to 157.5° from North**. If you construct your drain, for example to exit your compound in this direction, you will enjoy spectacular luck - considered the best kind of luck possible under this method. The indications are that there will be a great deal of money and wealth; there will be recognition, excellent reputations for every member of the household. In addition, this great good fortune and prosperity will last for a very long period of time.

There will also be excellent luck for the children of the household. Every child will achieve honours at school and later, at work, and will go on to achieve great heights in their careers. There is power and prosperity in their lives. If there are sons they could become Ministers, while the women of the household will benefit from a long and prosperous life. This water direction will also attract loyal and good mannered sons in law. Prosperity and happiness is therefore very much assured. Plus, long life is also indicated for all members of the household. Those with main doors facing this *ting wei* direction are strongly recommended to re-do their drains in a genuine attempt to create truly auspicious feng shui.

For those who live in a house with a South/SouthWest orientation at the front and are located near natural waterways, try to design your house in a fashion which has the waterway flowing in front of the door, moving from right to left, and make sure the door is facing the *ting wei* direction. Even if the river seems to exit in a wrong direction, *the flow of water right to left in front of your main door is deemed to be auspicious*. Where it does leave in the correct *shun tze* direction, then your prosperity truly knows no bounds !

The second exit direction:

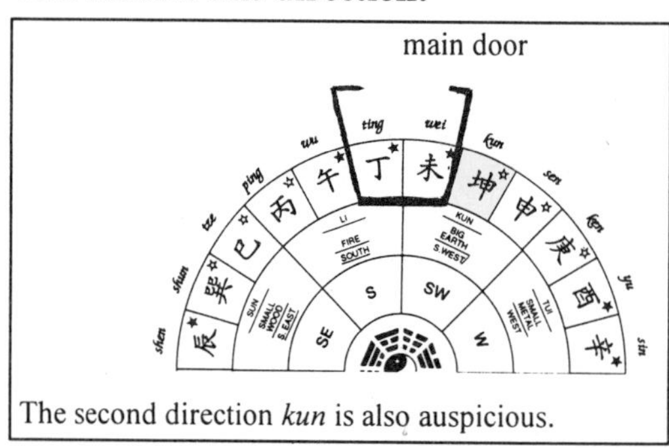

The second direction *kun* is also auspicious.

In this second exit direction, the water is again flowing from right to left; and it leaves the house compound in the *kun* direction (southwest). On the compass reading this is bearing between **217.5° to 232.5° from North**. If you are able to tap this direction correctly, you will become very rich indeed. You will have money in 10,000 cases. You will also become very noble and have the good fortune of having many sons and many descendants. All through your life you will enjoy good fortune, even during inauspicious astrological times, your feng shui luck will protect you from losses. In fact your luck is quite complete.

However when designing your exit direction, you must make very sure you do not touch either of the directions next to you i.e. *wei* or *sen*, as doing so will ruin your feng shui. It is therefore necessary to be very careful.

The third exit direction:
This is a very bad direction, which spells poverty and great misfortune. This third direction has the water leaving via the *ping* or *wu* directions, and it causes early deaths to the men of the household so that this is a house of widows. Where the men succeed in living to an old age, they will suffer from plenty of money problems, and in extreme cases could even become paupers. In addition to all this bad luck, if there happens to be a stone with an inauspicious shape (e.g. something pointed or resembling a fierce animal) in front of the *wei* direction of the house, then violence will befall the family and the head of the household could even lose his life in a violent manner.

The fourth exit direction:
This is not a particularly favourable direction, but it is also not very bad. This has the water leaving in the *yi* or *shen* direction. According to the manual, a household with this kind of water will not enjoy stable good fortune. Luck is erratic - sometimes good and sometimes bad, depending also on other factors. Members of such a household will experience a very average life.

The fifth exit direction:
Here the water leaves in either the *chia* or *mau* direction. This sort of water indicates a good beginning but a tragic ending. In early life, there could be some money and evidence of a certain amount of wealth, but in later years, the family wealth will be squandered, and property will be lost or sold. The second generation will also not come to a good end. Residents in homes which have this kind of water rarely enjoy career luck, and promotions will be hard to come by. There is definitely no money luck either.

The sixth exit direction:
This water leaves via the *gen* or the *yin* direction and it causes the family property and money to be reduced. It also causes a great deal of misfortune to befall the young children of the family, especially to the eldest son or daughter. This is an inauspicious direction of water flow and should be changed if you find your water flowing out this way.

The seventh exit direction:
The water here exits via *kway* or *choh* (North/Northeast) and this is probably the worst and most inauspicious direction. Those of you who diagnose this to be your water exit direction are very strongly urged to immediately make changes.

The eighth exit direction:
Here the water leaves via *chian* or *hai*. This is a direction which signifies a slow loss of money and property,until eventually all will be lost. Sons too will not survive and will die off young. A most inauspicious direction.

The ninth exit direction:
This has the water leaving via *sin* or *shih*, and it is an extremely inauspicious direction for those wishing to have children. This direction is one of those that cause couples to be barren. It is also a direction which signifies very poor money luck. Best avoided.

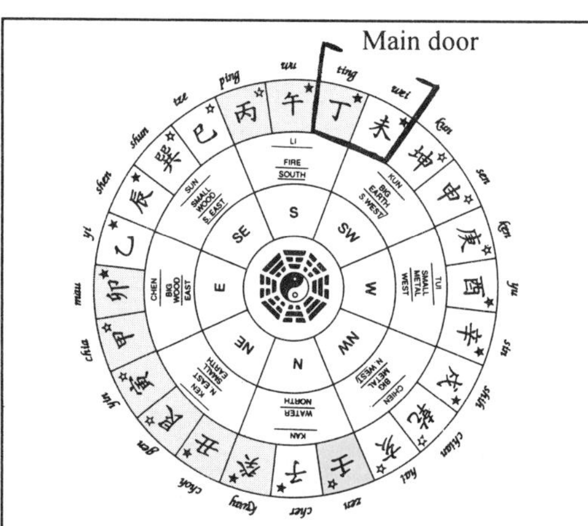

All the inauspicious exit directions of a house with a *ting wei* door are shaded grey.

The tenth exit direction:
This is an inauspicious direction, but it is not the worst. Here the water leaves via the *ken* or *yu* direction. This is a situation which spells unbalanced luck most of the time. There may be riches and even some wealth and moderately high position. However in the long run, the luck runs out and although certain members of the household may enjoy some success, once again, much of the good fortune is also short-lived. In the end the money and any good luck definitely does run out. It is a direction best avoided.

The eleventh exit direction:
This is a totally disastrous direction, with the water flowing from right to left and passing out through the *ting* direction. Avoid at all costs !

The twelfth exit direction:
here the water flows out via *zen* and it is flowing from left to right. This is an auspicious direction which can bring wealth and riches to residents. Prosperity and high position are on the cards, and there is the potential for a great deal of wealth. But this is also a direction which can be quite dangerous if done wrongly. The first thing to remember is that the neighbor direction *cher* must be avoided at all costs. If a mistake is made and the water flows out via *cher*, instead of the recommended *zen*, then plenty of bad luck will befall the residents. Also the flow of water must be on flat and low lying land. If the terrain is mountainous or has contours, all the good fortune turns into ill fortune.

CATEGORY THREE

Door faces *kun* or *sen* direction

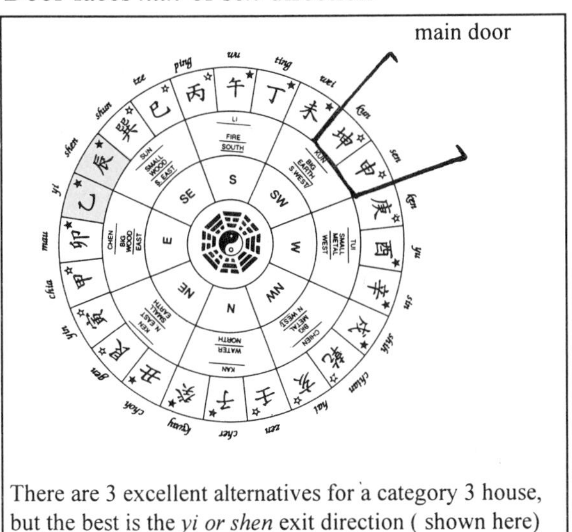

There are 3 excellent alternatives for a category 3 house, but the best is the *yi or shen* exit direction (shown here)

This house has its main door facing South/Southwest. To activate auspicious water feng shui, the water which flows past the main door should move from **right to left** (viewing it from inside the house). In this category there are three excellent exit directions for the water flow and those living in this house category should try to tap either one of them. It is useful to know also that while there is no indicated requirement that addresses the direction of the water entrance, the feng shui of the house does improve if the water flow is never allowed to dry up.

Thus while the source of the water is deemed to come from rain (i.e. from the heavens) and also from household use it is always a good idea to supplement this during dry periods with a running tap which feeds a regular and constant supply of water to the water flowing past the main door.

Also take note that the inauspicious exit directions are most dangerous, and should you find that your existing drains are flowing out via any of the unfortunate directions, you would be well advised to invest in some changes.

If you are careful with your compass readings, there is no need to get a feng shui master for this. Just be as accurate as you can with your measurements and your readings, and you will be able to undertake your own corrections.

The first exit direction:
The most auspicious exit direction for your household drain is for the water to leave via the *yi* or *shen* direction (i.e. East/Southeast). This direction bears **97.5° to 127.5° from North**. This exit direction spells tremendous good fortune for those in business as it attracts excellent luck for commercial ventures. This is also referred to as the *Golden City* direction, as it promises the path to great prosperity and abundance. Wives and sons will be supportive and filial, and prosperity will carry on for a very long time - as long as five generations. There is also the promise of high public recognition by the establishment with opportunities for rising to the nobility.

Second exit direction:

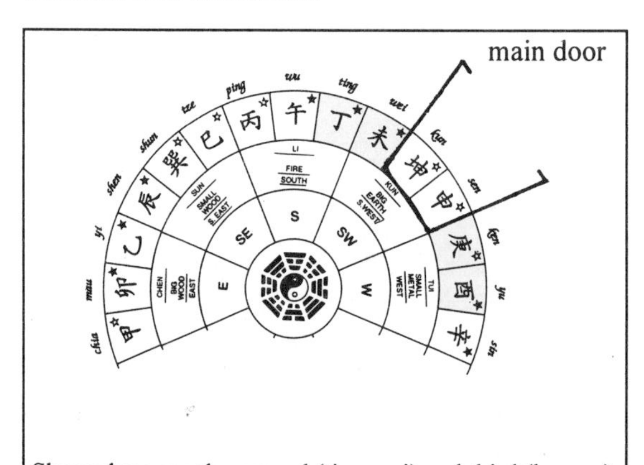

Shown here are the second (ting wei) and third (ken yu) exit directions for a category 3 house - both of which creates excellent feng shui.

If you find that for some reason you are unable to tap the first excellent direction, you can try the second exit direction which is also auspicious. This requires you to build your drain in such a way that all the water of your house leaves via the *ting* or the *wei* direction (i.e. South/Southwest) which is bearing **187.5° to217.5° from North**. The water should flow from right to left pass the main door and then collect the rest of the water from other side drains before leaving at an angle which flows in the *ting* or *wei* directions. If you do this successfully, you will definitely become prosperous. This direction is also extremely fortunate for those in politics as it spells success in political pursuits. You can attain a very high position in Government , described in the old books as Ministerial level. This direction is also very fortunate for the sons of the family especially the youngest son who will be the first amongst his brothers to attain great prosperity.

Third exit direction:
This has the water leaving the house compound or garden via the *ken* or *yu* direction (i.e. West). The exact angle is bearing **247.5° to 277.5° from North**. This direction is considered most auspicious, bringing great prosperity; enormous good fortune and plenty of excellent money making opportunities. Residents will be rich and will attain a high position in the commercial world.

Fourth exit direction:
If water from a third category house leaves via *ping* or *wu* direction, residents will enjoy moderately good fortune in the beginning, but this good fortune gradually turns bad. Despite initial success there will be failure in the long run. Reputations will suffer and the sons and daughters of the house will encounter a bad ending. This is not an auspicious direction.

Fifth exit direction:
A moderately inauspicious direction. Here the water leaves via *shun* or *tze* (in the Southeast). The reading on this exit direction is that residents will have no money luck. They will be taken advantage of, and are born losers - failing in most ventures and having a difficult time making ends meet. During the early years the children will fare well, but even hey will suffer from the bad feng shui of he house as they grow older. This is a direction best avoided.

Sixth exit direction:
This is a very unbalanced situation. Here the water exits via the *chia* or *mau* direction. It indicates a short life for the men of the household and residents will experience ups and downs in their work, career and business, sometimes enjoying good fortune and other times suffering from misfortune. There is definitely no prosperity possible and business ventures have no chance of long term success. Once again a direction best corrected.

Seventh exit direction:
A very inauspicious direction. Bad. No luck. This is when the water leaves via the *gen* or *yin* in the NorthEast. Residents suffer a great deal of sorrow and unhappiness. There are also indications of severe illnesses leading to disastrous traumas. Residents will encounter enormous difficulties to success. In fact success is most elusive.

A direction that should definitely be corrected.

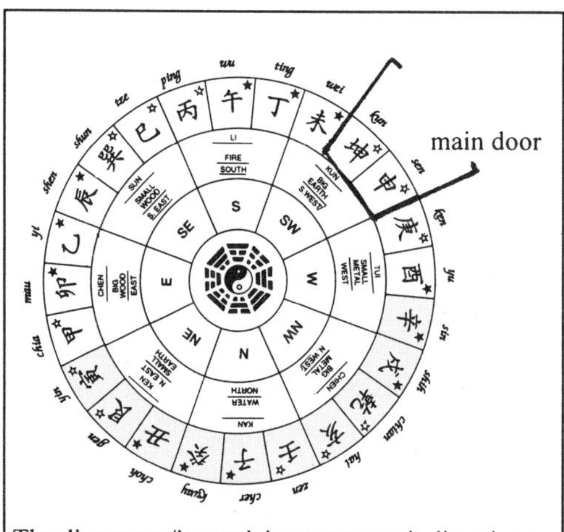

The disastrous/inauspicious water exit directions for a category three house are shaded grey.

Eighth exit direction:
This is the worst direction for this category of house. The water leaves via the *kway* or *choh* in the North/Northeast. Enormous bad luck and misfortune will follow the residents of this house. There is totally no chance for success!

Ninth exit direction:
A direction of abject poverty. Here the water leaves via either *zen* or *cher*. The family living in such a house will always be very poor, and be dogged by bad luck, Children of the household will suffer from illnesses and there is continuos discord amongst residents. Husband and wife can have no happiness.This is a direction which should definitely be corrected.

Tenth exit direction:
Here the water leaves via *sin* or *shih* in the West/Northwest. This direction has no prosperity but bad luck comes more in the form of tragedy rather than abject poverty. The household will lose its youngest or most intelligent son. Other young children could also get hurt either through illness or accident. There is failure and disaster. This direction should be corrected.

Eleventh exit direction:
This is as bad a direction as the previous one. The water leaves via *chien* or *hai* in the Northwest. In such a home, the eldest and most successful son will die. There will be loss of money and loss of blood. Most inauspicious.

Twelfth exit direction:
This is a very prosperous direction. If the water flows pass the front door from right to left and moves out of the compound via the direction *kun,* residents will enjoy great prosperity and riches. But it is vital that the outflow of water is done careful - it must not touch *sen* which lies just next to it. If done accurately this direction attracts enormous success for the older folk as well as for the children of the household. Just don't make a mistake with the direction.

CATEGORY FOUR

Door faces *ken* or *yu* direction

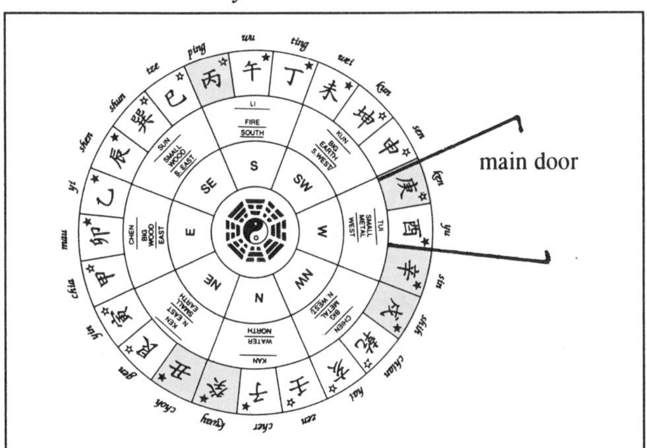

The most auspicious water dragon for a Category 4 house is for the water to flow out via *kway* or *choh* shown here.Other excellent directions are *sin/shih,, ping* and *ken* - also shown .

This house has its main door facing either of the first and second sub sectors of the west direction i.e. *ken* or *yu*. For such a house, any water passing the main door should flow from **left to right**, i.e. when viewed from inside the house. If yours is such a house you must first ensure that this direction of flow is achieved, especially in the water movement of your drain.
For this category of house, there are four excellent or auspicious directions for water exits, the last one of which (i.e. the last water direction where the water flows out via *ken*) must be practiced with great care as there are special features which also have to be incorporated for there to be excellent feng shui.

To build an auspicious water dragon in the garden, it is necessary to get the exit of the water as accurate as possible. There are no special requirements for the entrance of water - indeed the source of water is deemed to be the household itself, or the rain waters (deemed to come from heaven) so that it is the domestic drains which would best simulate the presence of the water dragon. Those who practice this method of feng shui can also try to tap into natural water flows outside the house, IF they happen to be available. In this connection, it is important not to ignore monsoon and public drains outside the house. Make certain any such drain is flowing in the auspicious left to right direction suitable for this type of house.

The first exit direction:
This has the water leaving the house compound in a *kway* or *choh* direction (North/Northeast), i.e. bearing **7.5° to 37.5° from North**. This exit orientation spells extreme good fortune for residents of the household. The metaphor used to describe this direction is three united precious jewels - big money, big position and excellent descendants. Family members will contribute to the honour of the family name, and every son will become prosperous in the long run. There will also be very long periods of business luck when everything will go according to plan. Money flows in continiuosly.This is the most auspicious direction for this type of house which is also very suitable for West group people. (Refer to the author's book on auspicious directions from birthcharts - Applied Pa Kua Lo Shu Feng Shui).

The second exit direction:
This is also a very auspicious direction of water exit, where it flows pass the main door in a **left to right** direction, and out of the compound in the *sin* or *shih* direction (West/Northwest) i.e. bearing **277.5 to 307.5 from North.** This is a very prosperous water dragon which spells long life and great respectability for the family patriarch. The boys of the family will be very smart, and even the girls will enjoy good fortune in their work and family life. Everything undertaken will meet with long term success. A very auspicious orientation.

The third exit direction:
This is also a very auspicious direction, but the water here flows in front of the main door from **right to left**, and flows out of the compound in a *ping* direction (South) i.e. bearing 157.5° to 172.5° from North. This direction will bring prosperity and nobility to the residents. There will be many children, most of whom will grow to enjoy a prosperous life style. There is however a need to be very careful, in that when you build such an exit direction it is vital that the exit flow must not touch *wu* (just next to *ping*) otherwise, the women of the household will suffer from a very flirtatious nature and come to a bad and even tragic end.

The fourth exit direction:
This is a very bad direction ! It describes the water flowing out of the house in a *sen* or *ken* direction ie almost in front of the main door in the Southwest/West direction. This is a situation of total loss and total disaster. The best and most promising son of the family could perish. There will be legal problems; loss of property, and a great deal of illness.

Members of the family could be seriously injured in an accident involving paralysis of limbs. The most vulnerable member of the family will be the second son who will be hurt first, followed by others. This is a direction which should definitely be corrected.

The fifth exit direction:
This is a loss direction and has the water leaving the compound of the house in a *ting* or *wei* direction (South/Southwest). This orientation hurts the youngest and most intelligent son. It also hurts the middle daughter or daughter in law. Residents will lose all their property, and descendants will be few. Difficulty therefore in getting children.

The sixth exit direction:
Once more, an inauspicious orientation. This is where the water leaves in *yi* or a *shen* direction (in the East/Southeast). There is danger of miscarriages, and the young son is vulnerable to hurt or illness. Not a good direction for the children of the household.

The seventh exit direction:
A moderately bad orientation; here the water leaves via *chia* or *mau* (in the east). The reading for this direction is that there is a good beginning and all seems well, but in the longer term, residents will lose. Money will flow out and children will leave the family. There is loss of descendants indicated as well. Better to correct such an orientation.

The eighth exit direction:
Here the water leaves via *gen* or *yin* in the Northeast. The children will be relatively healthy and lead average lives, but there is no money in this direction, and residents will suffer from long periods of financial difficulty. Even when the early stages of career and work look fine, in the long run, the luck is bad. This is a direction to be corrected.

The ninth exit direction:
An inauspicious orientation. The water leaves via the *zen* or *cher* direction in the North. Residents cannot live a long life. Illness and disease plague the family. Males die. There is widowhood. The third son will get hurt first, but most of the residents will suffer bad endings. There is moderate business success but luck is always in short supply. The rice urn can never be full - there is always something missing.

The tenth exit direction:
Here the water leaves via *chian* or *hai* in the Northwest. If the water leaves in this manner, men cannot live long in this house - they will either leave or suffer from debilitating disease. Children also cannot do well in such a house. Better to correct such an orientation of water flow.

The eleventh exit direction:
No money luck whatsoever in this direction of water flow, where it leaves the house via *shun* or *tze* in the Southeast. The eldest of the sons will suffer the most in such a house but everyone has their share of bad luck. It is not an auspicious direction and should be corrected as soon as possible.

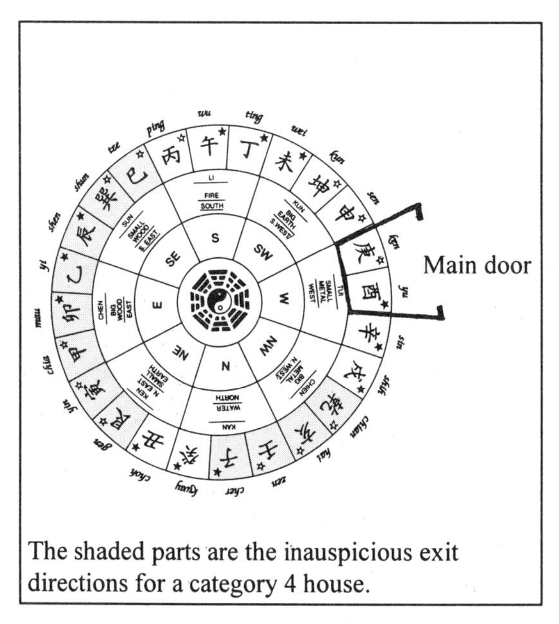

The shaded parts are the inauspicious exit directions for a category 4 house.

The twelfth exit direction:
A most auspicious direction where the water is supposed to leave via the *ken* direction in the West, i.e. bearing **247.5° to 262.5° from the North**. If the water flow is accurately constructed extremely good money luck will flow towards the residents.
However it is necessary to make certain that the exit flow of water does not touch the neighbor direction of *yu*; and also that the left hand water should be thin and small, i.e. smaller than the right hand water, otherwise much of the good luck could well dissipate. The water in this orientation should flow from **left to right**.

CATEGORY FIVE:

Door faces *sin* or *shih* direction

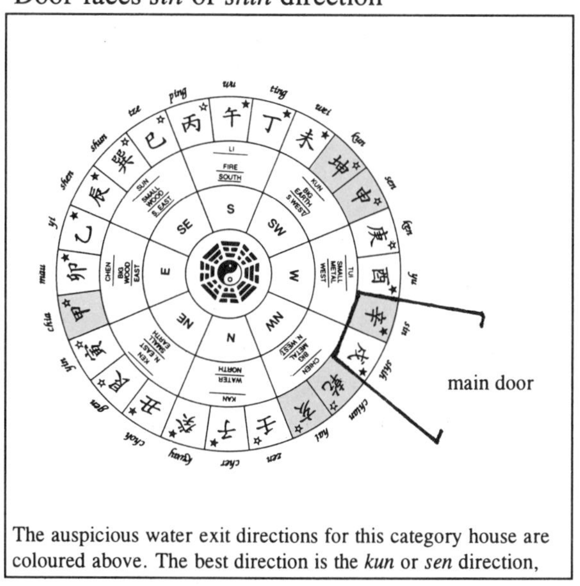

The auspicious water exit directions for this category house are coloured above. The best direction is the *kun* or *sen* direction,

This category has the main front door facing either *sin* or *shih*, i.e. the third sub sector of the West direction and the first sub sector of the Northwest direction. To establish good water feng shui, drains or any steams and rivers flowing pass the main door should flow from **right to left** (viewing from the inside of the house). This category house or building has three excellent alternative directions for their water to exit. Tap any of these directions effectively and they can be well assured of having auspicious good fortune for as long as they live there. The other orientations are inauspicious and some are totally disastrous so that by checking the water flow exit directions here with their actual flow, it is possible to make corrections, thereby transforming bad feng shui into good feng shui.

The first exit direction:

This is the most auspicious way for water to flow out of the house compound. It should flow from right to left when it passes the main door, and the requirement also states that the water must leave at an angle which corresponds to the *kun* or *sen* direction (in the Southwest) i.e. bearing **217.5° to 247.5° from North**. If done correctly, this orientation will lead to immense prosperity. Everything good will come to the residents; and the head of the household will even *get the chance to see the king* ! All the residents will benefit from the good fortune created by such a water flow.

The sons of the family will enjoy excellent reputations, have a very long period of good luck, and will develop uprightness and good moral character. Everyone in the house will prosper, especially the daughters who will be blessed with great good fortune, and the third son, who will create much wealth for the family.

The second exit direction:
This is yet another excellent direction for water exit. It is named the direction of *10,000 cases of money*, and it spells extreme great wealth and prosperity for the family. Here the water is expected to flow out via the *chien* or *hai* direction in the Northwest. In terms of compass directions this means bearing **307.5° to 352.5° from North.** There will also be good luck for residents keen on a political career, as residents will rise to a high position in Government. In addition there is also the promise of long life with a good many upright and successful descendants. An excellent direction to tap.

The third exit direction:
A direction which indicates extreme poverty luck. This is when the water flows out in the *ken* or *yu* direction in the West. It is a most inauspicious orientation as it is supposed to cause money to drain out of the house. If other feng shui indications are also bad the poverty aspects will be so extreme that residents could even become beggars. Indeed, the text warns that should there be a bad stone in the *shih* direction (i.e. the first sub sector of the Northwest corner of the house compound) , there could even be extreme violence experienced by certain members of the family, leading to a violent death. A bad stone is one which is pointed and sharp, or which resembles a fierce, unfriendly or hostile animal. It would be advisable to correct such a direction immediately, and most certainly to remove strange looking stones or structures coming from the Northwest direction.

The fourth exit direction:
This has the water leaving via the *ting* or *wei* direction and it signifies a good beginning with a very bad ending. There is loss indicated during the later years of career, and children will live apart from the parents. This is a moderately bad orientation.

The fifth exit direction:
A mixed orientation denoting a combination of good and bad, although on balance there will be more bad than good. Here the water is leaving via the *ping* and the *wu* in the South. Such an orientation should be corrected.

The sixth exit direction:
A very unlucky exit direction. Here the water flows out via the *shun* and the *tze* directions in the Southeast. When a house has this sort of flow, the indications are that there will definitely be loss of money. Young children will suffer from constant ill health, and the eldest son will bear the brunt of misfortune. Business ventures cannot succeed and even employment cannot be stable. Grave misfortune will come continuously.

The seventh exit direction:
A total disaster situation, where the water exits through *yi* or *shen* in the east/Southeast. The indication is that such a water flow causes extreme calamity and disaster to occur to the family. There will be plenty of tears and conflicts - altogether a most disagreeable state of affairs. If your water flow resembles this direction, do make some changes as soon as possible.

The eighth exit direction:
Another loss of money direction. Here the water leaves via the *gen* and the *yin* directions in the Northeast. Whatever money the family starts out with dwindle until the family goes into debt. Whatever property is inherited too will be lost. Grave misfortune of a financial kind will befall all residents.

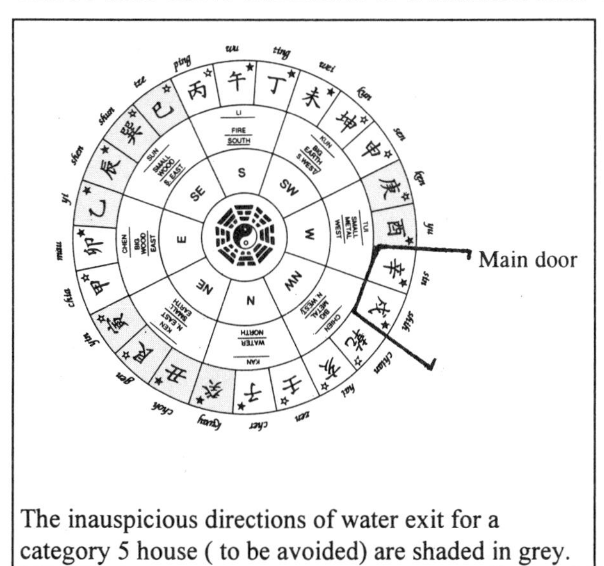

The inauspicious directions of water exit for a category 5 house (to be avoided) are shaded in grey.

The ninth exit direction:
Another inauspicious direction of water flow. Here the water exits via the *kway* or *choh* directions in the North/Northeast. It is once again a complete loss scenario. There is neither children nor wealth luck, and every business cannot succeed. Even when things appear good, something bad will occur to spoil matters. If the water presently leaves your category 5 house in this direction, your would be strongly urged to re construct your drains immediately so as to wash away the gross bad luck of this direction.

The tenth exit direction:
This is a mixed luck situation. The water departs via the *zen* or *cher* direction in the North. Here is a situation where the start is good and seems fairly lucky; however in later years the luck will turn bad and there will be grave misfortune unless other feng shui indicators are propitious. Nevertheless, it is far better to try to tap one of the auspicious directions than run the risk of bad luck befalling the family in later years.

The eleventh exit direction:
Here the water flow can be manipulated to be auspicious. The direction is to allow the water to flow past the main door from left to right, and then to let it flow out of the house compound in a *sin* direction, but it is vital to ensure that in flowing out it must not touch or encroach into the *shih* direction. Hence here the accuracy of the compass reading is vital. The water must leave at an angle bearing between **277.5° to 292.5° from North**. At all costs it must not go beyond **292.5° from North**. This is because encroaching into *shih* will cause there to be very grave misfortune.

After flowing in a *sin* direction for about 100 steps, the water should then return after; in other words, it should turn round after seeming to exit . This means it is necessary to build a loop for the water to flow out and then in again ! If these directions are followed to the letter, there will be abundant prosperity indeed. Nevertheless, feng shui experts in Taiwan are wary of this method since it is so easy to get it wrong, thereby causing the feng shui to be destroyed.

The twelfth exit direction

Opportunity for creating a very auspicious water dragon

This is a very auspicious creation of water flow which can be built only with certain categories of houses. Here what is suggested is that if your front door is in the *sin* or *shih* direction, you can build a water dragon.

To do so, the water flow of the house should originate or come from the direction of *sin* (i.e. the third sub sector of the West direction), flow from left to right pass the main door, and then circle round and up towards the East, and then exit in a *chia* direction. This water flow configuration creates a most auspicious water dragon which brings enormous prosperity. However it is necessary to build the flow of water correctly. The land on which the water is flowing has also to be totally flat. This water flow does not work on land that is contoured or where there are gradients and different levels.

CATEGORY SIX

Door faces *chian* or *hai* direction

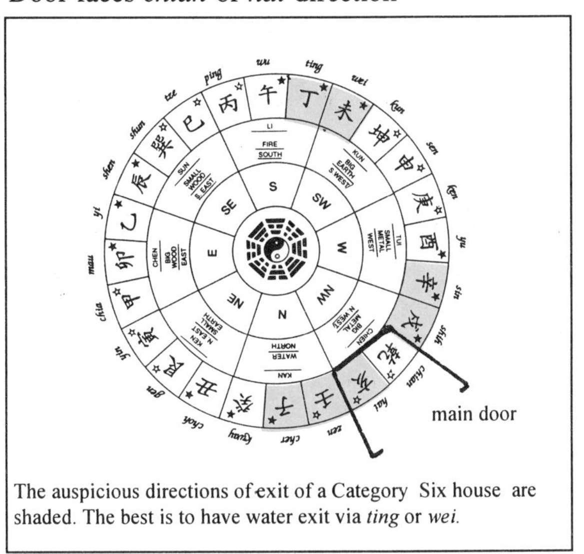

The auspicious directions of exit of a Category Six house are shaded. The best is to have water exit via *ting* or *wei*.

A Category Six house has its main door located in the Northwest sector and facing either *chian* or *hai* (the second and third sub sectors of the Northwest direction. There are three major directions of water exit which represent extreme prosperity luck for such a house, and these are the first, second and third exit directions. The direction of the water flow recommended differs depending on which of these three directions apply. The most auspicious direction however has the water flowing from right to left.

Apart from the three auspicious scenarios, there is also a fourth alternative which holds the promise of extreme good fortune, but which however can be difficult to apply. In looking for the best way to arrange the water flow, it is useful to read through all the exit directions and to note also the inauspicious directions. These latter situations can sometimes be very unfortunate and should they describe your existing drain flow, it would be advisable to do something to correct the situation immediately. Also, irrespective of exit directions, it is important to ensure that the water flow in your house never gets dry as this is inauspicious.

The easiest way to apply the water formula given here is to use it on the domestic drains which flow round your house or building, and the surest way of keeping them filled with flowing water is to allow a trickle of tap water to flow into the drains throughout the day, especially during dry spells.

The first exit direction:
This is the most auspicious direction of exit, and it requires the water to move out of the house in a *ting* or a *wei* direction (South/Southwest), i.e. bearing **187.5° to 217.5° from North.** The water should flow past main door from right to left (inside looking out). If these directions are properly applied and executed there will be brilliant prosperity luck for residents of the household.

Money and wealth will flow continuously into the house and residents will definitely become seriously wealthy. Business will prosper and expand with each passing year and both parents and children will achieve great success. Honour, fame and recognition will also come to the family, as will power and authority. The good fortune of the family will also last through five generations. This is thus an extremely auspicious water exit direction.

The second exit direction:
Once again a very auspicious direction of water exit. Here the water should again flow from right to left pass the main door, and then flow out of the house via the *sin* or *shih* direction in the West/Northwest. The angle of outflow has to be bearing between **277.5° to 307.7° from North**. When this is properly executed, there will be prosperity for a very long time for the residents. They will also enjoy a long and fruitful life and there will be plenty of filial and honourable sons to carry on the family name. Money luck is outstanding and good fortune comes again and again.

The third exit direction:
Completely auspicious ! Here the water has to flow past the front door moving left to right and exiting via the *zen* or *cher* direction in the North. The compass direction of the angle is between **352.5° to 7.5° bearing North**. This direction promises a great deal of extreme good fortune as everything undertaken will generate prosperity for residents. On the cards are every type of good luck - from a good life with plenty to eat as well good positions, with recognition and honour being bestowed on the family. Those in business will prosper and become extremely rich while those in Government will rise to a very high position and wield great authority.

There will also be many good and honourable descendants.
Sons and daughters will bring honour to the family.

The fourth exit direction:
This is a direction of water flow which brings early good fortune that later on turns into grave misfortune. Here the water is flowing out of the compound via the *ken* and the *yu* direction in the West. There is no money luck of any kind whatsoever; indeed there is precious little luck at all. Where there is money in the early days residents will find it difficult to conceive and have children. And should there be children, then money is sadly lacking. This is a direction which will cause the house to always suffer from financial difficulties.

The fifth exit direction:
This is one of the worse directions to have because it brings about a long life for residents, but there is also terrible poverty. Thus a very long life filled with suffering is indicated. Indeed, this direction of flow makes this a house for beggars. The water is flowing out via the *kun* or the *sen* direction in the Southwest. If your house drain flows out in this direction, do try to change it as soon as possible. Unless you do so you will get poorer and poorer and every member of your family will suffer from deprivation and illness.

The sixth exit direction:
Short life and poverty characterize this water exit direction which is *ping* or *wu* in the South. The men of the family will suffer from poor health and have to bear with difficulties associated with lack of money. There will be neither wealth creation luck nor employment luck. Children will suffer from inadequate opportunities and failure will attach to the family. This is a very inauspicious direction for water to flow out of the house.

The disastrous/inauspicious exit directions (of a category Six house)to avoid are shaded in grey.

The seventh exit direction:
Total disaster ! From beginning to end, there is one misfortune after another. This direction of water flow creates born losers. It has the water leaving in a *shun* or *tze* direction and is most inauspicious.

The women in the household will suffer from indignities and will not come to a good end. Far better to make changes as soon as possible.

The eighth exit direction:
This is also a bad exit direction. There will be total failure in all attempts to make money. Residents find it difficult to hold down employment. The eldest son will suffer and women residents will likely become widows. This has the water exiting via the *yi* or the *shen* direction in the East/Southeast.
The ninth exit direction:
A moderately bad exit direction. Here the water leaves via the *chia* or the *mau* direction in the East. In the early part of life there might be some money luck but in the end, residents will lose money and become much poorer. There is also ill health and many disappointments.
The tenth exit direction:
This is a direction which hurts the young children in the family, especially the youngest child. The women in the household will also be cheated and have a life of great suffering. There is very little money, and a terrible lack of opportunities. Residents will also tend to get cheated and betrayed. This is a most inauspicious direction, where the water flows out via the *kway* or the *choh* direction in the North/Northeast.
The eleventh exit direction:
Here the water flows out in the *gen* or *yin* direction in the Northeast. It is a direction which indicates extreme poverty. Very bad luck accrues to the residents. The smartest child in the family will get hurt, and there is absolutely no money luck whatsoever - in fact residents will perpetually suffer and worry from having to make ends meet.

The twelfth exit direction:
An opportunity to create the auspicious water dragon
This is a water dragon direction and when executed correctly is potentially an extremely auspicious direction. If the water ***flows from a height*** towards the main door, and then flows pass the main door from ***right to left***, and then flows outwards in a ***hai*** (in the Northwest) direction - which means it is right in front of the main door - and then after flowing for about 100 steps it **loops back** in whatever direction, an auspicious water dragon has been created. There will then be great good luck, and everything will succeed. Money pours into the household and every other kind of luck is also evident. This is a most auspicious feng shui indeed.
But it is vital that in flowing outwards, the flow of water must not touch the neighbour direction of ***chian***, otherwise the feng shui will be destroyed and the dragon turns pernicious.

CATEGORY SEVEN

Door faces *zen* or *cher* direction

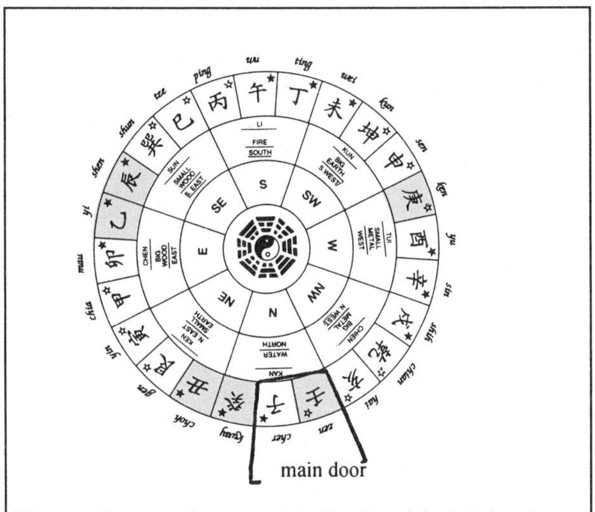

There are three excellent water exit directions (shaded above), with the best one being *yi & shen* in the East/Southeast. A water dragon with water flowing out via *zen* can also be created.

There are three potentially excellent water exit directions in this category house, as well as the possibility of creating an auspicious water dragon. The two most desirable orientations of water flow require the water to move from left to right, in full view of the main door (with the view taken from inside the house). When the door of the building faces *zen* or *cher* in the North as is the case here, a water dragon can be built such that the water flows out in the same direction of *zen*, not touching *cher* next to it and then looping back. This way the dragon is coiled in front of the main door thereby attracting auspicious good fortune into the household. The directions for building this dragon are given under the twelfth exit direction.

Apart from this, there are no specific requirements for the other three auspicious directions. There are also no specific requirements for water entrances, so that all the water of the house or building is deemed to be coming from the house or building itself, or from rain water.
As for the **in**auspicious directions, these are given as guidelines for investigation, and if the water of your house flows out via these inauspicious directions, it is strongly recommended that you make changes as soon as possible. Invest in a good compass when attempting to practice water feng shui as it is important to get the angle as accurate as possible.

The first exit direction:
This is the *unity of three priceless jewels* direction. The three jewels refer to great prosperity; achievement of a high and reputable position; as well as having many excellent and noble descendants. Here the water is supposed to exit via the *yi* or the *shen* direction in the East/Southeast i.e. the angle of flow bearing between **97.5° to 127.5° from North**. The water should also flow pass the main door from left to right before exiting. This flow and exit direction will bring enormous wealth to the household, and residents will benefit from long periods of good luck. Children of the household will enjoy excellent health and will achieve outstanding scholastic honours as well as become prosperous in their own right. This is a very auspicious direction.

The second exit direction:
This is a direction which signifies great expansion and great wealth. Business ventures will achieve success beyond imagination and will develop into large conglomerates. The master of the house will attain great heights of commercial achievement and become extremely powerful as well as having a long life. Descendants will be filial and loyal, bringing good name to the family. The women of the household will also experience a good life. This is truly a magnificent feng shui direction. To achieve it, the water must be made to flow pass the main door from **left to right**, and flow out of the house in either *kway* or *choh* direction in the North/Northeast i.e. at an angle bearing between **7.5° and 37.5° from the North**.

The third exit direction:
This is potentially an auspicious direction, but unlike the first two directions, the water has to flow pass the main door from right to left. It should exit the house compound thereafter via the direction *ken* in the West i.e. at an angle bearing between **247.5° to 262.5° from the North**. In building the water this way however, it is important to ensure that the exit direction is accurately taken, in that the angle of outflow must not veer outside of the angle given. This means it must not touch either *sen* or *yu,* the two directions on either side of *ken*. Otherwise there will be a great disaster. If you do get the direction correct however, you will enjoy tremendous good fortune.

The fourth exit direction:
This is the *death path* direction, and should be avoided at all costs. It describes water flowing out of the house via the *chian* or *hai* direction in the Northwest. This exit direction causes death in the family.

Disaster comes in the form of tragic loss of the best son of the family, severe legal problems and even accidents leading to loss of limbs and paralysis. This is an extremely fierce and very bad orientation for the water.

The fifth exit direction:
Also an inauspicious direction. Here the water leaves via *sin* or *shih* in the West/Northwest. This direction brings about loss of property and family assets, and bad luck to the children. The sons will get hurt or suffer from severe ill health while the daughters will be cheated and come to a bad end. This is a direction which should be corrected and avoided.

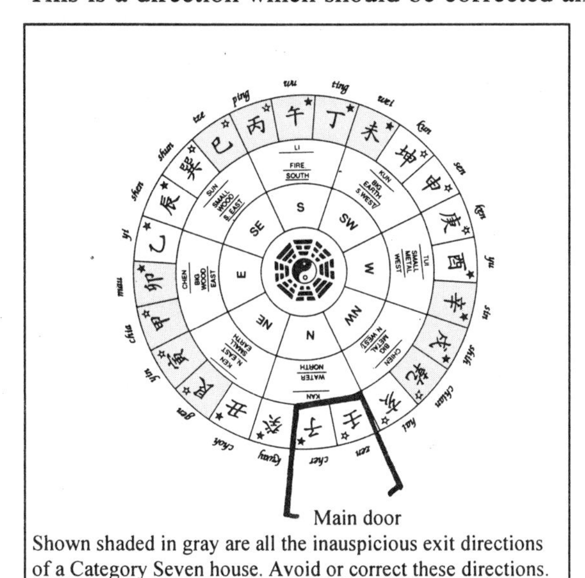

Shown shaded in gray are all the inauspicious exit directions of a Category Seven house. Avoid or correct these directions.

The sixth exit direction:
This is a direction which is especially damaging to those who want to have children. If the water exits out of either *ting* or *wei* in the South/Southwest couples will find difficulty in conceiving, or there could be miscarriages or if there are young children, they will be easily hurt or suffer from poor health. There is also no money in this direction.

The seventh exit direction:
A direction of mixed fortunes - with fortunate beginnings but a very poor ending. Here the water exits via the directions *ping* or *wu* in the South. Residents of such a house will enjoy some good fortune at the start. But over the long term, there is loss of money and property. There will be long life for residents, but it will also be quite a hard life. Not a good direction.

The eighth exit direction:
There is very little money in this exit direction. Again, the beginning may seem auspicious but in the end there is bad luck and a major loss of the family fortunes. Here the water flows out via the *shun* or *tze* direction. Inauspicious.

The ninth exit direction:
Very "sway" luck. Totally inauspicious and bad luck. This is a death direction which cause grave harm to the third son. Health is bad - can vomit blood. Money luck is bad and even when things seem to work well, there is hidden loss. If money manages to come to the house, someone will die ! here the water flows out via *chia* or *mau* in the East. This is considered a very bad exit direction and should be corrected.

The tenth exit direction:
Once again bad luck orientation. Here the water exits via *gen* or *yin* in the Northeast. If this is the way the water leaves, the men in the household will have short lives. The women will become widows. Property will be reduced. Health is bad and residents are susceptible to lung diseases. The third or youngest son will be the first to suffer.

The eleventh exit direction:
This is a direction where there is some moderate money luck, but there is no descendant luck. Children will be very sickly or be prone to accidents. Or worse even die. The water leaves via the *kun* or *sen* direction in the Southwest.
A direction that is best avoided or corrected.

The twelfth exit direction:
Potential for creating a water dragon.
This direction describes the instructions for creating a a water dragon. First the water must **flow from right to left** pass the main door, and then appear to flow out through the direction *zen* in the North, just in front of the main door. Let this water flow for about 100 steps, and then let the water urn round on the left, and end anywhere in the rest of the left hand side of the garden. The water on the left hand side of this loop should be small water, i.e. the drain on the left hand side should be smaller. Also, the water when appearing to flow out must not touch the *cher* direction(on the right). If you get these instructions correct your house and all the residents in it will have huge success and a great deal of money luck. But should you make a mistake, there will be no luck for anybody. Instead the dragon becomes weak and even pernicious.

CATEGORY EIGHT:
Door faces *kway* or *choh* direction

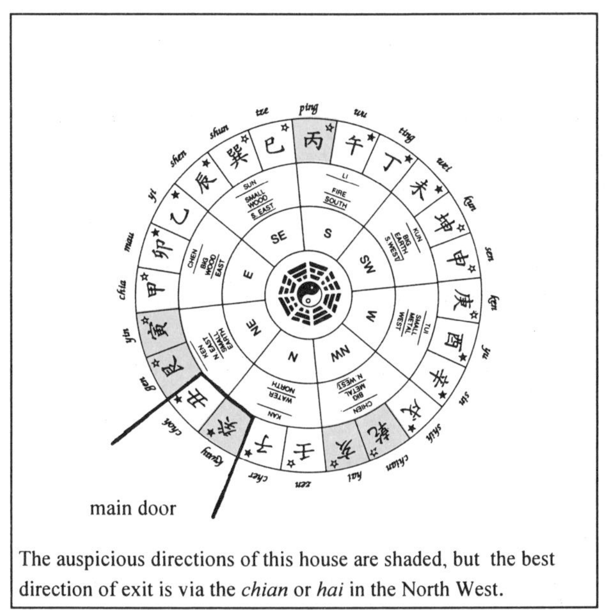

The auspicious directions of this house are shaded, but the best direction of exit is via the *chian* or *hai* in the North West.

There are two excellent directions of exit for this category of house. There are also two potential water dragons which can be created if your main door faces *kway* or *choh* in the North/Northeast. These are given in exit directions eleven and twelve. For this category, please note the water flow left to right or right to left carefully as they are different for the two directions.

There are eight inauspicious directions of exit, some signifying worse luck than others, but all suggesting a sorry lack of money or wealth luck. Thus if yours is such a house you should either adopt exit directions one or two, or build a water dragon carefully, taking note of the special directions given.

First exit direction:
This has the water flowing out via the directions *chian* or *hai* in the Northwest, i.e. **307.5° to 337.5° bearing from North**, and flowing pass the main door from **right to left**. This is an excellent and auspicious flow of water and if well positioned according to these indications, residents of the house will have extremely good money and wealth luck. Every kind of success will visit the household including a great deal of business success as well as plenty of political success luck. The master of the house could well become a Minister or have a significantly high title conferred on him.

His family will attain nobility rank and the children will be very successful. This direction is especially fortunate for the women of the house - and all the daughters will have outstanding careers as well plenty of money luck.

Second exit direction:
Another extremely excellent feng shui direction. Here the water flows pass the main door from **left to right**, and flows out of the house in either a *gen* or *yin* direction, at an angle **bearing 37.5° to 67.5° from North**. The excellent benefits everyone. There will be plenty of money and each of the children will expand the family wealth. The house also attracts a great deal of recognition and business success indeed this direction suggest a lot of business acumen. However the patriarch of the house will suffer from rheumatism and the more severe and serious this becomes the richer the family will get ! This is regarded as a very auspicious direction of water flow, favouring the descendants of the family.

Third exit direction:
Inauspicious ! Here the water flows out via the *Zen* or the *cheer* direction in the first two subsectors of the North corner of the house. This is a <u>no money</u> direction; and there is also ill health afflicting the men of the family, sometimes with tragic consequences. The men of the family will have a tendency to die young. At best this direction brings irregular luck, At worst it brings death and great poverty. If there is a bad stone (something sharp or hostile looking) facing the *choh* direction i.e. in the Northeast, near the main door, it could cause a great deal of violent harm to the family, or denote violence within the family. Certainly it will cause a major loss of wealth.

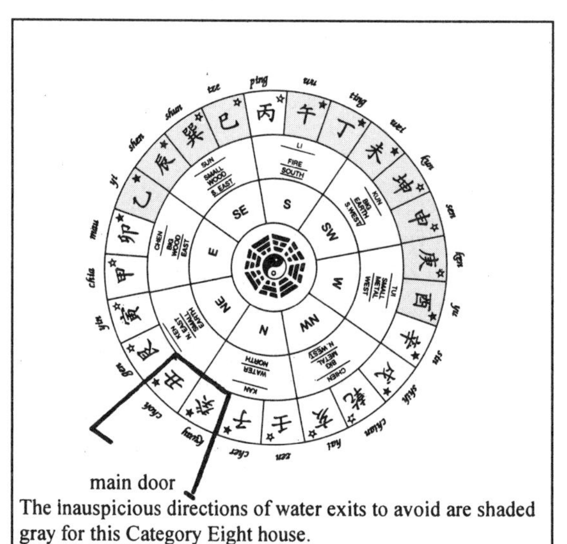

The inauspicious directions of water exits to avoid are shaded gray for this Category Eight house.

The fourth exit direction:
A moderately bad direction. There are no bad or major disasters indicated, but there is no money luck at all. The family will enjoy a long and peaceful life, but there is neither any big success or recognition of any kind. Here the water is flowing out via the *sin* or *shih* direction in the West/Northwest.

The fifth exit direction:
A direction which signifies a gradual but sure loss of wealth. Money and good luck slowly dissipates over time so that despite promising beginnings, in the end, life will be quite difficult. Here the water is flowing out via the *ken* or *yu* direction in the West.

The sixth exit direction:
This is an exit direction with indications of poverty! There is no chance of getting rich if the water flows out via this *kun* or *sen* direction in the Southwest. There is also no descendants luck. There might be daughters but there will be very few sons, and children of the household are susceptible to illnesses. This is a direction which should be corrected if you wish to have good feng shui luck.

The seventh exit direction:
A most inauspicious direction. There are indications of grave misfortune from this direction of water flow which has the water leaving in either the *ting* or the *wei* direction in the South/Southwest. Residents will meet with bad luck frequently and there is grave misfortune, and even death to the male members of the household.

The eighth exit direction:
Also an inauspicious direction of water exit. Here the water flows out via either the *shun* or *tze* direction in the Southeast. Residents will gradually lose any good fortune they might already have, and suffer great losses. Big money cannot enter this house and there is also unfortunate descendants luck.

The ninth exit direction:
A terrible feng shui direction ! This is when the water flows out via the *yi* or the *shen* direction. Luck is most unfortunate. Businesses cannot succeed; careers cannot flourish, and there is disappointment for most of the residents. There is also no money luck whatsoever. Children will also not flourish.

The tenth exit direction:
This is a moderate exit direction. Residents of this type of house and having the water flow out via the *chia* or *mau* direction in the East will have a sprinkling of good fortune mixed with bad fortune. The luck of the house is not balanced and tends to be irregular.
Money luck too is only moderate.

Creating the water dragon in a Category Eight house

The eleventh exit direction:

A potential water dragon configuration. This is when the water flows from left to right pass the main door and then flows out in a *kway* direction, just in front of the main door. The water should flow in this *kway* direction i.e. at an angle bearing between **7.5° to 22.5° from North**, (but without touching the *choh* direction) **for about a hundred steps before turning around** towards the right. It is necessary to be very careful. If the directions are correctly implemented, the residents of the house will enjoy tremendous good fortune. Big money luck is especially indicated with this sort of water flow. There will be cause for celebration. Children will be filial and will prosper. Business will expand and there will also be elevation of rank for the head of the household. Extremely good fortune is the result !

The twelfth exit direction:

A second water dragon configuration is indicated with this direction. Here the water flows pass the main door again from left to right , and the water is coming from a *kway* direction; it then turns right, goes around the land (or compound) and flows out via the *ping* direction in the South (at the back). When exiting the compound the water must not touch the *wu* direction, which is next to ping. Thus the water must flow out at an angle bearing between **157.5° to 172.5° from North**. If this is achieved residents will enjoy five generations of good fortune ! Money flows in easily, and everything attempted by the residents will meet with success. But this particular water dragon cannot work on hilly or mountainous land. The surface area of the land must be flat. Otherwise the direction cannot come alive, and there cannot be good fortune.

A special note on water dragons

When constructing a water dragon, you must first investigate the terrain of the land. Often the water manual states that hilly land is not suitable, and ceratin angles of flow are to be strenuously avoided, in which case it is better not to attempt it, and instead try to tap one of the auspicious directions. Accuracy of compass readings is also extremely vital.

CATEGORY NINE:

Door faces *gen* or *yin* direction.

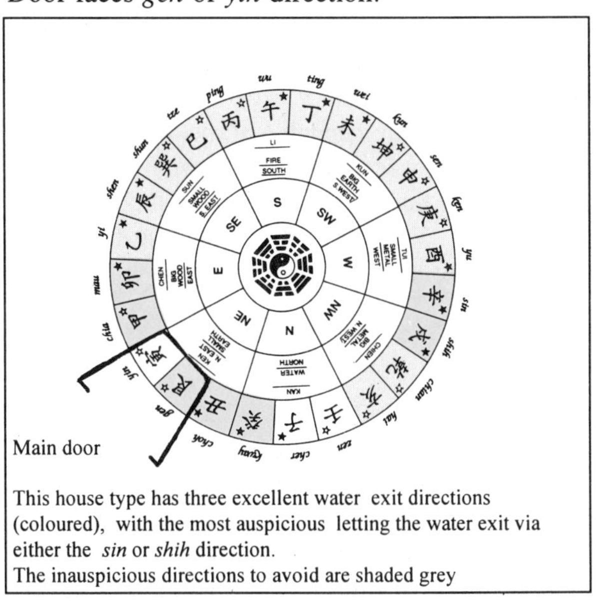

This house type has three excellent water exit directions (coloured), with the most auspicious letting the water exit via either the *sin* or *shih* direction.
The inauspicious directions to avoid are shaded grey

If your house has its main door facing the *gen* or *yin* directions i.e. the North East second and third sub-sectors, there are three excellent water exit directions you can choose to use to bring prosperity and wealth flowing into your house. These are the exit directions one, two and three, and if the indicated angles of flow are scrupulously followed then the excellent attributes of each of these directions will be felt over time.

For the first two directions the flow of water pass the main door is **right to left**. This flow brings auspicious luck which gets activated each time there is water moving slowly pass. This has led some feng shui experts to recommend that a continuos flow be maintained by turning on a tap that allows water to flow into a drain flowing pass the main door. The author regularly keeps one of the taps in her garden flowing in this manner during the dry periods, although with so much rain these days, this is rarely necessary.

Rain water is especially auspicious as it is deemed to come from heaven; although feng shui experts also attest to the potency of the water that has been used to wash the rice before cooking. Let this rice water flow pass your main door in an auspicious direction and it is supposed to activate good luck for the household.

The first exit direction:
This very auspicious water direction requires the water to flow out via the *sin* or *shih* direction in the West/Northwest, and pass the main door moving from right to left. The angle of flow outwards is bearing between **277.5° to 307.5° from North**. This is an all encompassing direction of excellent good fortune. Wealth, Money, Prosperity - is assured for the residents of the household. The family living in such a house will enjoy recognition and command great respect, and they will live in luxury. The master will attain a high position while children will be plentiful and filial. There is also excellent health luck. This is the *Golden pathway* direction as it leads to great abundance for everyone and in everything.

The second exit direction:
If for some reason you are unable to exit in the first direction you can also try letting your water flow out via the second direction which is via *kway* or *choh* direction in the North/Northeast. The angle of flow out is bearing **7.5° to 37.5° from North**. The water should flow from right to left pass your main door. This configuration of water flow signifies extreme good fortune for the young members of the family. If the landscape or terrain of the house is also excellent, the eldest will also prosper; otherwise most of the good luck will flow to the more junior members of the family. Nevertheless this is a house with money and success luck; and there is also laughter and cause for celebration.

The third exit direction;
Here the water is flowing pass the main door from left to right, and is flowing out via the *chia* or *mau* direction in the east. The angle of flow out is bearing between **67.5° to 97.5° from North**. This is an extremely auspicious direction of water configuration. When constructed correctly according to specifications indicated, the family living in such a house will enjoy tremendous good fortune. Bad luck turns to good luck. Anything lost will be recovered. Business will succeed. Careers will flourish. Health is good. Money will expand slowly but steadily, and the everyone will have a good ending. There are also a great many money making opportunities which will come your way, and children will achieve honours in their undertakings.

The name of the family will spread far and wide.

The fourth exit direction:
A moderate direction. The water flows out via the *zen* or the *cher* direction. Good beginnings and poor endings is the general rule, but if the terrain is good, then residents will be favoured with better luck. Otherwise there could be a lack of money luck. And children will suffer. At any rate if you have a choice try to avoid this direction.

The fifth exit direction:
Water flows out via the *chian* or the *hai* direction. There is no money in this direction. Children cannot flourish and indeed will suffer from headaches and poor grades. In some cases they may even perish or get mixed up in bad company. Careers cannot take off, and promotions are hard to come by. There will also be a shortage of opportunities for advancement. Altogether a most inauspicious direction.

The sixth exit direction:
This is an extremely bad feng shui configuration of water. This is when the water flows out of the house via the *ken* or *yu* direction in the West. There is totally no money luck whatsoever. Everything fails. When you are thirsty you do no get water and when you re hungry there is no food on the table ! There could also be law suits, and if the landscape feng shui is also bad, the effect will be disastrous. This is a direction to be changed.

The seventh exit direction;
A total disaster direction ! Here the water moves out via the *kun* or *sen* direction in the Southwest. What is indicated is extreme bad luck for the male members of the family. Accidents, illnesses of the blood and lungs, and even death could occur. Thus there are indications of widow hood for the women of the household. If there is no health problems, there will be financial difficulties coming frequently to bother the family. There can also be no success in undertakings, and members could also get cheated. A direction to avoid.

The eighth exit direction;
An equally inauspicious direction for the family . If water flows out via *ting* or *wei* directions in the South/Southwest, there is nothing much to look forward to. Tragedy associated with financial loss and death will plague the residents. Property will be sold; children will either leave the family or cause a great deal of problems and everything just cannot succeed. A most inauspicious direction.

The ninth exit direction:
A direction with a great deal of bad luck and unfortunate developments. Once again there is no wealth look and residents just cannot make any kind of money. Here the water is leaving via the *ping* or *wu* direction in the South. Mothers will have occasion to grieve and the women in general will be dressed in mourning.

The tenth exit direction:
This direction hurts the children and younger members of the family. Here the water flows out via the *yi* or *shen* direction in the East/Southeast. The women in the house will tend to be flirtatious and come to a bad end. There can be no happiness and no prosperity. In fact opportunities are difficult to come by and the table is often bare. A direction to avoid if possible.

The eleventh exit direction;
There are indications of death to he most successful son in this direction. Here the water flows out via the *shun* and *tze* direction in the Southeast. It denotes poor descendants luck, and a state of poverty. Money cannot come in and most ventures undertaken will fail.

The twelfth exit direction
A potential water dragon configuration
This can be an extremely auspicious configuration if the water flows pass the main door in a **right to left direction**, and then exits via the *gen* direction in the Northeast i.e. near the main door. The angle of outflow is bearing between **37.5° to 52.5° from North**. When flowing out, the angle must not touch the *yin* direction. After flowing in the *gen* direction for 100 steps, the water should then turn round towards the left thereby forming a loop or curve. This creates an auspicious water dragon for the house and will bring great prosperity and abundance. Everything good will flow into the house. There will be good business luck and many opportunities for making money. If the terrain is also favourable, the family will enjoy great respectability - with the family patriarch achieveign Ministerial status. The children of the family will prosper and bring great honour to the family name. All the residents of the house will benefit.

CATEGORY TEN

Door faces *chia* or *mau* direction

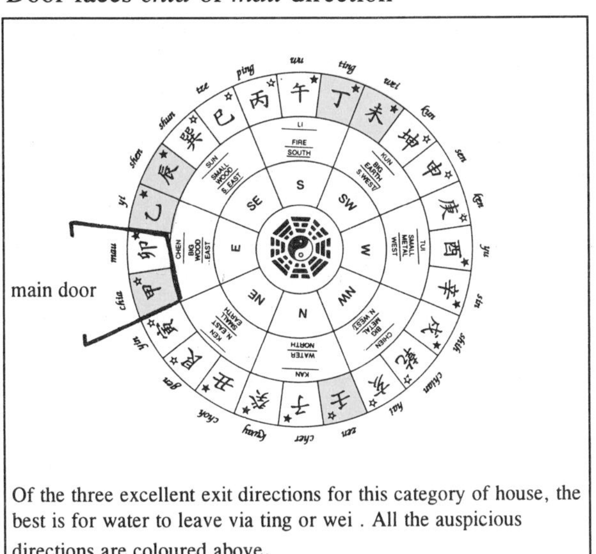

Of the three excellent exit directions for this category of house, the best is for water to leave via ting or wei . All the auspicious directions are coloured above.

This category house has its main door facing either the *chia* or mau direction in the East. It is suitable for an East Group person (**Please refer to my earlier Feng Shui books to determine if you are an east or west group person according to your date of birth**). To activate excellent money feng shui for the house, thereby complimenting other auspicious features already undertaken, it is recommended that attention be focused on the water drains which surround the house. This involves making sure they flow pass the main door in an auspicious direction, and most important, that the water of the house exits in a direction that brings great good luck to the family.

There are all together twelve possible directions for the water to flow out of the house compound, and of these only three are really auspicious. There is also a fourth possibility, and this involves creating a water dragon with special requirements for the water flow. The water dragon also brings prosperity and abundance. All of the other directions of exit are inauspicious and some are extremely dangerous in that they bring about great misfortune and financial loss. To practice water feng shui, you must first investigate your main door direction accurately. Once you know this you can examine the auspicious and inauspicious directions suitable for your house, and make changes accordingly. You do not require the services of a feng shui expert for this. Besides only very few of them posses this formula, so try doing it for yourself.

The first exit direction:
For a Category Ten house which has its main door facing *chia* or *mau* in the East, the best water exit direction is the South/Southwest i.e. the directions *ting* or *wei*. The angle of out-flowing water should be bearing between 187.5° to 217.5° from North. The water should also flow pass the main door from left to right. The other direction spells disaster. If you undertake these instructions carefully, then according to the Water Feng Shui formula you and your family will enjoy the *triple precious jewels luck*, which is translated to mean extreme good luck that includes great wealth and prosperity, good and many descendants and an honourable and noble position in society. This prosperity will also last for a very long time. Residents will enjoy long life and good health and will live in luxury, getting more and more wealthier as the years pass. This is the most auspicious direction of water exit for this house category.

The second exit direction;
This is also a very auspicious direction which can be considered an alternative to the first exit direction. Here the water flows pass the main door from left to right, and exits at an angle equivalent to the *yi* or *shen* direction in the East/Southeast. This means an angle bearing between **97.5° to 127.5° from North.** If the water originates from a Northeast direction, it will be stupendous good luck ! This is one of the rare directions where *the entrance direction* is also stated, and if it is possible to also tap the entrance direction, the family's wealth will be truly enormous ! Everything achieved and attained will be the best and business luck will be especially good. But there is also family and descendants luck as well, and children will enjoy honours and excellent careers. This direction is excellent feng shui.

The third exit direction:
Again an auspicious direction. Here the water should flow out in a *zen* direction i.e. bearing between **337.5° to 352.5°** from North. Extra care must be taken to ensure that in using this direction you do not touch the neighbour direction of *hai* - otherwise whatever good feng shui created will be neutralized and lost. With the water exiting via *zen* brings good fortune in that there will be many opportunities for advancement and money success. The family will have a peaceful co existence, and there is gradual improvement of income. This is not a millionaire class sort of money feng shui direction. However if other aspects of the land terrain and compass directions are also auspicious this sort of water flow will do much to enhance the family fortunes.

The fourth exit direction:
This is not a good direction as it hurts the children of the family, especially the most successful and brightest child. The third child will be vulnerable. Here the water is flowing out via *gen* or *yin* in the Northeast. There is illness and poor health indicated and money luck is absolutely non existent.

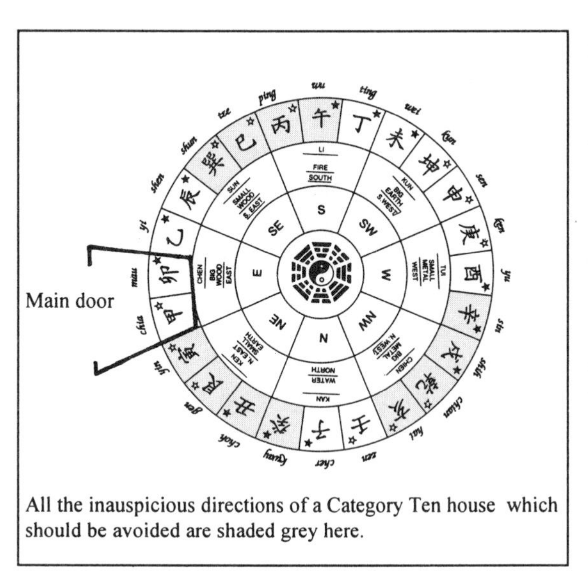

All the inauspicious directions of a Category Ten house which should be avoided are shaded grey here.

The fifth exit direction:
A very bad orientation of water flow. Here the water goes out via the *kway* or *choh* directions in the North/Northeast. This direction of exit is extremely unfortunate for the women and children of the family. The men cannot stay home, and will also suffer from illness. The children could be influenced negatively by outsiders, and everything will go wrong. There is one problem after another.

The sixth exit direction:
Once again a direction which is inauspicious and could even be termed dangerous for the children of the household. Here the water is leaving via the *sin* or *shih* directions in the West/Northwest. There is totally no money luck in this direction.

The seventh exit direction:
A moderate direction of flow where the water exits via the *ken* or *yu* direction in the West. The indications for this direction are that in the beginning there is some money luck, and sons will benefit from good luck; but with the passage of time, the *chi* created gets exhausted and good fortune will slowly turn into misfortune. This transformation of luck could lead to the early demise of one of the sons. Best to avoid this direction.

The eighth exit direction:
This is a water exit direction with mixed good and bad effects on the feng shui luck. Here the water flows out via the *kun* or *sen* in the Southwest.

What the texts imply is that with this kind of exit water flow, you cannot have everything. Thus if you have healthy sons (descendants luck) you will not have much money luck; and if you are successful with money matters and in business, then you will not have much children luck.

The ninth exit direction:

This is the death path direction and should be avoided at all costs. Everything will suffer misfortune. The exit direction has the water flowing out via the *ping* or *wu* direction in the South. Prosperity is elusive; Commercial enterprises cannot succeed and one thing after another goes bad. If residents do well in their careers, they could fall ill with problems relating to the heart or lungs. The older generation will not live long enough to see their children turn out well. There is very little to recommend about this direction.

The tenth exit direction:

This is also a very inauspicious direction. It suggests a very short life for the man of the family. Children of the family are vulnerable to ill health and women could become widows. There is also no money luck, and ventures cannot take off. Everything is bad. Here the water flows out via the *shun* or *tze* direction.

The eleventh exit direction:

This is a direction which suggests grave misfortunes for the sons of the family especially the eldest son. The younger sons will also find it difficult to succeed. There is no money and few opportunities to make anything worthwhile. The water is flowing out via *chian* or *hai* in the Northwest.

The twelfth exit direction

A potential water dragon configuration.

For a house with the *chia* or *mau* main door, the drains of the house can be transformed into a water dragon . Let the water flow from **right to left** pass the main door. Let it flow out in the *chia* direction in the East, at an angle bearing between **67.5° to 82.5° from the North**, just in front of the main door. Flowing in this angle let the water move along for about 100 steps, then let the drain turn round towards the left. In flowing outwards, the angle of flow must not touch the *mau* direction. If properly executed, this is a configuration which attracts big big money into the household. There will be great wealth attracted to the house which will benefit all the residents. Such a water dragon should be built on flat land and there should not be any bad stone which resembles a hostile animal or structure that is situated in the vicinity of the drain, otherwise, the feng shui will be affected.

CATEGORY ELEVEN

Door faces *yi* or *shen* direction

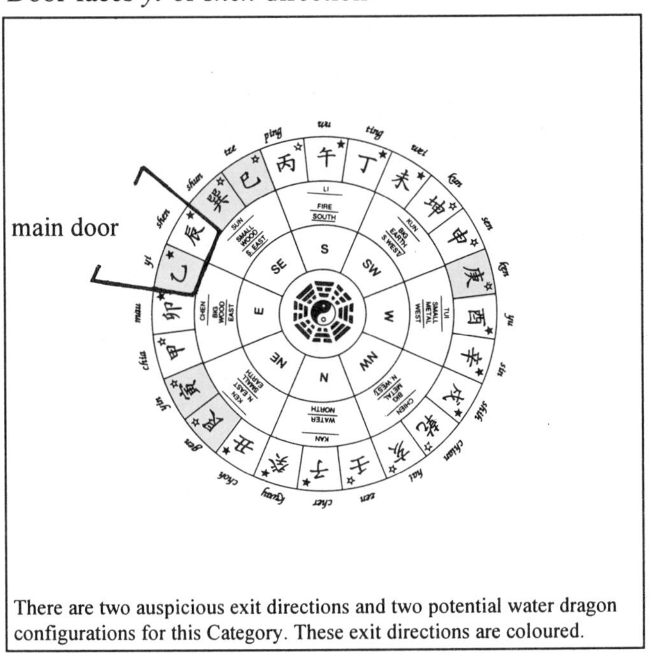

There are two auspicious exit directions and two potential water dragon configurations for this Category. These exit directions are coloured.

In a house whose main door faces *yi* or *shen* in the East/Southeast, there are two extremely exit directions for water. There is also the potential to create two water dragon configurations which spell excellent feng shui. All four of these possibilities of water flow is said to bring enormous wealth and prosperity luck to the family.

Almost all the rest of the directions will bring enormous bad luck, with some being almost disastrous and fierce in their effects, causing death and tremendous loss of property and assets. These bad exit directions should be avoided, and if this category describes your house, then you should make sure your drains do not flow out of your house in an angle deemed to be inauspicious.

As for the building of the water dragons, do be very accurate in your compass readings, and follow the instructions explicitly. A bad stone refers to a boulder which resembles a hostile animal or a pest like a rat or has a fierce configuration. A hundred steps refer to your footsteps or approximately a hundred feet.

The first exit direction.

This is supposedly the most auspicious water exit direction. It has the water flowing pass the main door from right to left, and it flows out of the house at an angle corresponding to the *gen* or *yin* direction, i.e. bearing between **37.5° to 67.5° from North**. With this sort of configuration, residents will benefit from the three jewels luck i.e. prosperity and wealth; good and filial descendants and noble rank for the patriarch. There is plenty of money luck and everything will succeed. Family members will live in luxury, and the direction will be especially beneficial to the women of the household.

The second exit direction:

If you find it impossible for some reason to activate the first direction, there is a second alternative. Let the water flow pass the main door from left to right, but let it flow out of the house at an angle which corresponds to the *shun* or *tze* directions in the Southeast. This means bearing between **127.5° to 157.5° from the North**. With this sort of water flow around the house, residents will enjoy extreme good fortune. There will be very big money flowing to the family and everything will be successful. There is political success as well as business success. Nobility can be attained with the conferment of honours and children will benefit.

The third exit direction:

This is a mixed configuration. Here the water flows out via the direction *chia* or *mau* in the East. By itself this configuration indicates a mixture of good and bad with average money luck. Success will be sprinkled with some misfortune. However if there is a bad stone facing the direction *shen* (i.e. near the vicinity of the main door in the Southeast) there will be extreme misfortune caused by violence, and leading to most tragic consequences. The house will also attract unsavoury characters who cause big problems.

The fourth exit direction:

Also a mixed indication given. Here the water flows out via *kway* or *choh* in the North/Northeast. There is no money luck at all, and children tend to suffer from ill health and poor motivation. Not a good direction and best corrected.

The fifth exit direction:
Here the water exits via the *zen* or *cher* directions in the North. With this flow, life for the residents will appear fortunate in the beginning - there is money, some success and happiness. But gradually the family will suffer from severe losses in investments, and the men in the family will have short lives. Children will also bear the brunt of the bad feng shui in that they will either leave home and not return or come to a bad end.
Not a very good configuration to have over the long term.

The sixth exit direction:
The death path direction. Here the water flows out via *chian* or *hai* in the Northwest. It signifies misfortune resulting in death for the family and is most inauspicious. The residents will be accident prone, and have difficulties with finances or have legal problems. This direction should be avoided.

The seventh exit direction:
Total disaster. Here the water flows out via *sin* or *shih* in the West/Northwest. Misfortune is grave and there is perpetual bad luck. Nothing succeeds. Best to avoid this direction.

The eighth exit direction:
Another total disaster direction. Here the water flows out via either *ken* or *yu* in the West, and it spells difficulties, problems and tragedies. Nothing succeeds. Everything goes wrong. Feng shui experts knowledgeable about water strenuously warn against this water exit direction.

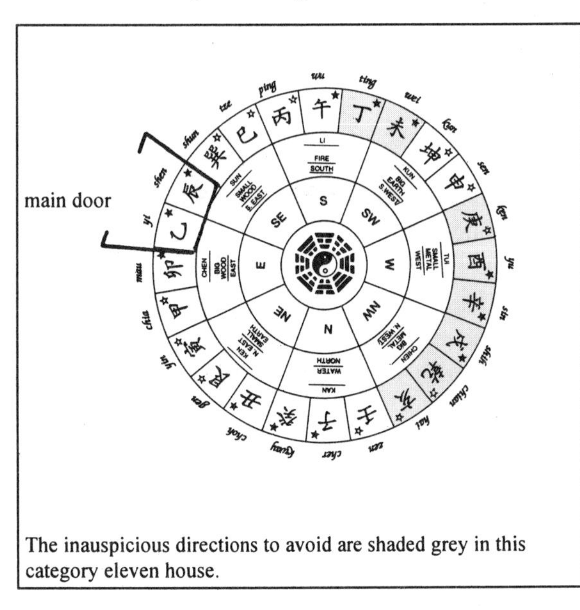

The inauspicious directions to avoid are shaded grey in this category eleven house.

The ninth exit direction:
Here the water leaves via the *ting* or *wei* directions in the South/Southwest. Again it is a very bad direction for the water flow and is best avoided. Grave misfortune befalls residents of a house with this sort of water flow.

The tenth exit direction:
An average water direction. Here the exit is via the *ping* or the *wu* direction in the South. This direction spells average good fortune for the residents of the household, with a mixture of good and bad. There is some money, but it is not big money; just as there is some small success. Children will have good health but will tend to fly the nest early. If other feng shui factors are bad however there could be violence which cause heartache and problems for the family.

The eleventh exit direction:
A potential water dragon configuration
This can be a very prosperous configuration as it is identified as a water dragon direction. Here the water moves pass the main door from left to right, and moves outwards in a yi direction (similiar to one of the door directions). The angle of the flow outwards bears between 97.5° to 112.5° from North. It flows for about 100 steps, and then turns round again on the right. If you can get these directions correct, there will be great prosperity luck !

This is known as the wealth bringing dragon.

The twelfth exit direction
A potential water dragon direction
Here the instructions tell you to have the water originating from *yi* i.e. it flows in at an angle bearing between **97.5° to 112.5° from North**; then **it turns right** and moves to the back of the house until it reaches the West sector, and then it flows out of the house via the *ken* direction there i.e. at an angle bearing **247.5° to 262.5° from North**. But in doing so the water must not touch *yu*, just next to it. In other words it is vital that the angle of flow is accurately done. The requirement for this water dragon is that the land must be flat, and then there will be fantastic good luck.
Prosperity and wealth will be assured .

CATEGORY TWELVE:
Door faces *shun* or *tze* direction.

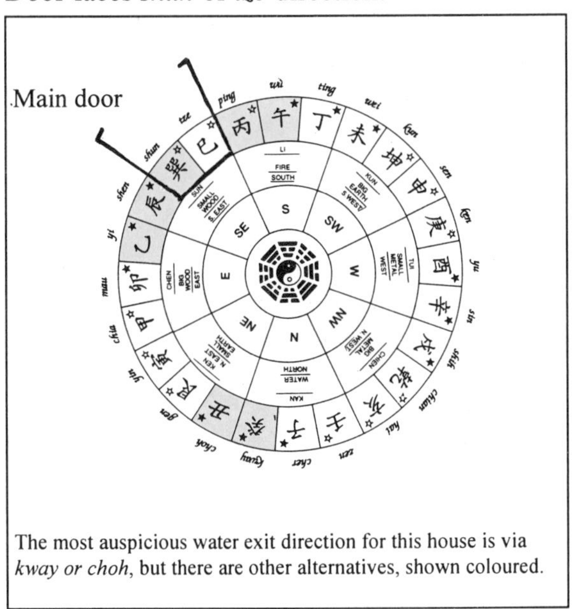

The most auspicious water exit direction for this house is via *kway or choh*, but there are other alternatives, shown coloured.

This is the final category of house based on the direction of its front /main door. In this case the door is facing either shun or tze direction in the South East. With the directions given in this section, the water formula will be complete. In this category there are three excellent configurations of water flow, and there is potential to build one water dragon. Any of these alternatives will create auspicious water feng shui thereby enhancing the wealth potential of the house. However it is also important that I stress the danger of misfortune of some of the other exit directions.

In water feng shui, when the flow of water is auspicious, the luck generated can be quite enormous, but in the same way if one is unfortunate enough to have the drain or water flow out the wrong way, it can also cause very grave misfortune.

The first exit direction:
This is a very auspicious exit direction and brings enormous good luck, one comparable to the wearing of a jade belt. This spells a very high and respected position for the family patriarch and wealth luck is also enormous.

Here the water flows pass the main door in a **right to left** direction, and flows out of the house compound via either the *kway* or *choh* direction in the North/Northeast. The angle of flow is bearing between **7.5° to 37.5° from North.** Residents of such a household will enjoy easy success with few worries. Children attain high ranks and the women benefit from the family wealth enormously.

The second exit direction:
If the first alternative is not possible, this house can also tap the second direction which has the water flowing pass the main door in a **right to left** movement, and exits the compound via the *yi* or *shen* direction in the East and Southeast. The angle of outflow is bearing between **97.5° to 127.5° from North**.If undertaken correctly this direction attracts prosperity for the house and it is especially beneficial for the youngest son, although all the children will benefit from the good fortune. Money luck is forthcoming; businesses prosper and opportunities for advancement are forthcoming. This is an auspicious direction.

The third exit direction:
Also a very good configuration. Here the water flows pass the main door in a **left to right** direction and exits via the *ping* or *wu* direction in the South. The angle of outflow is bearing between **157.5° to 187.5° from North**. When done correctly this direction attracts wealth luck which will benefit the women of the household. There is also descendants luck in that children will be loyal and filial and will also succeed in attaining good careers. Everything is successful and although the prosperity of this direction of flow is not as large as the first direction it is considered very auspicious as well.

The fourth exit direction:
This is an inauspicious configuration of water. A state of poverty is indicated and other manifestations of misfortune will also occur. During the early days, things may not appear to be bad; sons will be born and careers move along steadily but after several years, problems get more and more severe. There could even be tragic consequences in the form of severe illness or accidents. Here the water exits via the *chia* or *mau* directions in the east.

The fifth exit direction:
No reputation can be gained from this exit direction which sees the water flowing out via the *gen* or *yin* directions in the Northeast. Life will be difficult. There are few opportunities and everything seems to go wrong.

There will also be harmful people around and assets lost cannot be recovered. A most inauspicious direction.

The sixth exit direction:
A disastrous direction. Here water exits via the *zen* or *cher* direction. Everything spells misfortune in this direction and should you have such a configuration of water flow, it must be corrected as soon as possible.

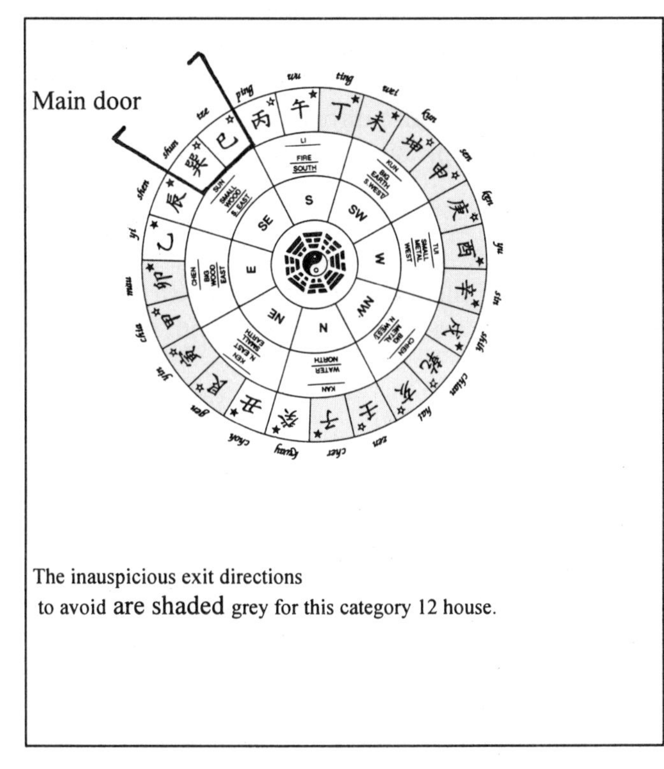

The inauspicious exit directions to avoid are shaded grey for this category 12 house.

The seventh exit direction:
This is a very inauspicious direction of water flow which cause death and grave misfortune to the children and the women of the household. The man of the house will stay out for long periods or could meet with violence. There are also indications of widow-hood. Children will suffer from sickness and poor performance. Very bad luck indeed and best avoided. Here the water is flowing out at an angle corresponding to the *chian* or *hai* directions in the Northwest.

The eighth exit direction:
Once more a most inauspicious direction. Here the water moves out via the *sin* or *shih* directions in the West/Northwest. Disaster comes in the form of grave misfortune befalling the sons of the family. There is little money luck and problems occur again and again. Everything is difficult to succeed. The women of the household will also meet with misfortune and could get cheated, thereby coming to a bad end.

The ninth exit direction:
This direction spells enormous poverty and great losses. The family will always be in debt and nothing moves smoothly.
This is when the water flows out via the *ken* or *yu* directions in the West. It is best to avoid this direction as it causes sorrow and tragedy fort he family.

The tenth exit direction:
here the water flows out via the *ting* or *wei* directions in the South/Southwest. This is a configuration which hurts the youngest son and the daughters of the family especially beautiful women. Though blessed with good lucks, they will encounter betrayal and heartbreak. There is also difficulty in achieving success in business or careers. Most inauspicious.

The eleventh exit direction;
Once again a bad direction of water flow. Here the water exits via the *kun* or a *sen* direction in the Southwest. Young members of the family will get hurt with this direction. There will be scandals and even problems with the law, and nothing succeeds.

The twelfth exit direction:
A potential water dragon configuration
For a house with the main door facing *shun* or *tze,* there are instructions on how to build a water dragon thereby activating great prosperity luck for residents. To activate the dragon, the water must flow from **right to left** pass the main door; and flow out in a *shun* direction, very similiar to that of the main door. But in exiting it must not touch the next direction which is *tze*. After flowing outwards for a hundred steps, the water should then turn around towards the left and then slowly trickle into a smaller water flow. If this can be done, there will be great prosperity luck created. Everything will seem to happen with ease and money will flow into he household. The good fortune will last for a very long period of time, and the family will attain nobility status. This is considered a most auspicious configuration of water, which can be equally applied on flat or undulating land.

CHAPTER FOUR
CONSTRUCTING THE WATER DRAGON

He strikes the golden bell,
The sound is heard
around the world ...
His fame is like the sound
It reaches everywhere
Good fortune comes
continiously...

"A spring wells up
at the foot of the mountain
The image of ***youth***
The superior man fosters his character,
And practice thoroughness
In all that he does"
from the **I Ching**, on the Trigram Meng

CHAPTER FOUR

Now that you understand the components of the water formula, we can proceed to address the practical aspects of constructing the water dragon. Even if you do not build a water dragon, the formula must be applied correctly. This is because mistakes can easily be made.

Before you start building your water dragon or alter the water flows of your drain, list out the various options you are seriously considering. In other words start first by eliminating the exit directions you do **not** wish to have. Usually you will narrow it down to two or three options.

Next investigate the dimensions and orientations of your house and your compound. See which of the options is the most suitable for your land and your house. Decide whether it is easier to change your main door direction thereby giving you additional options, or whether it is easier to change your drains. Don't forget the formula applications can be approached from two viewpoints. If you decide to change your door direction however, do not forget the effect of the Pa Kua Lo Shu formula. Also check whether the new direction you are planning for your door will be auspicious for you and your family. Unless you cannot help it, **do try to get both your best door direction as well as your best water exit flow direction.**

Employ all specifications given as precisely as possible. Explore problems which may have to be confronted. These usually have to do with **irregularity** in the shape of the land; in the **unsuitability** of the contours of the land to your particular exit direction. Sometimes the effect of **outside features** like public drains and rivers, and so forth can cause practical difficulties. Remember that the practice of feng shui is not *just* about knowing the formulas - applying the formulas correctly often require a certain amount of ingenuity. *What is difficult is trying to apply what has been determined as auspicious onto your particular house and garden.* There will be instances where it may seem to be truly impossible to tap the best exit direction, thus forcing you to compromise and accept second best. This does not mean that you cannot enjoy prosperity - merely that the quantum of good fortune may be diffused a little bit. But good or bad feng shui is relative. Depending on one's circumstances, quantum of losses and gains have different effect on different pockets !

PRACTICAL APPLICATIONS OF THE FORMULA

Before proceeding to the worked examples of application, consider the following solutions you can employ under different circumstances.

USING DRAIN COVERS There may be times when you absolutely cannot help water flowing out of the house in a direction that is inauspicious, due to the sitting of the public drain into which your drains flow. Or it can be because your house has been built in a way which does not give you much flexibility in re orienting your drains. If such instances, one way of overcoming the problem is to use cement drain covers which completely close up *offending* drains. See the example given here.

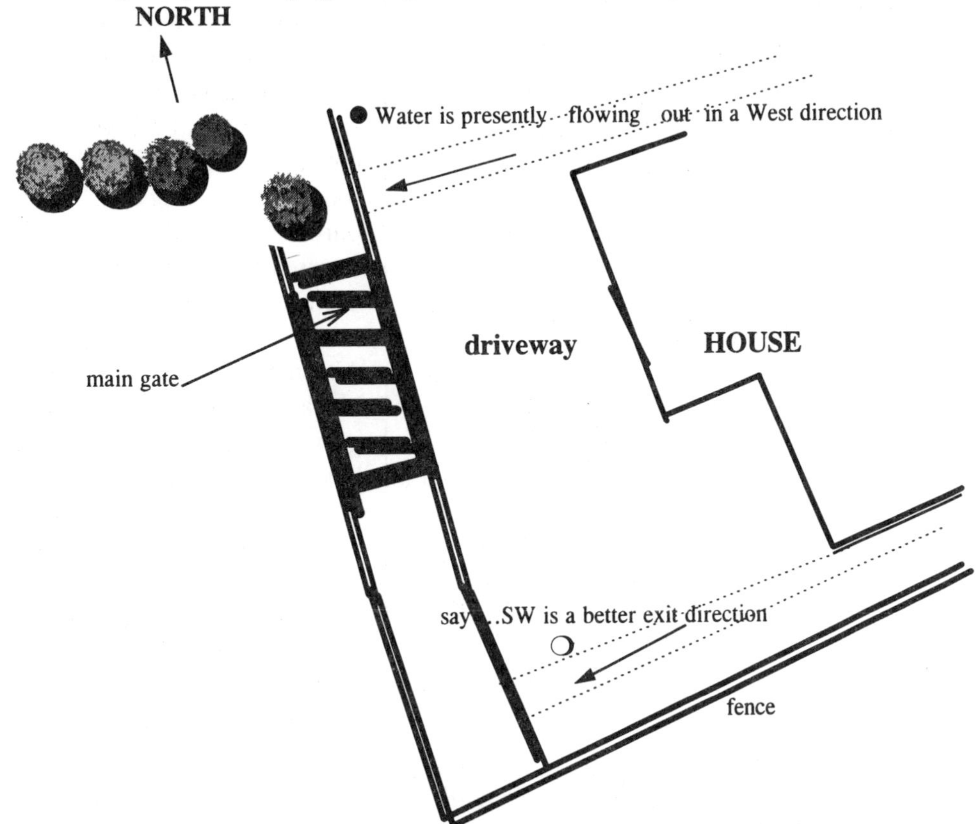

Suppose the more auspicious direction of flow is for the water to exit at ❍ , i.e. in the *Southwest* direction, then the new drain built will be more favourable, and the existing drain at ● should be *covered up with cement*

When constructing your drains according to the formula, let only those drains that flow in an auspicious direction be visible. Drains that are necessary - or which have already been constructed but which are inauspicious, and you do not wish to demolish must be covered or camouflaged. Once made *out of sight* they do **not** affect the feng shui of new drains constructed according to the formula.

Camouflaging with drain covers:

In the example sketched here, the drain is deemed to be flowing in the wrong direction. But because it already exists, and does serve a drainage purpose the owner does not wish to have it demolished. Cement slabs have thus been used to cover the drain so it looks like a footpath. For feng shui purposes, once the drain is covered in this manner, it is deemed no longer there.

Camouflaging with plants:

Alternatively, it is possible to block a drain from view by growing some hedge plants or bushes. This causes the drain to be out of sight of the main house. Ideally this method is ideal if the drain to be blocked is near the fence. In Malaysia, frequency of heavy downpours and tropical rain showers require homes to have good drainage, and it is not always possible to design them in a way that creates good feng shui. Hence practical methods of camouflage are useful to know.

BUILDING WELLS Another important and useful tool in the practical application of the water formula is the construction of a *well* which collects *all* the water of the household before allowing it to flow out in the correct and auspicious direction. In fact this is the most efficient method of ensuring that *the water exit direction* is correctly followed. In using wells there are several useful points to note:

Firstly, its Shape:
Round/Oval shaped wells are preferred to square/rectangular shaped wells. This ensures that there are no inadvertent corners that may be created to cause unnecessary creation of *shar chi* or poison arrows. In any case circular wells are more easy to manage when you have several drains flowing into it.

Secondly, its Dimensions:
Although not vital, the dimensions of the well should correspond to excellent feng dimensions. These dimensions refer to the diameter and depth of the well. In this context readers may wish to refer to the table of auspicious dimensions reproduced on the following page.

Thirdly, its Size:
The well should not be too small as to make the outflowing drain too small to have an effect. Nor should it be too big, thereby causing imbalance. Two very good sizes to use are **32" by 35" or 25" by 18".** At any rate do be guided by the size of your house and the size of your garden when determining the size of the well.

Fourthly, its Depth:
While adhering to feng shui dimensions, it is also advisable to make the well just one inch deeper than the inflowing drain levels. This allows water to flow in from these drains. The outflowing drains should then be slightly lower than the depth of the well. This ensures water flows out by the correct drain. Remember that **the outflowing drain must be oriented absolutely correctly.** This will be the most crucial part of the exercise.

Finally, the safety feature:
To make the well safe for residents, they should ideally be covered by grating or grills. They must **not** be covered up with cement slabs or blocked out of view. The water must be shown flowing into the well, and more importantly, the water must be seen flowing out of the well. When the well is blocked from view, the effect is that it is deemed to be *not there*.

Table of Auspicious Feng Shui Dimensions

Chai *(Money Luck)*

between 0 **to** 2 and1/8 inches
between 17 **to** 19 and 1/8 inches
between 34 **to** 36 and1/8 inches
between 51 **to** 53 and1/8 inches

Vi *(Helpful People Luck)*

between 6 and1/4 **to** 81/2 inches
between 23 and 3/8 **to** 25and1/2 inches
between 40 and3/8 **to** 42 and1/2 inches
between 57and3/8 **to** 59 and1/2 inches

Kwan *(Career & Power Luck)*

between 8 and1/2 **to**10 and5/8 inches
between 25 and1/2 **to** 27 and 5/8 inches
between 42 and 1/2 **to** 44 and 5/8 inches
between 59 and 1/2 **to** 61 and 5/8 inches

Pun *(Capital and Wealth Luck)*

between 14 and3/4 **to** 17 inches
between 31 and 3/4 **to** 44 and 3/8 inches
between 48 and 3/4 **to** 51 inches
between 65 and3/4 **to** 68 inches

❀ *The above summary of feng shui dimensions may be supplemented with more detailed meanings of dimensions contained in the author's second book on feng shui entitled APPLIED PA KUA LO SHU FENG SHUI*

Constructing a well

The best way to ensure that all the water of the house flows out in one auspicious direction is to construct a well. All the drains of the house should flow into this well which thus serves to collect the water in a single place. Another drain should then convey the water out of the house compound. An example of how two drains bring the water into a well, and then another taking it out is shown in the example sketched on the following page.

Constructing a well:

In the example shown on this page, the water flow in front of the main door was flowing from left to right, and this was ascertained to be inauspicious. For the residents to tap into auspicious water feng shui luck, the flow had to be changed such that it was moving from right to left.

The water exit direction recommended was that the water should be flowing out of the garden via a drain *bearing 148 degrees from North*. This would ensure fabulous good luck for the residents.

Thus **a new drain was built to flow pass the front door** moving from right to left. This drain was allowed to also flow pass the garage before making its way into a specially constructed well. Meanwhile another drain carrying water from the back of the house was also **diverted to deposit its water into the same well**. Thus the well is receiving water from two drains.

Then a third drain was built to drain out water from the well in the recommended auspicious direction. This is shown in the sketch below.

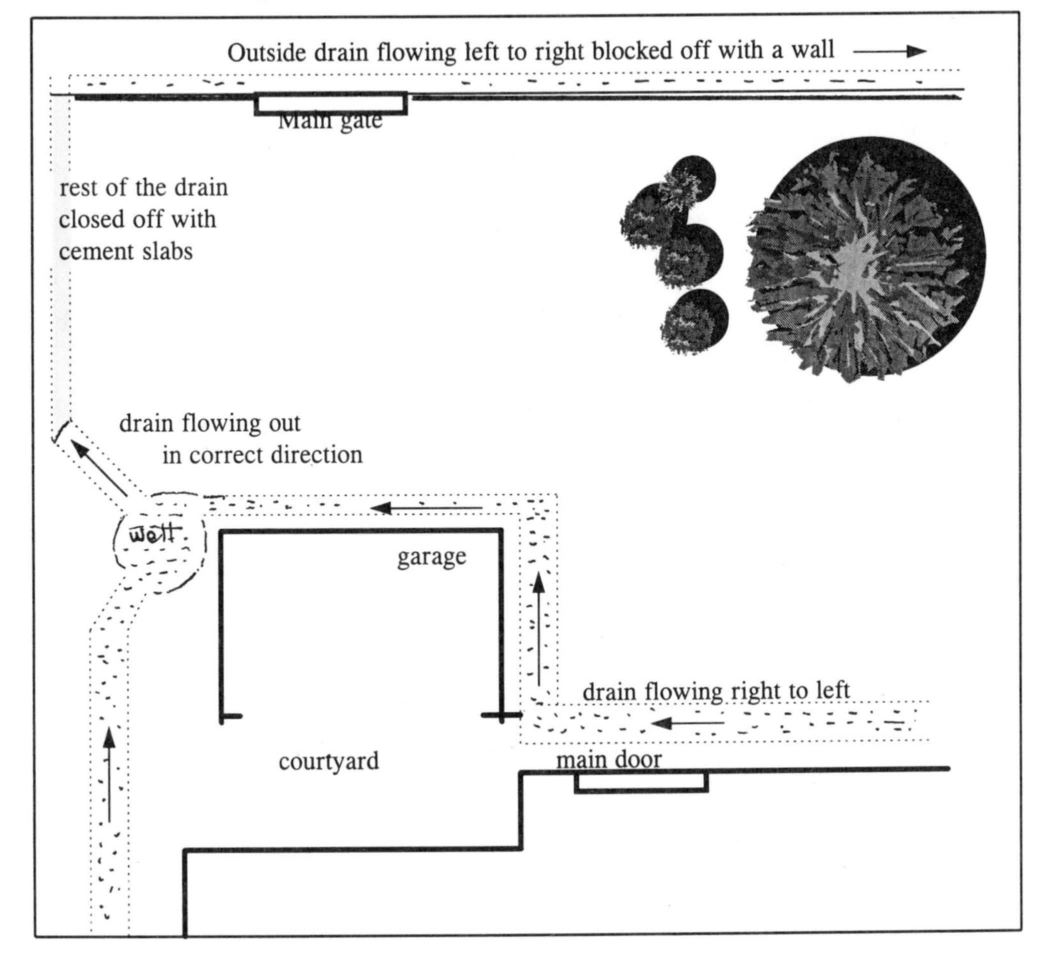

Constructing a well:

Here is another example showing a well being used at the back of the house. The reason for doing so may be to tap the best exit direction. Or it may be due to the fact that the public drain for this house is located at the back of the house. Note in this case how the water from the drain flows into the well allowing the recommended exit direction to be adhered to but *without the need for a sharp turn in the drain*. So far no specific auspicious directions are being given according to formula. These examples merely illustrates application methods.

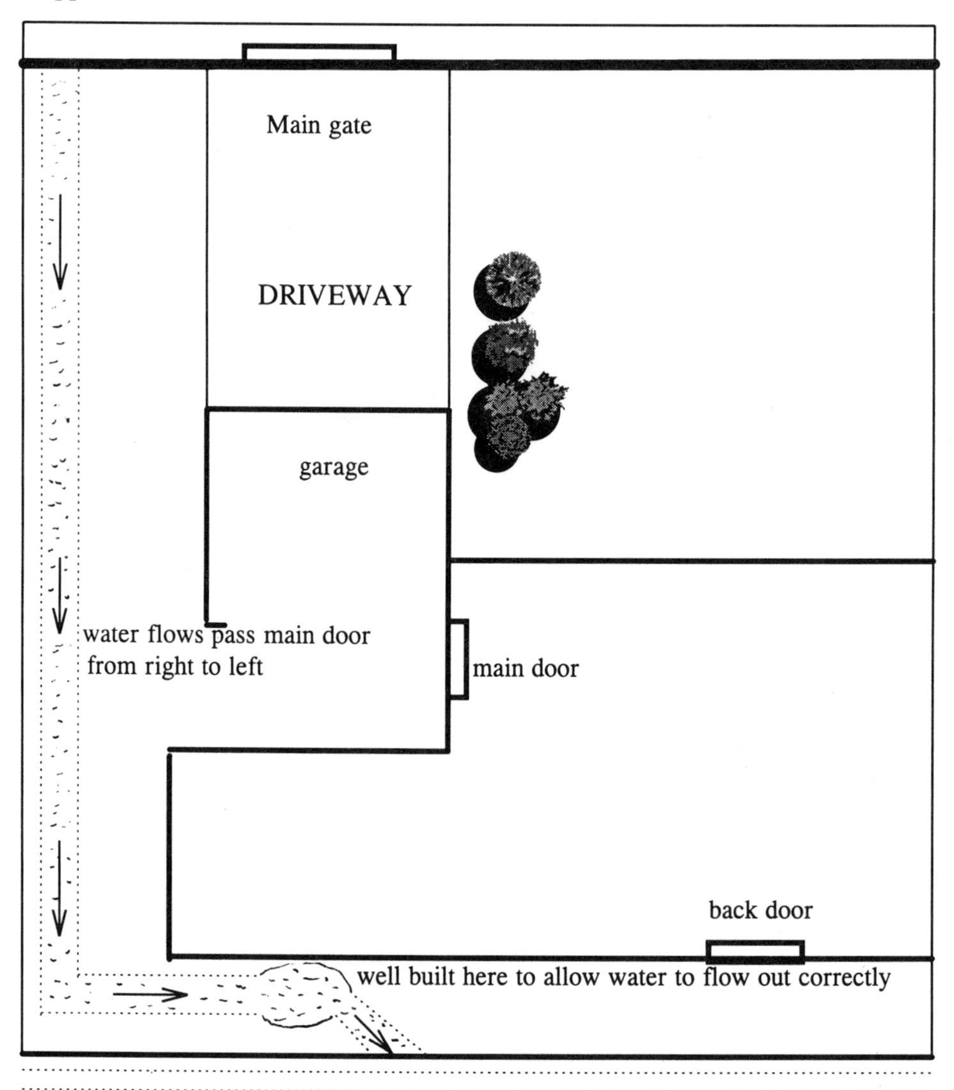

Constructing a well

A third example shows a small well constructed at the corner of a link house. Here the drain goes pass only the front door before exiting at the front left hand corner of the garden in a suitable direction. Note this way, the well allows resident flexibility of exit directions.

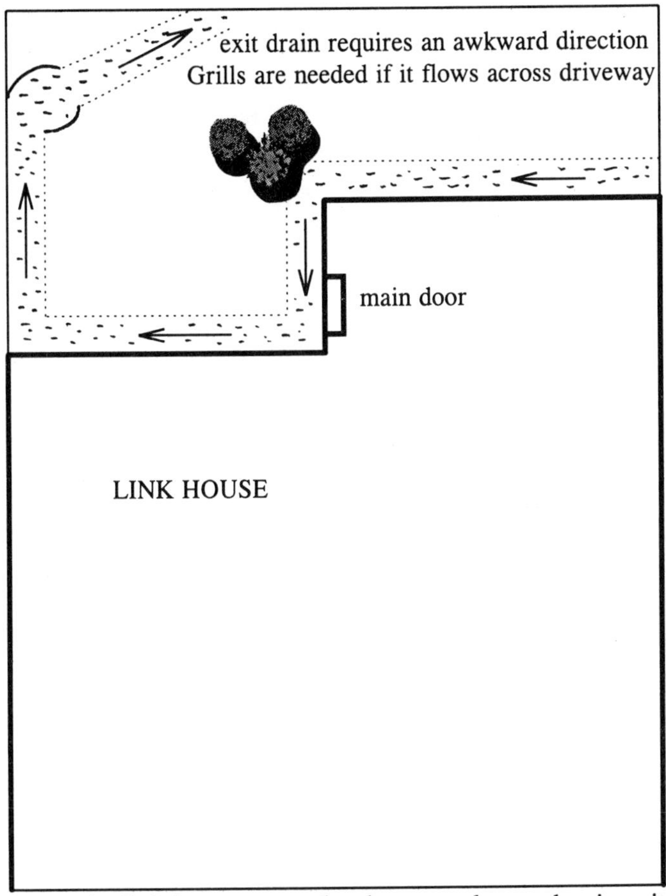

In this example of a link house, note that because the garden is quite tiny, and the drains cannot flow pass the sides of the house, water flows are necessarily quite tight. **This does not matter as long as the water flows pass the main door** in the correct direction, and exits via the correct direction according to the formula. Do try to make sure that any well that gets built is not too large, as it could then overwhelm the house. Also, it is preferable for the well to be located on the left hand side of the main door (looking out) . In this case, however, it is not possible.

WORKED EXAMPLES FOR DIFFERENT DOOR DIRECTIONS

The worked examples presented in the rest of this chapter are based on each of the twelve categories of door directions. Bearing in mind that each door category has two possible door directions at least two examples are being given for every door category.

Readers are strongly advised to follow through all the examples given as they will collectively assist the amateur practitioner. Most of the practical difficulties that are usually encountered will be discussed, with possible solutions offered. These problems, as we have seen have to do with constraints imposed by contours, levels and shapes of the garden and house.

Several tips are again repeated here:

Firstly do make very certain that direction of your main door is accurate. This is because it is the main door that determines your house category. The water dragon formula is not based on your birth date. Instead it is based solely on the direction of the main door, and any auspicious results of the water feng shui implemented benefits everyone in the house irrespective of their birth dates, and also irrespective of whether they are family or not. The water feng shui formula benefits every resident - although of course in varying degrees. Depending on which of the auspicious exit direction is used, different members of the family will benefit more than others.

Secondly, be absolutely accurate when plotting the exit direction. Use a good compass, and check several times before aligning the exit drain. It is easy to make mistakes, and certain parts of the formula can be tricky in that what separates a good direction from a bad one is sometimes a matter of only a few degrees. So do supervise your contractor very closely.

Thirdly, when determining size and length of drains, always bear in the mind the need for balance. Drains should never overwhelm by being too large or too deep. Nor should they be so small as to be rendered useless for practical purposes.

Fourthly, it is strongly advised that you keep the water flowing. During dry spells, turn on the tap for part of the day. This simulates the flow that is so necessary to activate the good effects of the formula.

Fifthly, never allow the water in the well to get stagnant and dirty. The drains should also be kept clean. Otherwise the auspicious *chi* could well turn into *shar chi*. This is one of the cardinal rules of feng shui. Water should never be allowed to stagnate, or get smelly and dirty. Keep your drains clean.

Finally, sketch out your options and study them carefully before arranging for your old drains to be altered or new ones to be constructed. You will find that during the construction stage your contractor will have some difficulty in being exact and accurate. You will have to help him along, and supervise him. Otherwise you could inadvertently make mistakes.

Example 1.
<u>Category One House</u>
Main door faces ***ping*** or ***wu*** direction.(first and second sub sectors of South)
Water needs to flow pass the main door from ***left to right***.
Best and most auspicious exit direction is via **sin/shih** direction
(ie. Bearing **277.5° to 307.5° from North**)

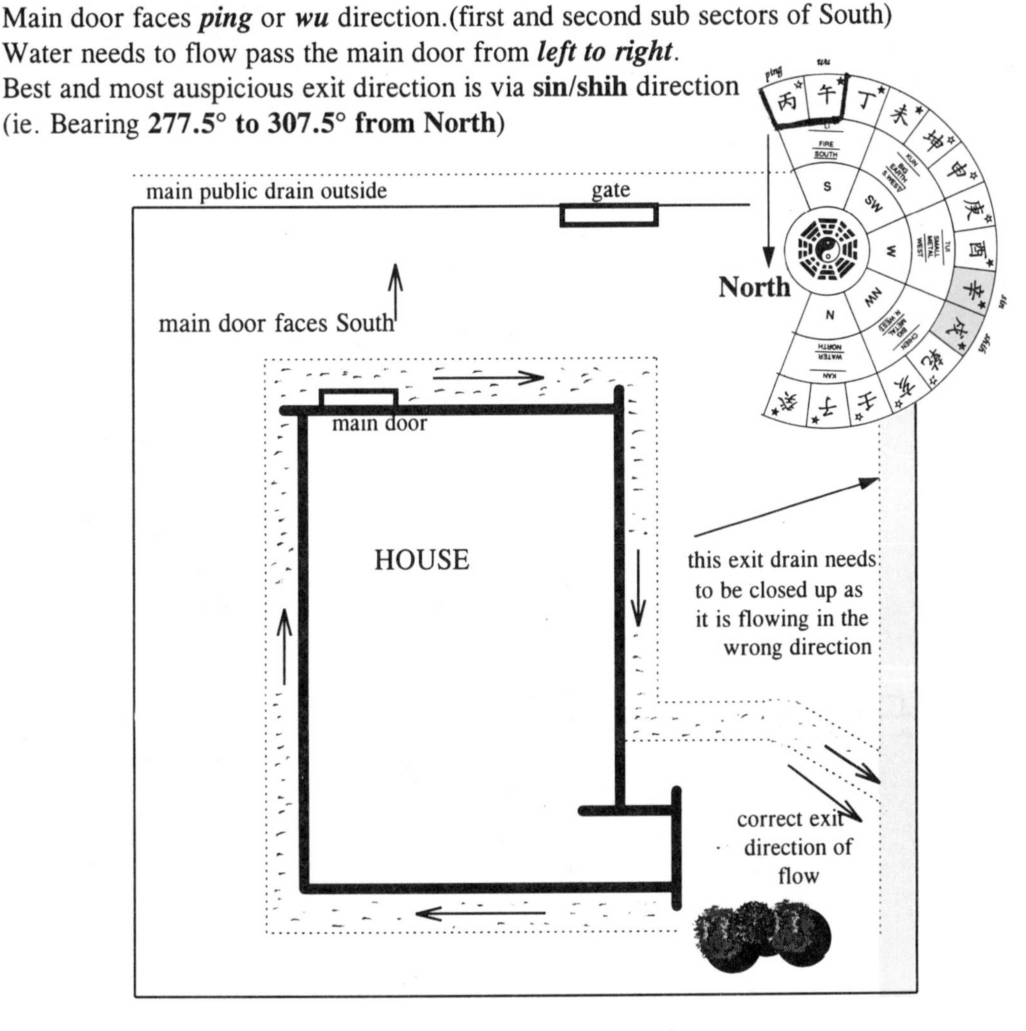

Example 2:
Category One House

Main door faces *ping* or *wu* direction but this house is a link house and water thus has to flow out in the front part of the house. Thus it is not possible to tap the best direction. The alternative is therefore to try and tap the second best exit direction which is for the exit drain to flow out via the *ting/wei* direction, ie bearing **187.5 to 217.5 from North**. Since the gate and driveway are not in the way, it makes things easier. Also, unlike the previous example 1, the exit drain can flow directly onto the main public drain outside. Again, unlike Example 1, there is therefore no need for any connecting drain which would have to be covered.

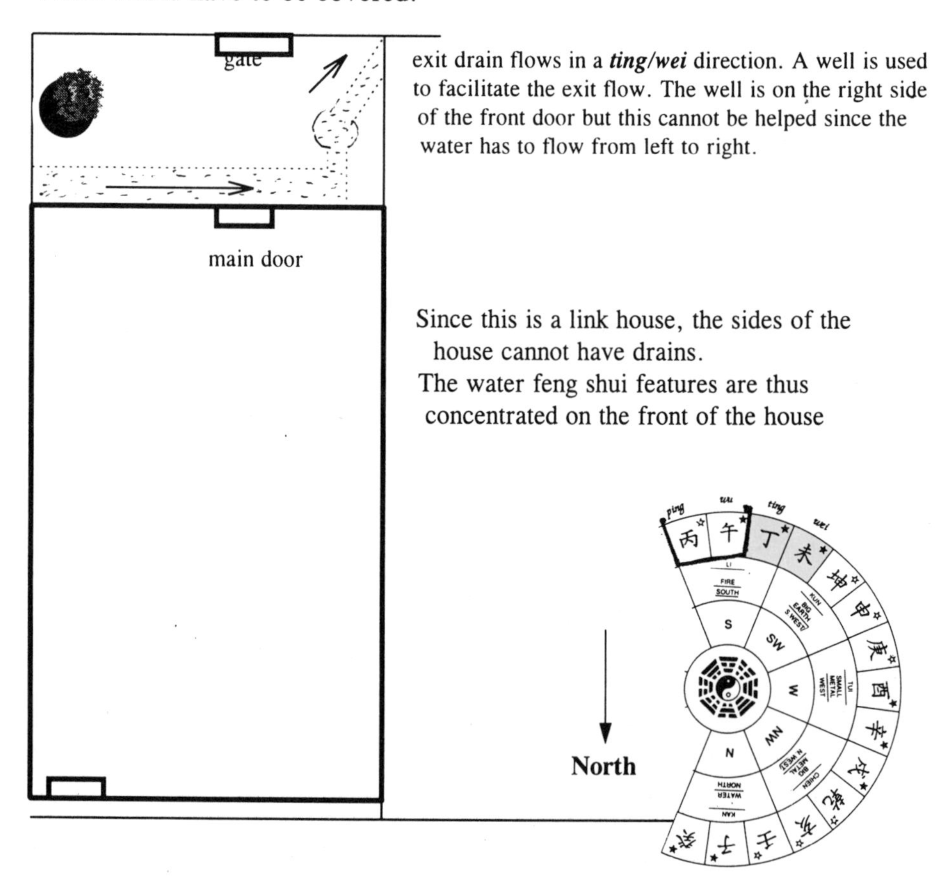

Example 3
Category Two House

Main door in this bungalow house faces a *ting wei* direction. This is the third subsector of the South direction or the first subsector of the Soutwest direction. The best exit direction for such a house is via the ***shun tze*** direction, which is in the Southeast of the house. This means the water has to flow out through the front of the house. Unfortunately there is no public drain in front of the house. The only public drain is at the back of the house. Such a situation requires ingenuity. Also the water needs to flow pass the main door in a ***right to left*** direction. In the example given, the *visible* drain has been built to flow out in a ***shun tze*** direction from the well that has been placed in the Southeast sector of the garden. It then flows into a another drain which carries the water to the back, except that this drain is covered (shown in the sketch as the shaded portion). The compass sketched alongside should assist you to get your bearings.

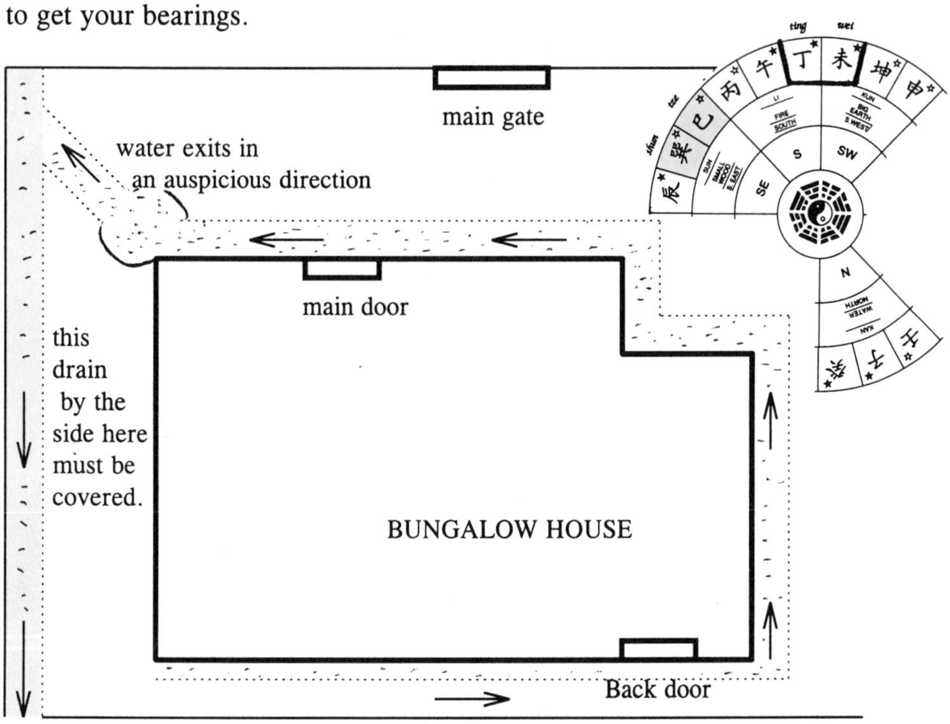

water from the house is deposited into public drain at the back of the house

Example 4
Category Two House

Main door is again facing the ***ting wei*** direction. In the case of this example, the house is a semi detached bungalow with the left side of the house attached. It is thus difficult for the house owner to tap the best exit direction for this category house. However because the second best direction also holds out the promise of wealth and prosperity, he has decided to make do with the second best direction. This is for the water to flow pass the main door in a ***right to left direction*** as required. It then flows out to another drain located in front of the garden in a ***kun*** direction ie bearing between **217.5° to 232.5°** from North. **This is regarded as the exit drain**. The drain into which it flows must absolutely be covered because apart from the wrong compass direction, it is flowing from left to right which is inauspicious. This drain takes the water all the way to the public drain at the back of the house.

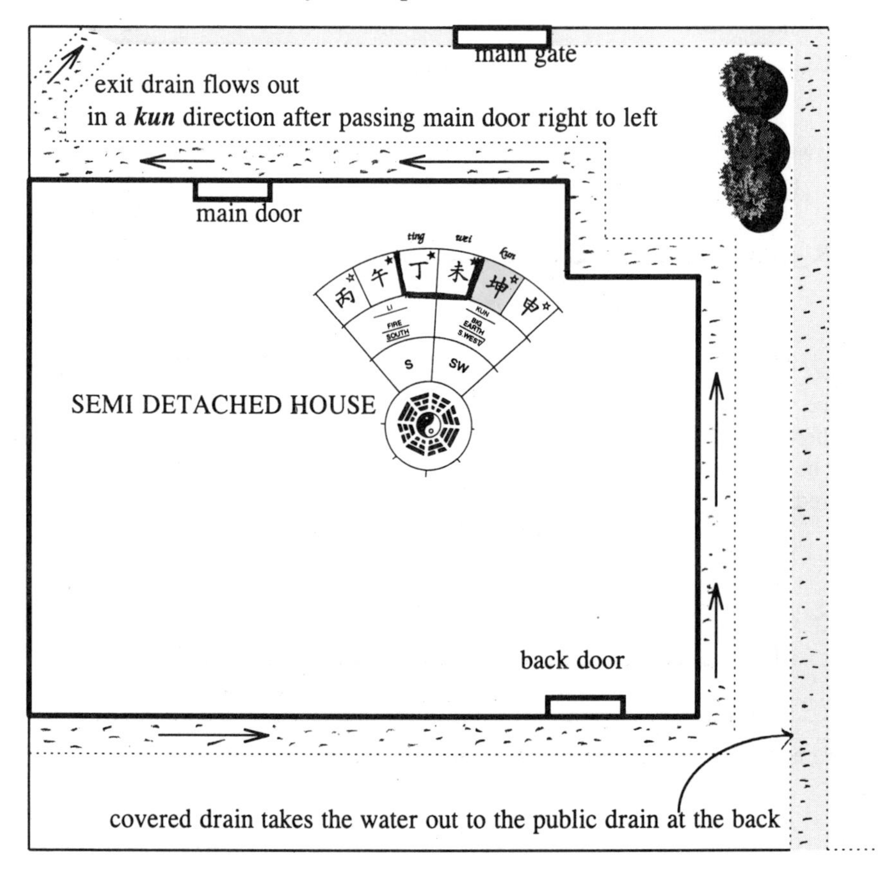

Example 5
Category Three House
Main door faces Southwest in this example, specifically in the second or third subsectors of the Southwest - named ***kun*** or ***sen*** in the Feng Shui compass. The best exit direction for such a house is East/Southeast, or more specifically via the ***yi or shen*** direction bearing between **97.5° to 127.5°** from North. ***The water has to flow from right to left pass the main door***. This means that the household water should ideally be seen to flow out at the left side of the house. In this example because there is a lot of land on the left side, it is easy to tap the best exit direction. If there is not, the solution will be to use the next best direction, or follow the previous example of building another drain to transport the water, and then, to cover this drain.

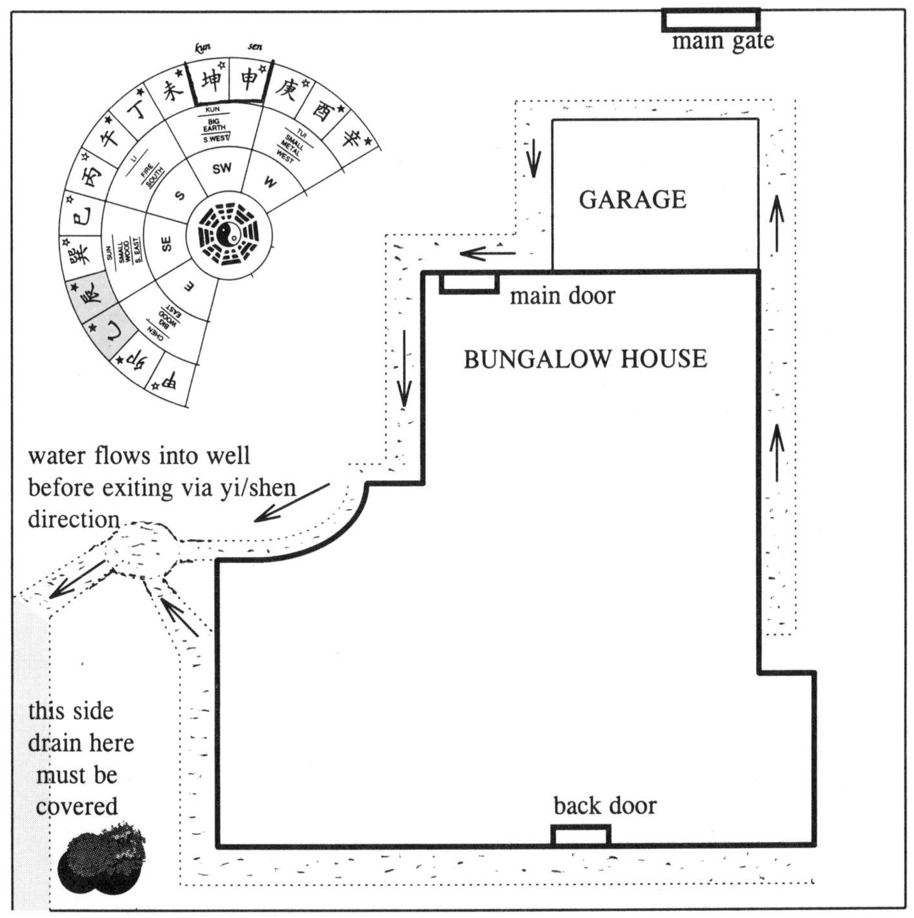

water flows into public drain at back of house.

EXAMPLE 6
Category Three House
This is a link house whose main door faces **Southwest** ie the ***kun/sen*** direction, ie similiar to the previous example. However because it does not have enough land, residents can utilise the next best direction, which is for the water to flow out via the ***ting/wei*** direction **ie South/Southwest**, specifically, bearing between **187.5° to 217.5° from North** on the compass; which is what has been shown here. The water flows into the public drain in front of the house, but a well has been built because the driveway makes a direct flow out difficult.

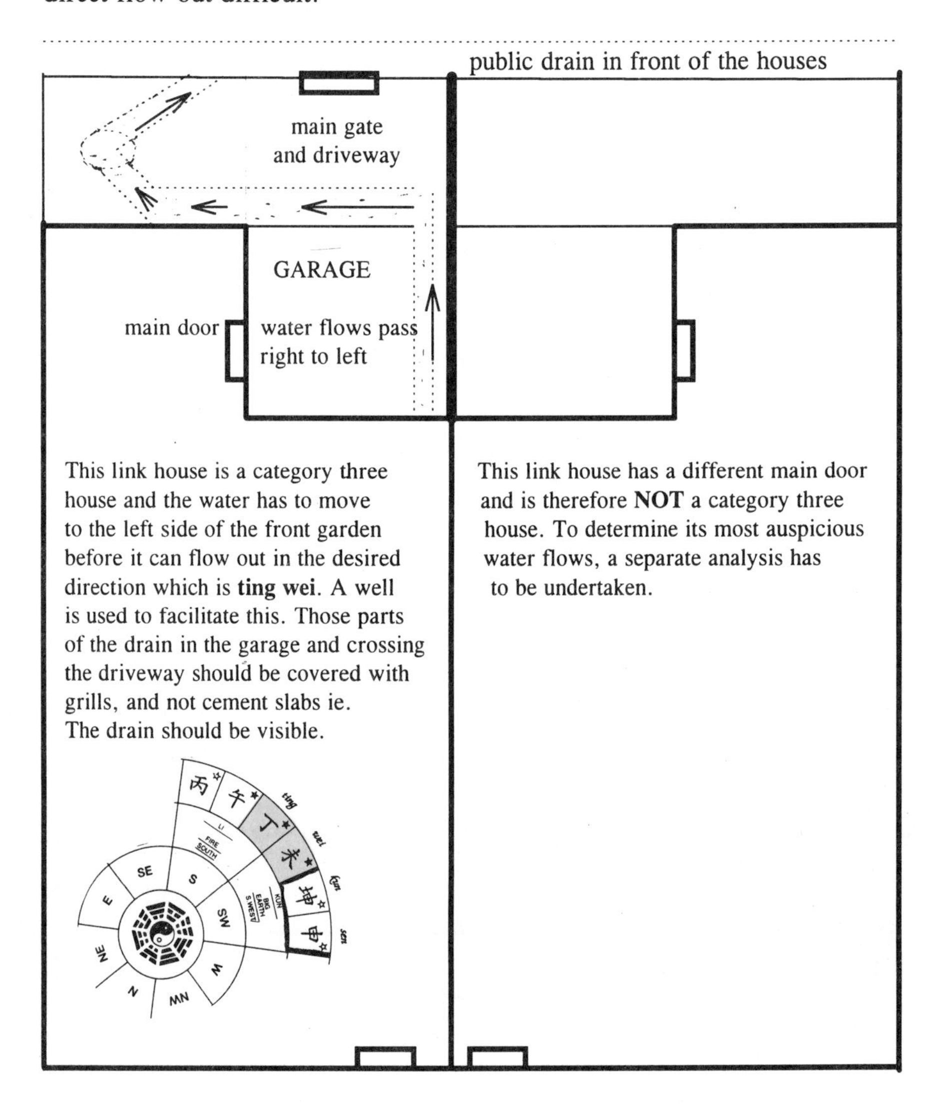

Example 7
Category Four House

Main door faces **West**, more specifically the first or second subsectors of West named ***ken and yu*** respectively in the Feng Shui compass. For this category house the most auspicious direction of water exit flow is between **7.5° to 37.5° from North**, referred to as ***kway or choh*** directions in the compass. This is shown in the sketch of the compass simultaneously reproduced here. Because it is a West facing house the water must pass the front door moving a left to right direction. This makes it easy for this particular house to arrange its water flows. The drains have been designed for the water to collect in a well located on the Northeast sector of the house before exiting via the drain flowing out into the covered drain alongside the fence. Because the public drain is at the back this side drain goes to the back.

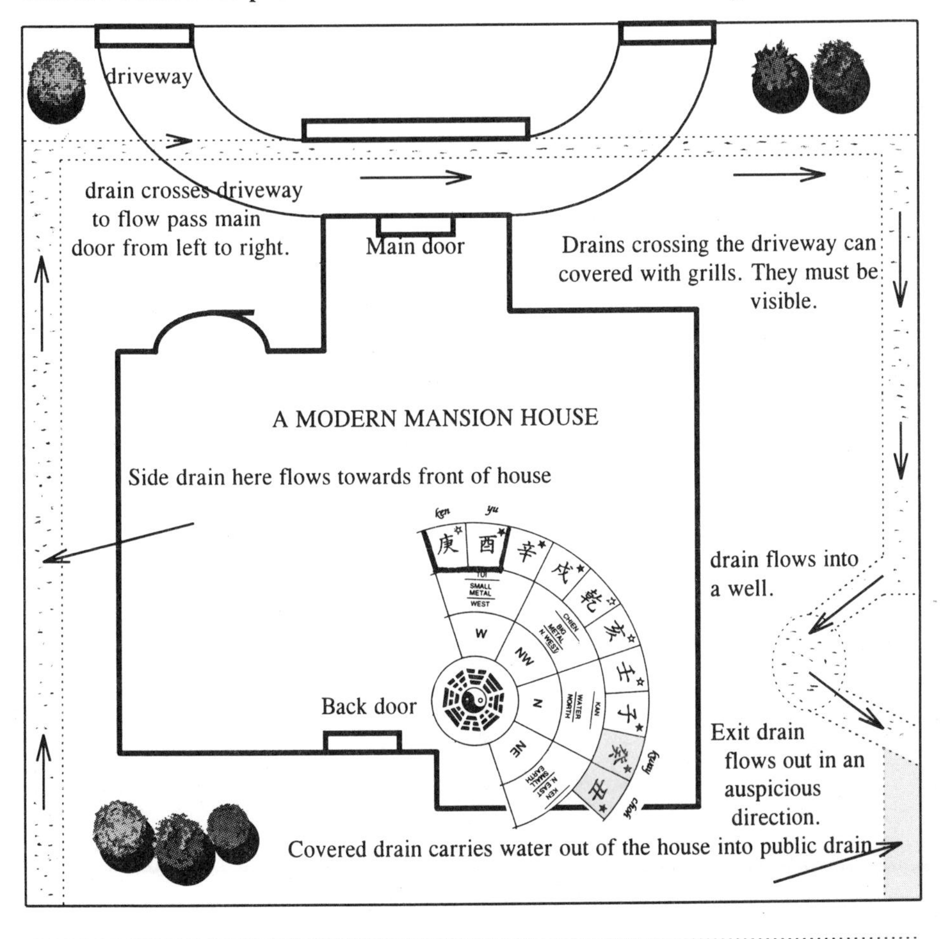

Example 8
Category Four House
The Main door of this house faces directly West, i.e. in the second sub sector named ***yu*** in the Feng Shui compass. The recommended exit direction for this link house is via ***sin or shih*** i.e. in a direction slightly to the right of the house. To be exact, the direction of exit flow should bear between **277.5° to 307.5° from North.** Because this is a West facing house, the water must flow pass the main front door in a left to right direction for it to be auspicious. A well is used to facilitate the water flow.

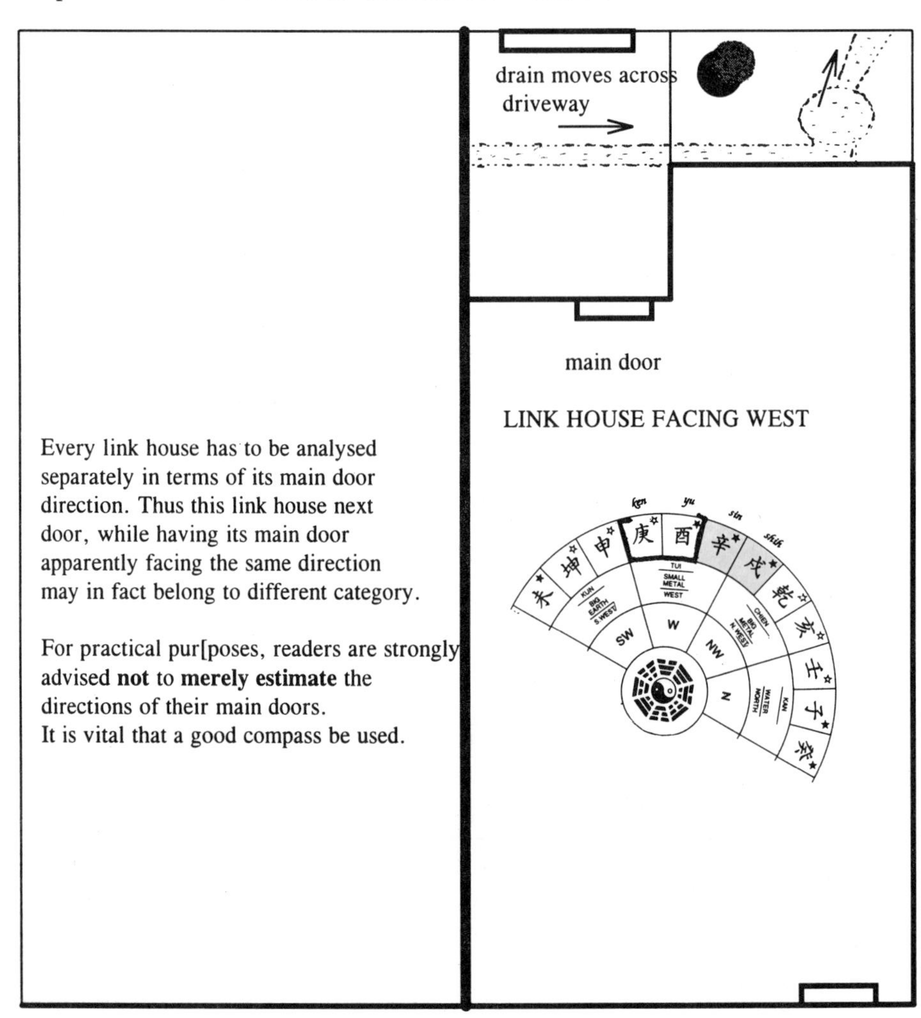

Example 9

Category Five House

This mansion house has its main door facing the West/Northwest direction, what the Feng Shui compass refers to as the ***sin/shih*** direction. As such its most auspicious water exit direction according to the water Dragon Classic formula is for it to leave bearing between **217.5° to 247.5°** from North. This is called the ***kun*** or ***sen*** direction and it corresponds to the Southwest. The water should flow from **right to left** pass the main door. Some problems have to be overcome. *Firstly,* the land slopes down from left to right. The water must flow in the other direction. To overcome this problem the depth of the drain must slope deeper towards the left so as to facilitate he flow. *Secondly,* the house has utilised so much land that it is difficult to build a well. The exit drain thus turns rather sharply. To counter the angle formed small bushes are planted to camouflage it. *Thirdly* the shape of the land is slightly irregular.

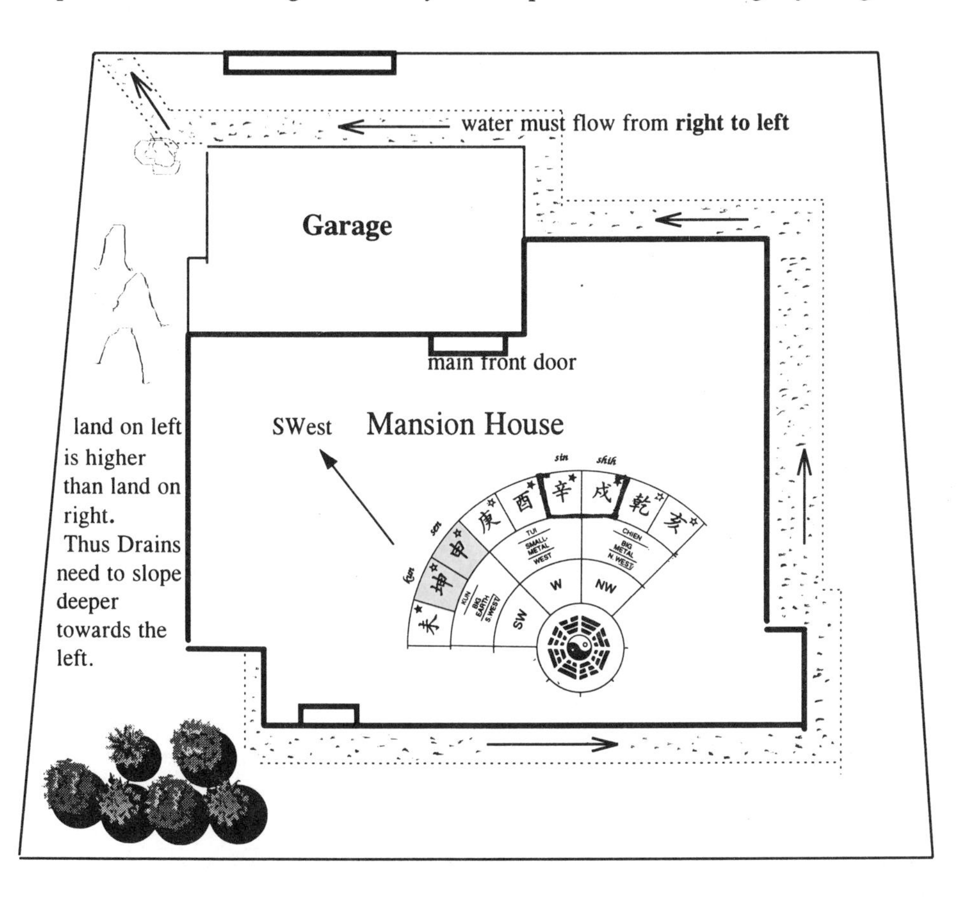

Example 10
Category Five House

In this example, we shall see how a **an auspicious water dragon** is constructed. According to the Water Dragon Classic, if your house faces the direction ***sin*** or ***shih***, i.e. in the last sub sector of West or the first subsector of Northwest, it is possible to build a water dragon. The instructions for building a water dragon must be followed very carefully, since getting the instructions wrong will cause you to inadvertently tap into an inauspicious direction.

The instructions for building a water dragon are very explicit for a category Five House.
Firstly the water must originate, i.e. it must seem to come from the ***sin*** direction. ***Sin*** is in the West part of the garden. Thus it is necessary to build a drain in that sector, and to let the water start flowing from that direction towards the house. During dry spells, it is suggested that you might even want to artificially create water by turning on a suitably located tap !

Secondly, the water **must then flow pass the main front door in a left to right direction**. This is a variation from what is normally recommended for the other auspicious directions of a Category Five House. Normally, the recommendation is for the water to flow from right to left. Thus it is important to note this major difference, when constructing a water dragon.

Thirdly, the water must then **circle round the house, and flow towards the east sector** of the house. To ensure that maximum good *chi* is created, it is recommended that the drain be built to flow towards the extremity of the sector. This can be seen in the sketched example.

Finally the **water must then be seen to exit the house in a *chia* direction**. This corresponds to the first sub sector of the East, and to ensure that there are no sharp bends created, using a well is a good idea.
Remember that when building a water dragon, it is preferable that no other drains be built to flow into the well. Let the exposed drain which is simulating the dragon be the only artery of water flowing round the garden of the house. You will see from the sketch on the next page that the water dragon is seen to be hugging the house in a most auspicious way. Also, it is recommended that all drain corners be rounded off to simulate the dragon.

Creating a Water Dragon for a House with *sin/shih* main door

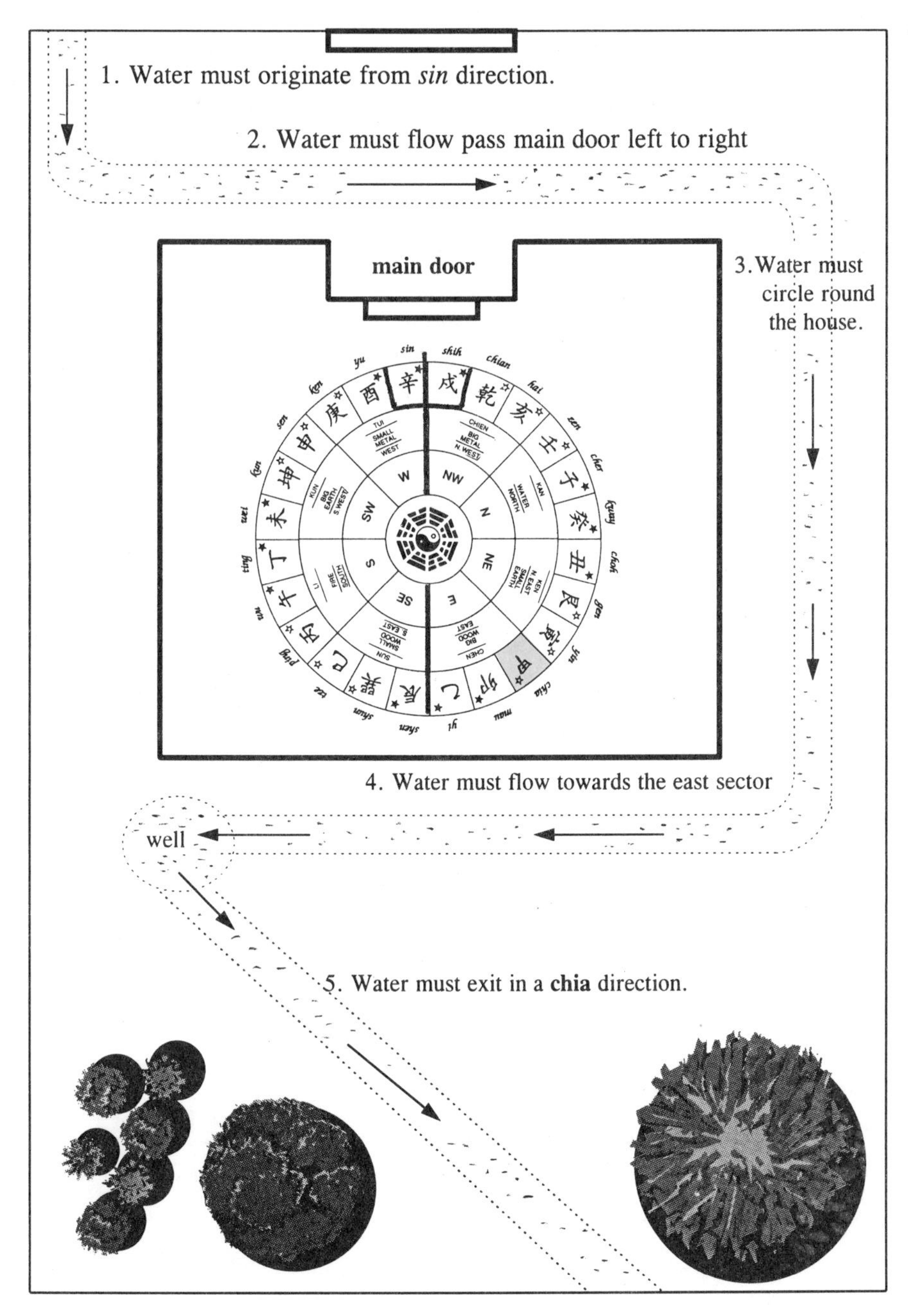

Example 11
Category Six Apartment Block
The Main Door of the building is facing either the second or third subsector of the direction **Northwest.** These directions are named ***chian*** and ***hai*** respectively in the Feng Shui compass. The most auspicious exit direction for this building is to have the water **flow out bearing between 187.5° to 217.5°** from North - which is in the South/Southwest direction. These directions are named ***ting*** and ***wei*** respectively. In addition, the water must first flow pass the main front door from **right to left**. If these directions are correctly applied the building will enjoy a great deal of money luck. The example shown here is an apartment block which has an auspicious river flowing past its main entrance in a right to left direction. This alone will bring the residents of such an apartment abundant money luck. But to enhance it further, the developers have also cleverly introduced additional water features by making certain the drains are built according to the Water Dragon Classic formula.

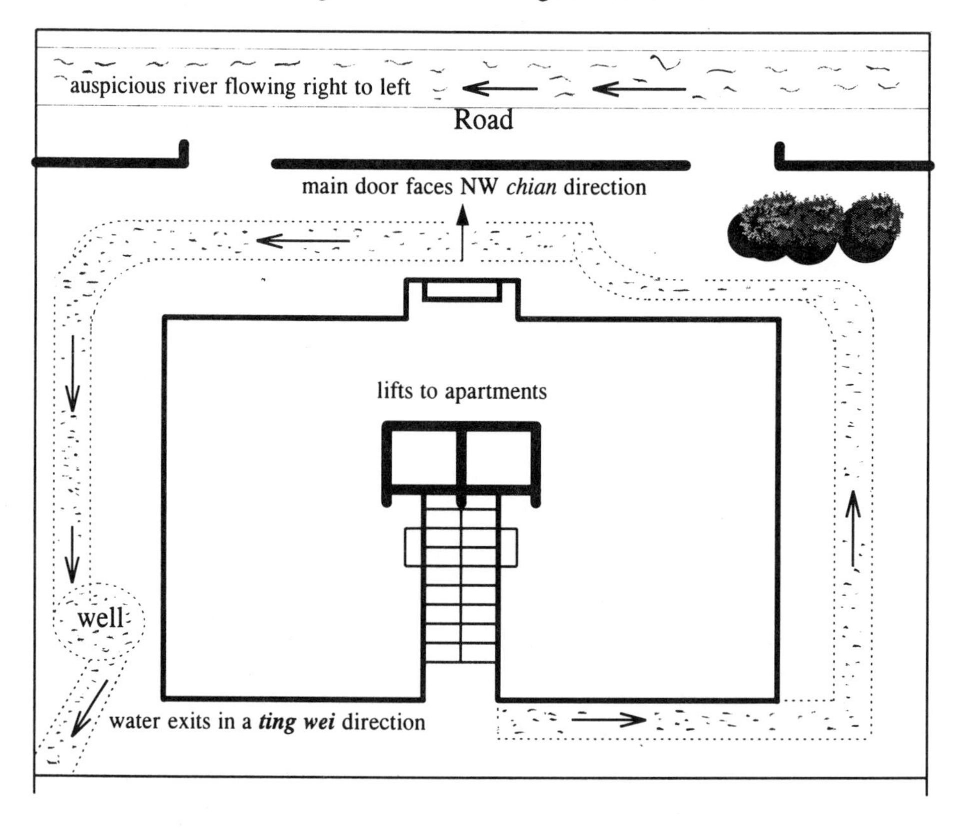

Example 12
Category Six House

This house also faces the Northwest, in the direction ***hai.*** In this example the house owner has decided to tap the second best exit direction which is to let the water flow out in a ***sin/shih*** direction. This means bearing **between 277.5° to 307.5° from North**. This direction promises long term prosperity for residents, and although, it may not be as auspicious as the first exit direction, it is nevertheless acceptable, especially since the house does not lend itself easily to tapping the first exit direction. This is because of the irregular shape of the land which is narrow at the back.

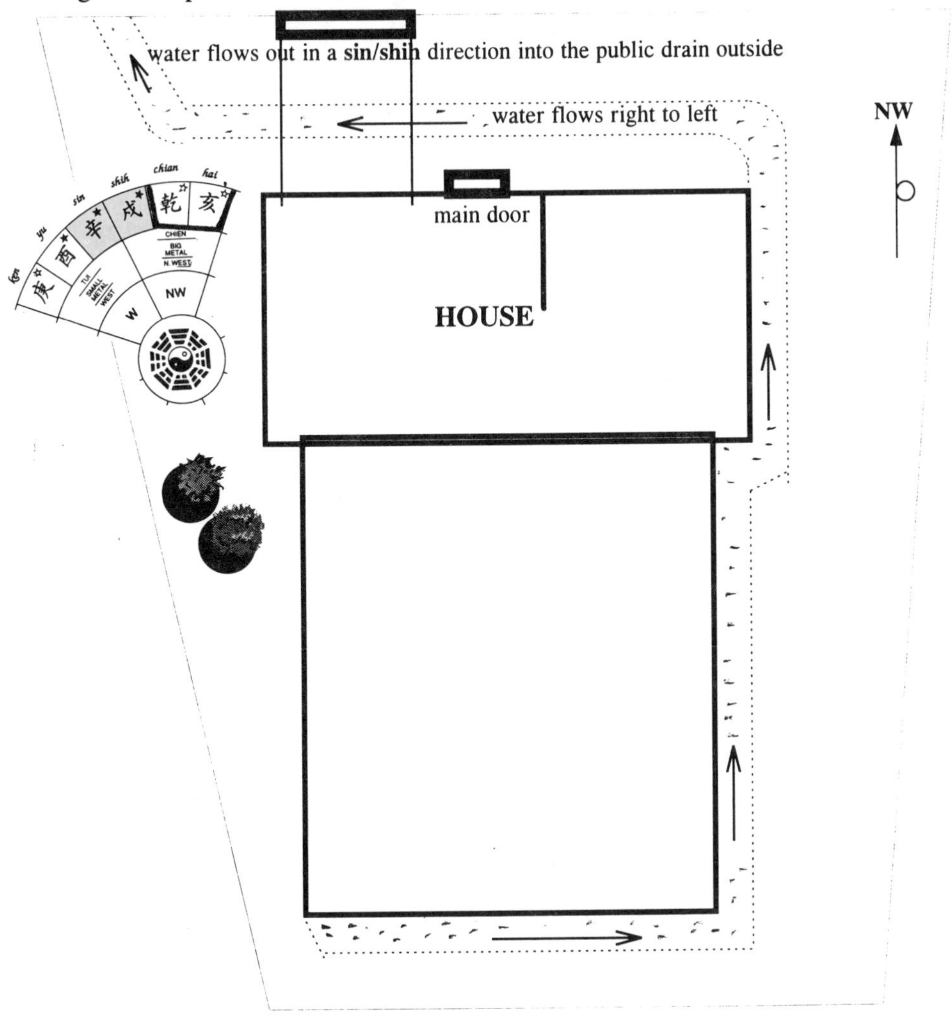

Example 13
Creating a Water Dragon for a Category Six House

In this category house, the main door faces the *chian or the hai* direction ie the *second and third subsectors of the **Northwest*** direction. To create the kind of auspicious feng shui which cause money to pour into the household, owners of such a house can seriously consider building a water dragon. To do this successfully requires that there be enough of a garden, since this particular dragon requires the land in the front of the house, to be large enough to at least accomodate the need for the drain to flow for at least a hundred steps - equivalent to a hundred feet in terms of dimensions.

The detailed steps to follow are as follows:

1. Water must ***flow from a height towards the main door.***
2. Water must also flow pass the main door in a ***right to left direction***. This means that the water will be flowing from the North or East sectors of the garden to the West. This also means that the North side of the garden should be higher than the South and West sides in view of the first requirement.
3. Water must be seen to exit the house in a ***hai*** direction. This is a Northwest direction that corresponds to one of the door directions of this category house. The exact direction is vital - practitioners **MUST** get the direction absolutely correct. The ***hai*** direction is bearing ***between 322.5° to 352.5° from North***. It is advisable to get a good compass when actually constructing this exit drain. The ***hai*** direction is also directly in front of the main door. The most important thing to remember is that the water in this exit drain must not touch ***chian***, the neighbour direction on the left of ***hai***. ***Chian*** bears between 307.5° to 322.5°. Thus it would seem safer, when building the exit drain to veer more towards 352.5° than 322.5° This is because if the exit drain touches ***chian***, it will cause tremendous bad luck.
4. The exit drain must flow for at least **100 steps** in the direction indicated.
5. The water must then **loop back in any direction** towards the house, like a dragon coiling itself towards the house in a tight embrace.
6. The water then may exit in any direction except that the drain must then be covered with cement slabs.

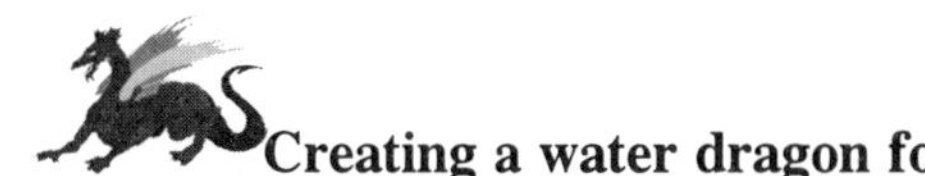

Creating a water dragon for a house with *chian/hai* main door.

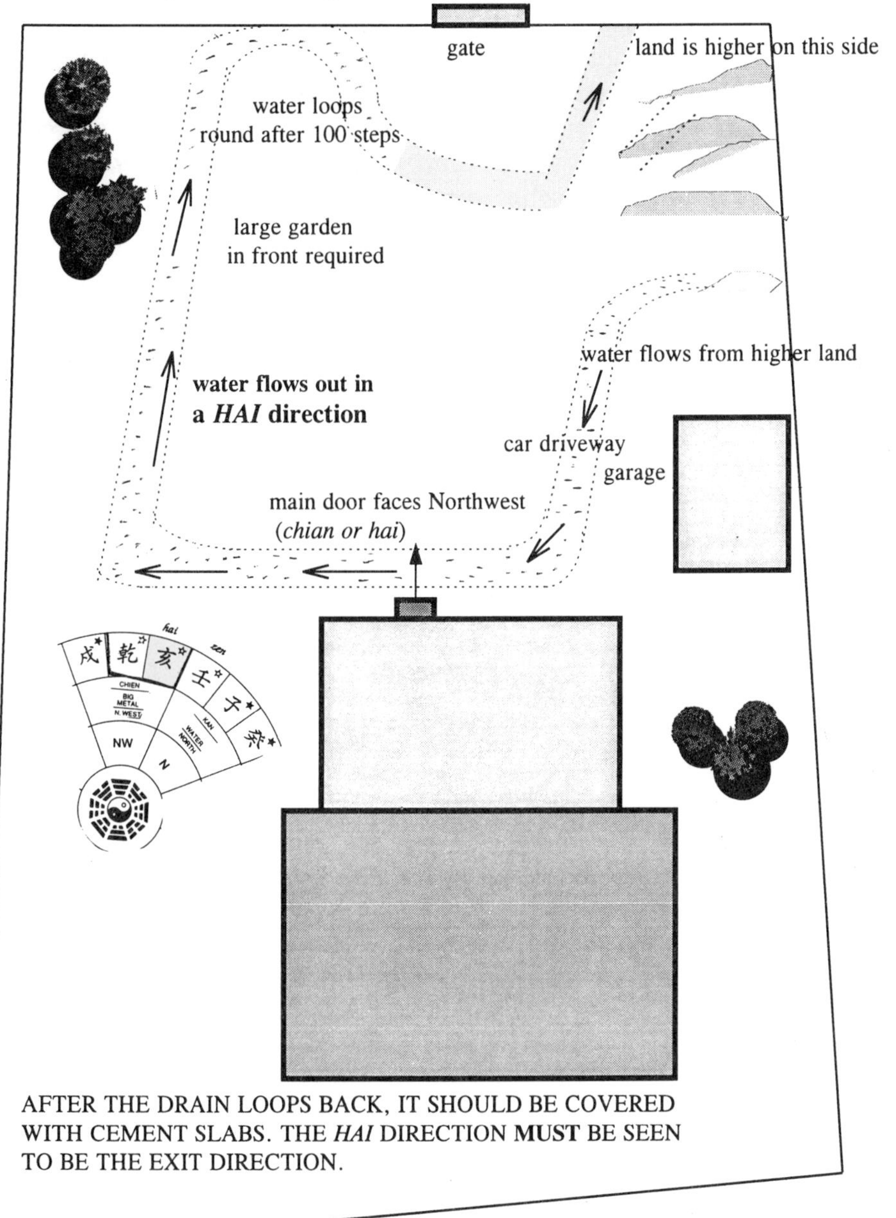

Example 14
Category Seven House
This house will have its main front door facing North, and more accurately the first and second sub sectors of North, named *zen* and *cher* in the Compass. In this example, we show the water flowing pass the main door in a left to right direction, and exiting via the ***yi*** and ***shen*** directions (in theEast/Southeast). This means the water is visibly flowing out in a direction that bears between **97.5 to 127.5 from North**. This is known as ***the three priceless jewels*** direction and is extremely auspicious. If your house is configured this way, you can use this example, and if undertaken accurately you will enjoy tremendous feng shui luck !

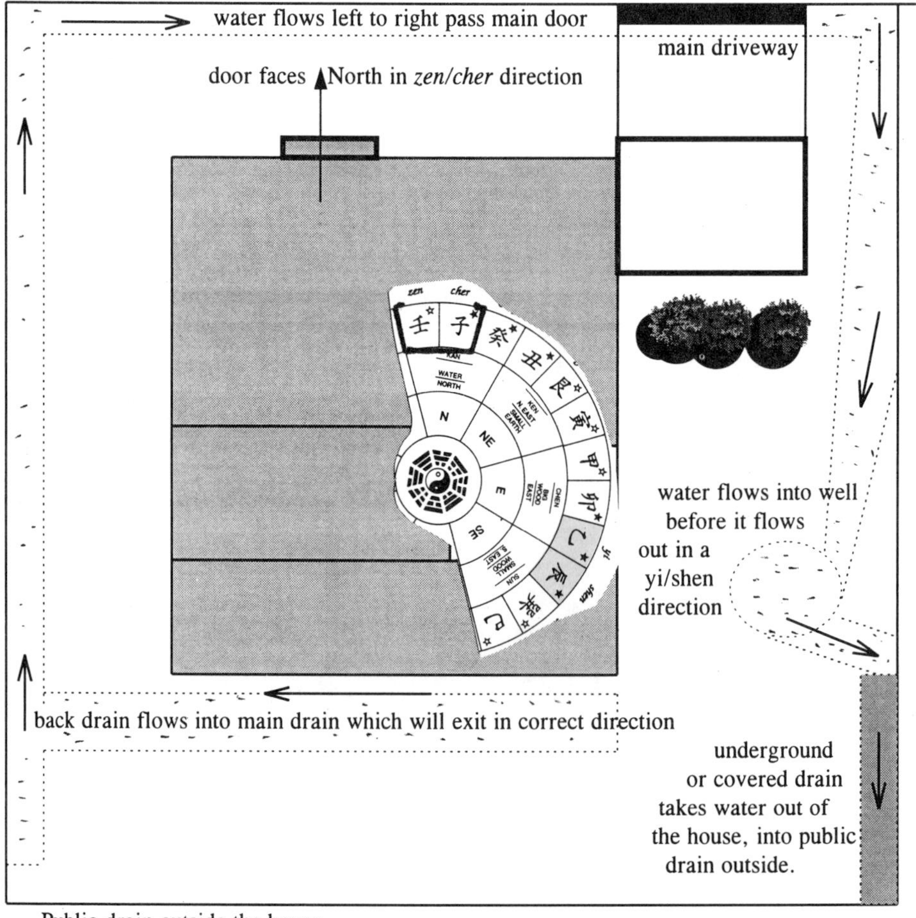

Example 15
Category Seven House

Here is a house facing a similiar direction as the previous example ie zen/cher in the North. However because this is a link house which does not have any garden at the back of the house (and thus I am showing only the front portion of the house together with the front garden), residents would be advised in such an instance, to selecet the second best exit direction - which also promises excellent prospects for harnessing good fortune luck. This requires the water to flow **left to right pass the main door** and then for it to exit via ***kway*** or ***choh.*** In the example given here ***the main door of the house has been changed to facilitate the water flow.*** Thus the original main door which was actually facing West has been closed up and a new main door has been installed to face the North thereby making it easier to design the water flow.

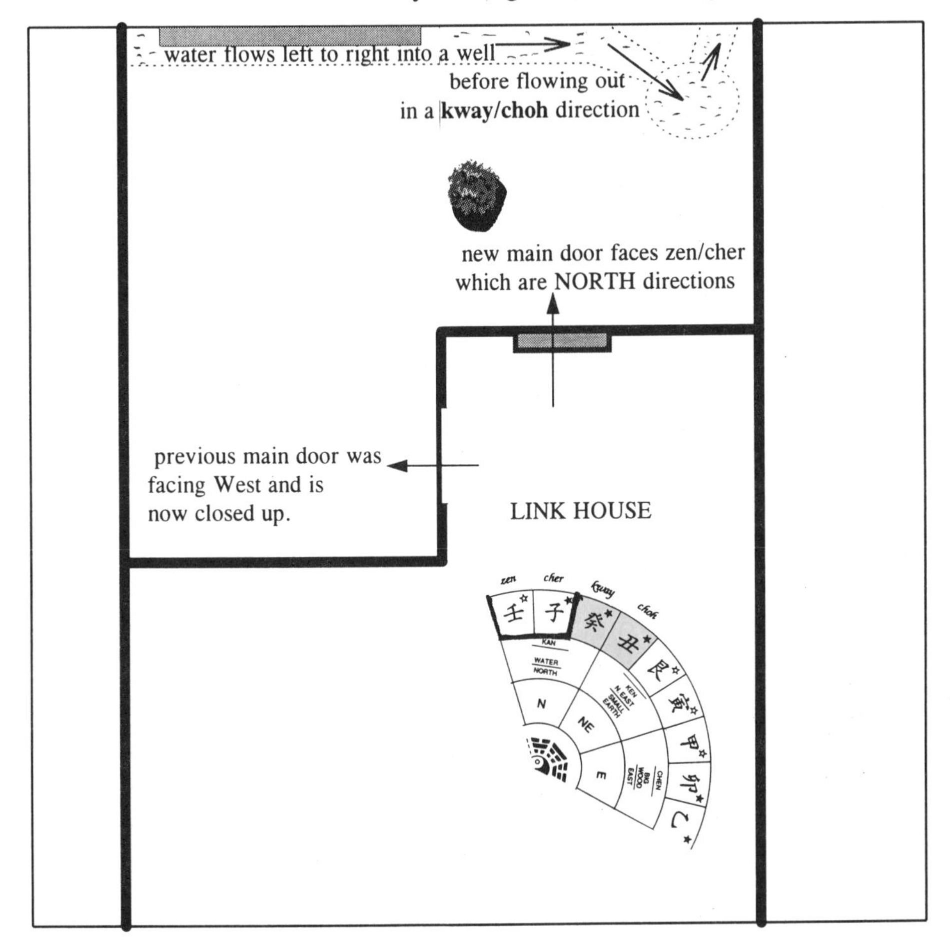

Example 16
Creating a Water Dragon for a Category Seven Apartment Block

This luxury Apartment Block has an irregular **U - shape** with the main entrance facing North, the **zen** and **cher** direction, which makes it a Category Seven Building. Because it does have land around it, residents can attempt to build a water dragon around the compound, thereby benefiting all the residents living in the apartment block.

For a Category Seven building, the water dragon is built according to the following specific instructions:

1. Firstly, the water (drain) should flow around the block, collecting water and then it must flow pass the main entrance from **right to left.**

2. It must then appear **to flow out through the *zen* direction** just in front of the main entrance. The water must **flow for a hundred steps, before turning round on the left hand side of the compound.**

3. The water flow must **end anywhere on the left hand side** of the compound. (ie **left** is taken from inside the apartment looking out).

4. The water ie the **drain on the left hand side should loop a little, and it must be smaller than any water ie drain anywhere else in the compound**.

5. The water can then flow out of the compound in any direction except it **must not touch the *cher* direction.** This is the direction just next to *zen*, on its right. ***Cher*** is also a North direction except that it is the second subsector of North.

6. When these instructions for building the water dragon are followed without mistakes, residents will enjoy huge success and benefit from a great deal of money luck. However, should there be mistakes made, residents will experience a great deal of bad luck. So do be very careful !!

The fountain in front of the main entrance is auspicious.
It does not interfere with the water dragon.

Creating the water dragon
for the Category Seven Apartment Building.

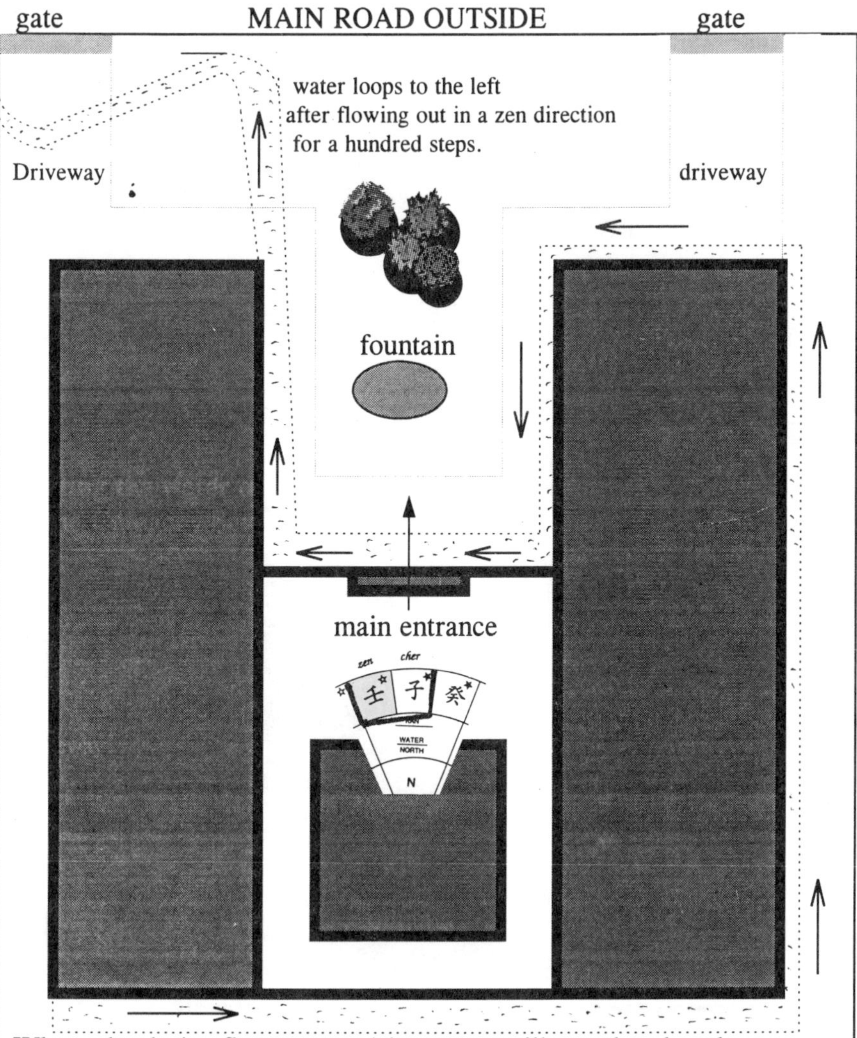

Where the drains flow across driveways, grills can be placed over them. It is important that drains constructed specifically for feng shui purpose should be visible. Thus only grills can be used, not cement slabs. Where the drain is exiting the compound, it is vital that it must not flow out in a ***cher*** direction. Otherwise the water dragon turns pernicious, bringing bad luck to residents.

Example 17
A Category Eight Building

Main Door of this building faces either the ***kway*** or **chor** directions, which correspond to the third subsector of North, and the first subsector of Northeast respectively. This is a Category Eight House and the best direction for such a building is known as the *jade belt* direction ie the patriarch (men) residents living in this building will wear a jade belt. At the same time everyone else will also enjoy auspicious money luck. The drain must flow pass the main door **from right to left**, and it must visibly exit from the compound in either a ***chian*** or a *hai* direction. This is bearing between **307.5° to 337.5° degrees from North.**

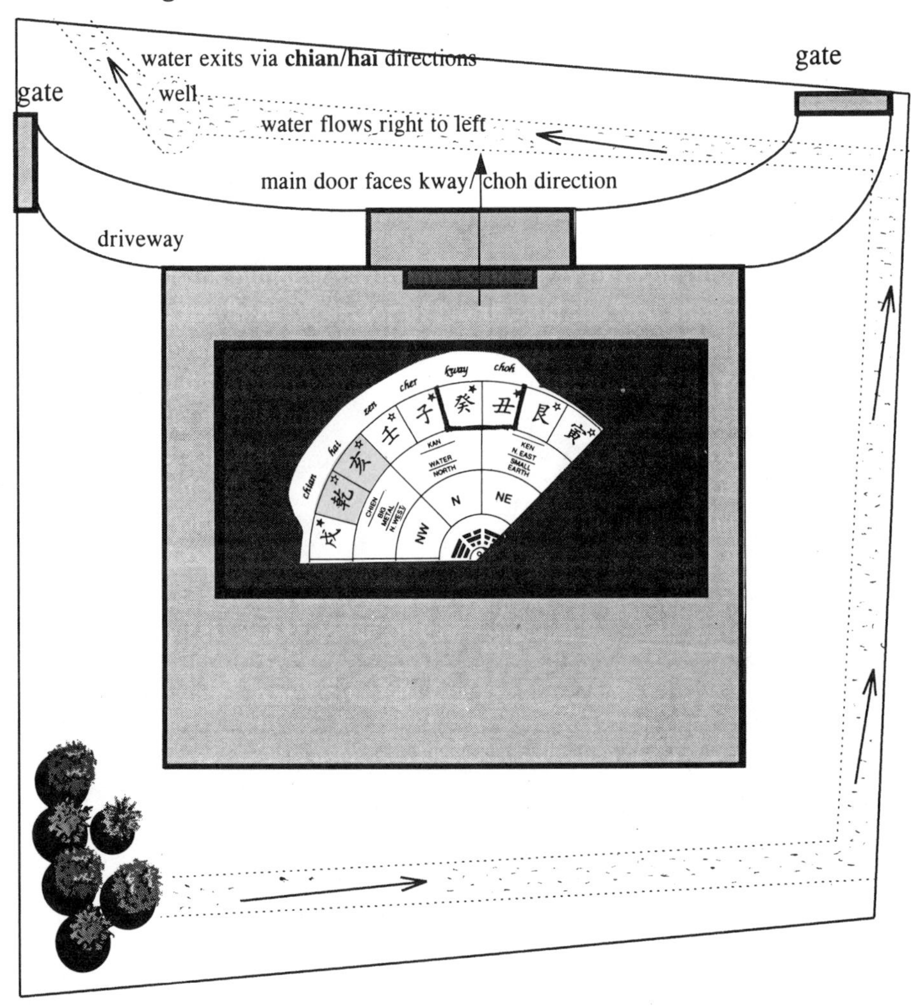

Example 18
A Category Eight House

This example features a link house where the main door has been changed to face the North direction of ***kway*** (third subsector of North) - which therefore makes it a category Eight House. This enables residents to tap into an auspicious water flow direction very easily. The original door which faces East has been closed off. In practising water feng shui, readers would do well to remember that the main door is a vital component of the formula- and this can always be altered to make the practice easier. Here he water flows out via the ***gen/yin direction*** ie bearing between **37.5° to 67.5°** from North. This exit direction brings plenty of money to residents and business luck is especially excellent.

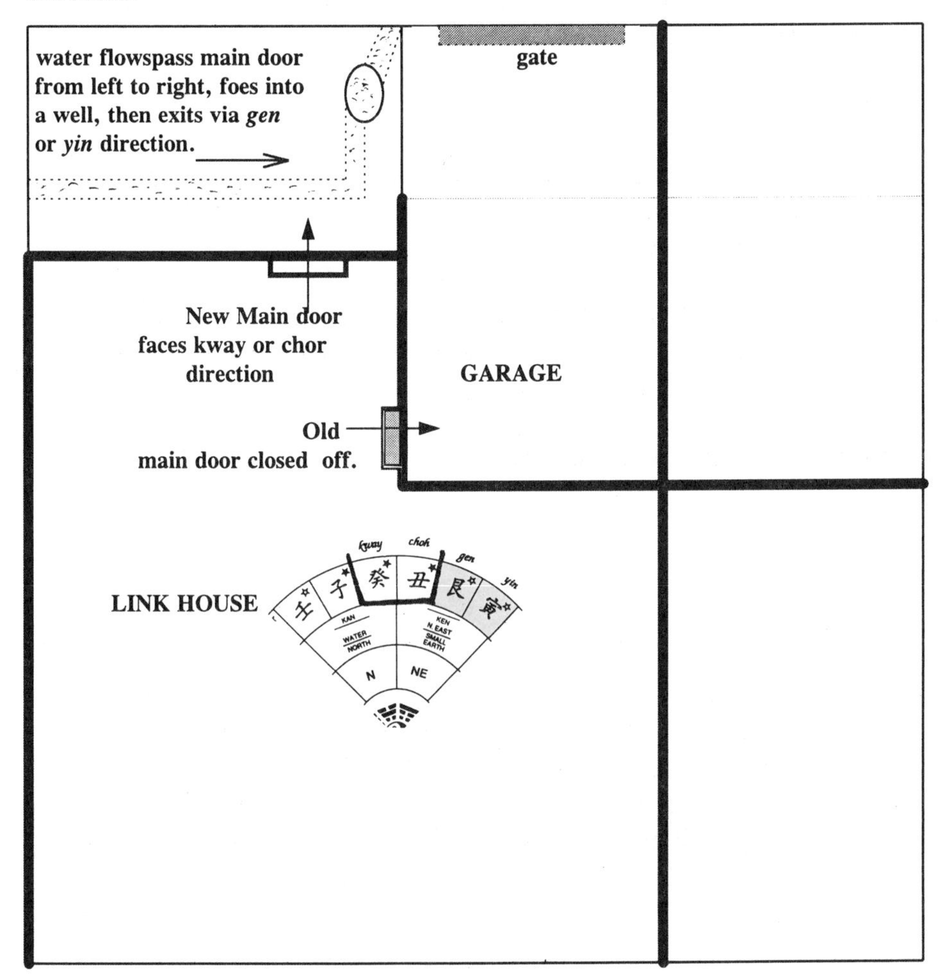

Example 19
Creating a water dragon for a Category Eight House

If your live in a house where the main front door is facing either a ***kway*** or a ***choh*** direction (North or Northeast - but be exact with the sub sectors), and you have a large enough piece of land **AND** your land is completely flat, you can attempt to build a ***golden water dragon*** which will bring you and your family five generations of the most auspicious wealth luck !!
Money will flow to the residents easily, and every business venture attempted will meet with success ultimately. The main thing to remember about this water dragon is that it must be constructed on level land, and that when exiting the garden, it must not encroach on the direction ***wu***.

Here is how you can do it.

1. First, check the terrain of your land to make very certain the **land is completely flat.** If necessary, work at getting totally flat by levelling off any slopes that may exist in the garden.

2. Next, design the drain such that **water seems to originate from the *kway* direction.** This is the third sub sector of North and is exactly the direction which your main front door is facing.

3. Then let the **water turn right** before it flows pass the main door.

4. Make certain that it is passing the main door in a **left to right** direction.

5. Then let the drain **flow right round the house**. This is going to be a very long water dragonwhich seems to embrace the house.

6. The exit direction required is ***ping,*** which is in the South ie the first sub sector of South; But there is a major warning that in exiting via ***ping*** you **MUST NOT let it touch the next door direction of *wu***, which is the second sub sector of South. Thus you must make very sure that the exit direction is located exactly between **157.5° to 172.5°** from the North.

Creating the golden water dragon in a Category Eight House

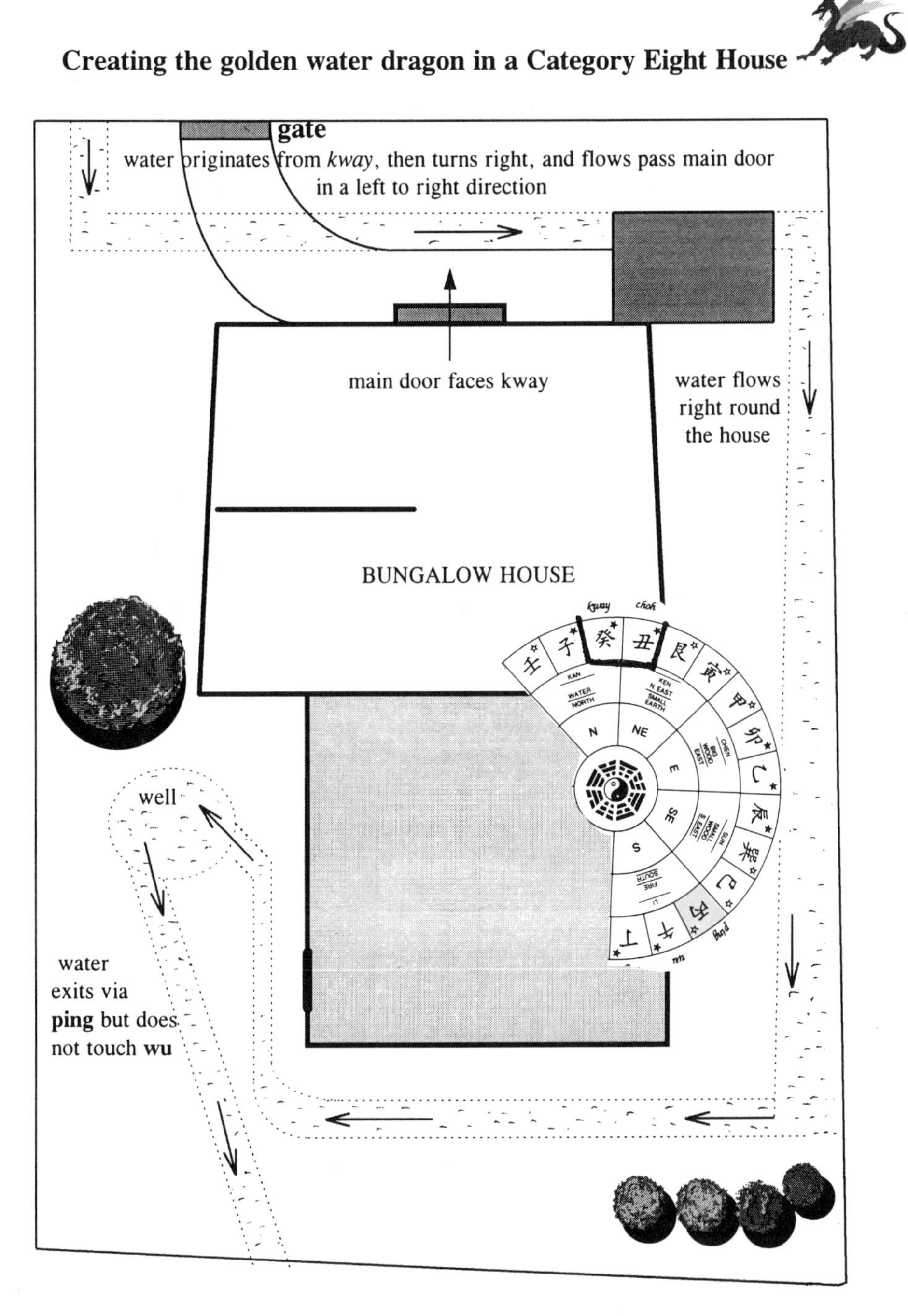

Example 20
A Category Nine House

In this example, the house sits on a very small piece of land with its door facing the second and third sub sectors of Northeast - these are the ***gen*** and ***yin*** directions respectively - thereby making it a Category Nine House. Because of the way the house has been laid out, the owner finds that he is able to tap the most auspicious water feng shui direction for this category. This is the ***Golden Pathway*** direction which requires the drain to flow pass the main door from right to left, and then to exit via the ***sin/shih*** directions ie bearing between **277.5° to 307.5°**.

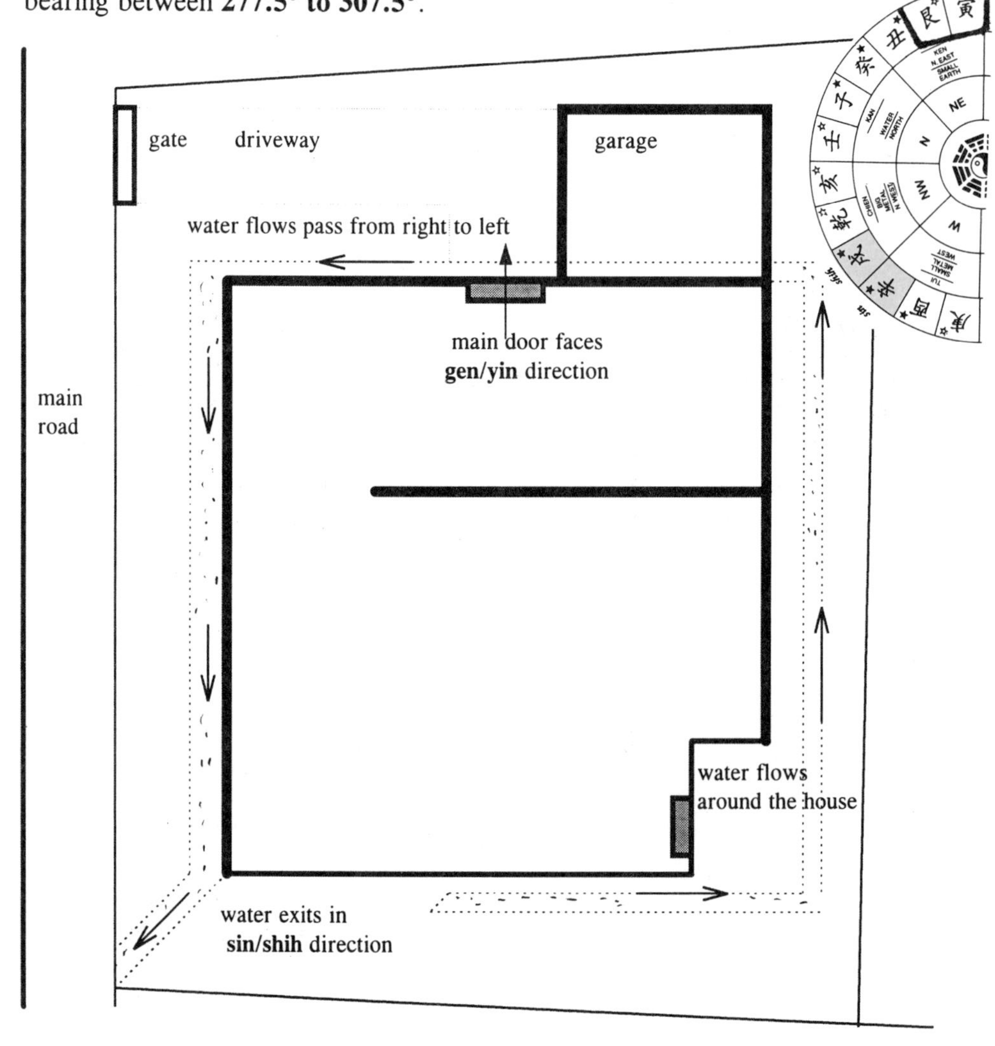

Example 21 

Creating the water dragon in a Category Nine House

The instructions on how to build a water dragon for a house whose main door faces ***gen*** or ***yin*** are simple. Let the drain flow **right to left** pass the door, then let it **flow outwards** in a ***gen*** direction **for a hundred steps**, making very sure it **does not touch the *yin*** direction. The water then **curves back towards the left**, forming a loop or curve. This configuration of water brings enormous good fortune - money, power and fabulous recognition.

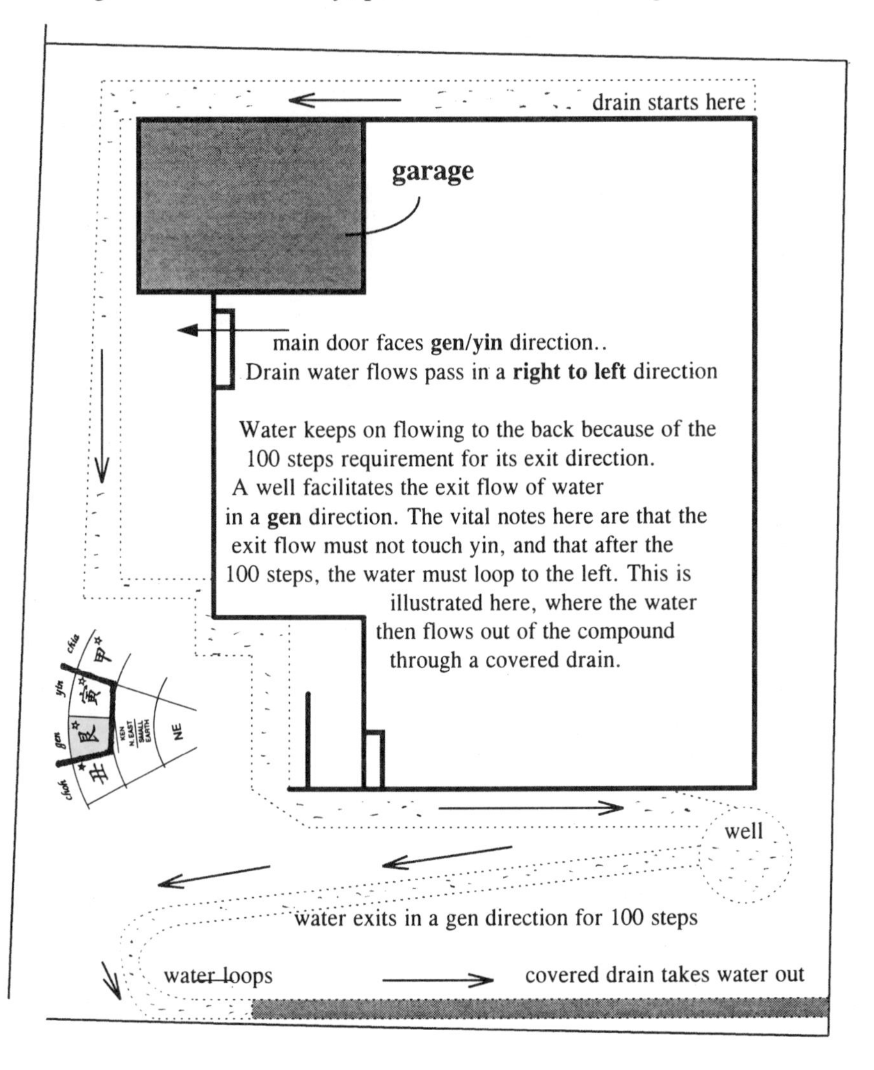

Example 22
A Category Ten Office Building
This office building is facing East. Its main door directly faces the ***chia/mau*** direction. If the Tai Pan of this building arranges the drains around the building to flow pass the front of the building in a **left to right** direction, and if the drain is then allowed to exit into an underground drain via the ***ting*** or ***wei*** direction in the South/Southwest, then if he has his office in the building, he will enjoy the ***triple precious jewels luck*** which brings enormous success for his company ! The exit direction is all important, and it must have an angle which bears between **187.5° to 217.5°** from North. This is shown in the sketch illustrated here.

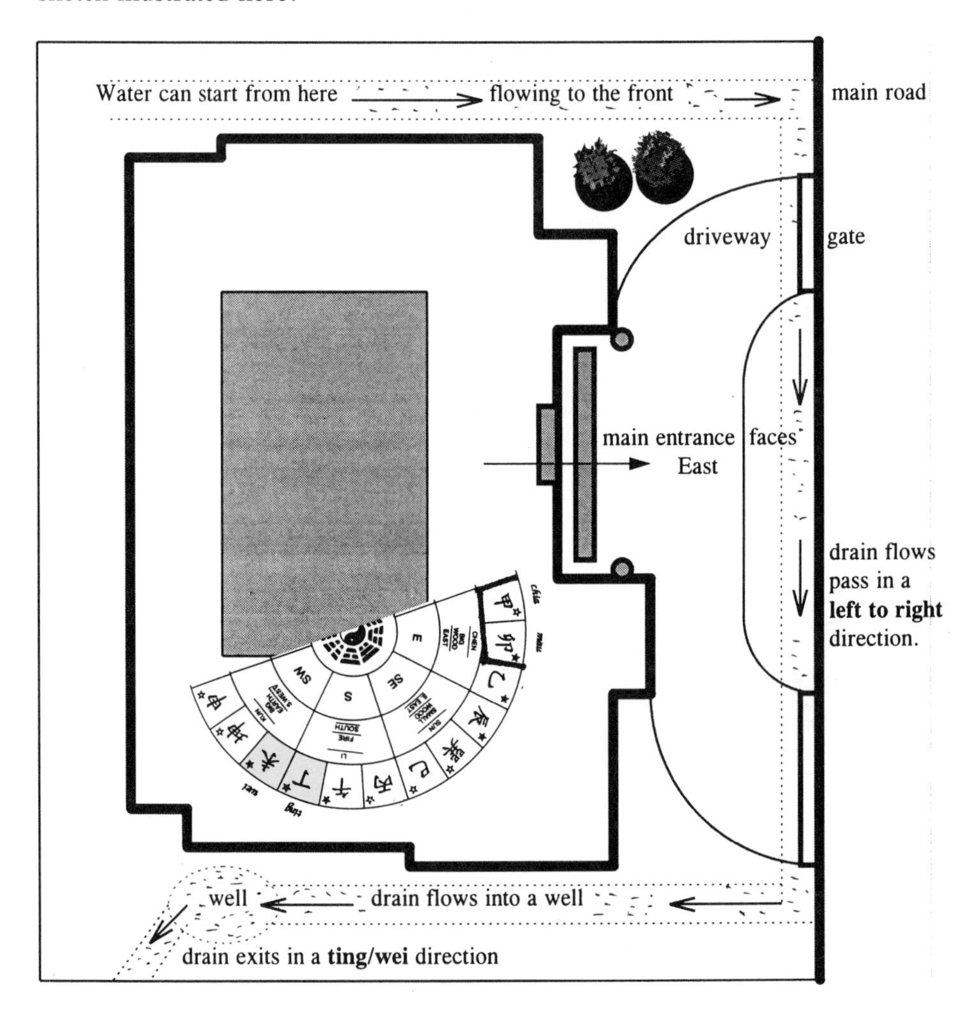

Example 22

Creating a water dragon for the same Category Ten Office Building

This office building facesEast. Its main door directly faces the ***chia/mau*** direction. If the Tai Pan wishes, he can try to create a water dragon round his building. To do so the drain must flow pass the front of the building in a **right to left** direction, and it must exit via the ***chia*** direction for 100 steps **without touching the mau** direction. And then it must loop to the left ! The angle of outflow must scrupulously be between **67.5° to 82.5°** from North. The suggested way of creating the dragon is illustrated below.

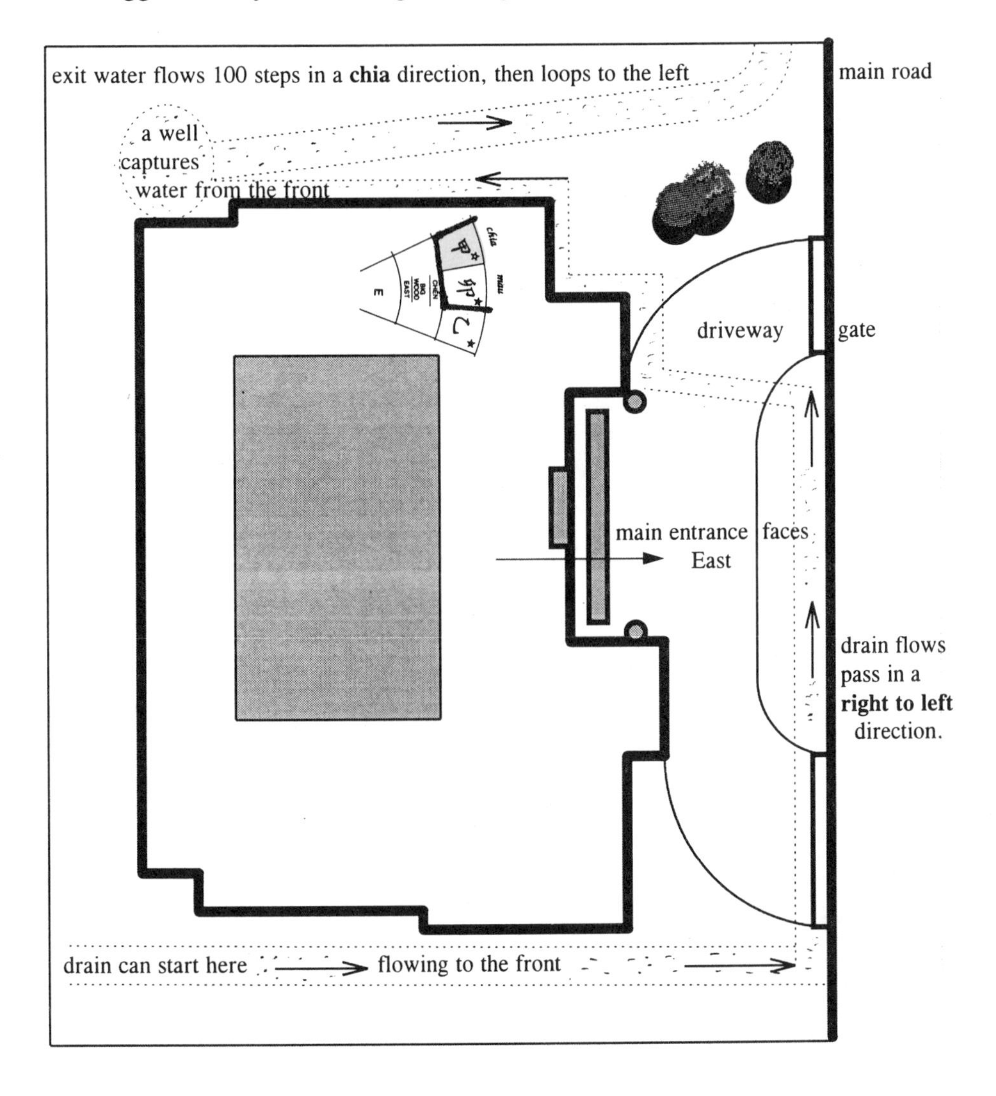

Example 23

A water dragon for a Category Eleven House

This house faces the ***yi/shen*** direction which is East/Southeast, making it a Category Eleven House. This kind of house has two water dragon configurations, and both are illustrated to highlight the auspicious possibilities which can be tapped. In the first example shown on this page, the drain is constructed for the water to flow pass the **main door from left to right**, before it then runs into a well, for it to position itself to flow out in a ***yi*** direction for **100 steps**. At which point it then turns **right in a curve**. This is a wealth bringing dragon and all residents will benefit, if it is constructed correctly.

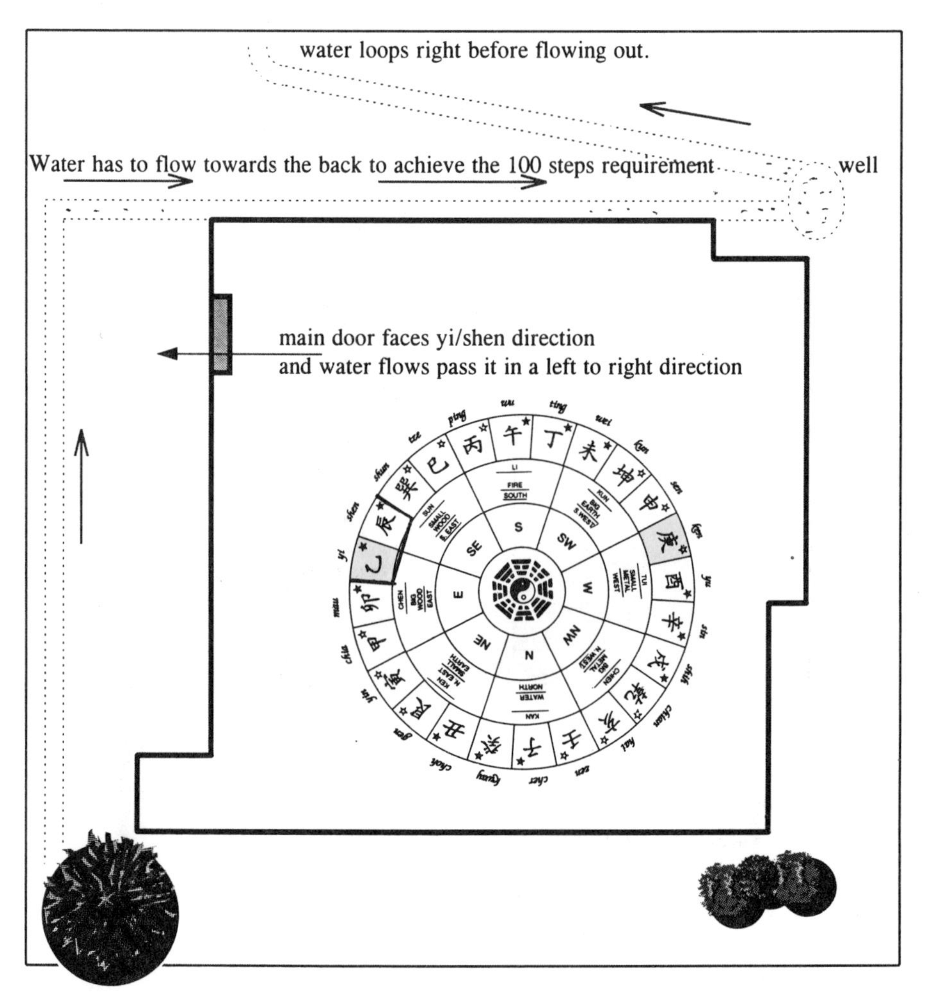

Example 23 

A different water dragon for the same Category Eleven House

It is possibe to consider another equally auspicious water dragon for the same house. As sketched below, readers will note that this dragon is different from the previous one. Here water is ***originating from a specific direction*** ie. the direction ***yi***, which is the direction the main door is facing. It then turns right, moves pass the main door, and ***flows towards the back*** - round the house until it reaches ***the WEST sector*** of the compound. The water then flows out the garden at an angle which corresponds to ***ken*** ie bearing between **247.5° to 262.5° from North**. The taboo to note is that the exit direction must be very accurate. It must NOT touch the direction next to it, ie the direction ***yu***. Both ***ken*** and ***yu*** are West directions and it is necessary to be careful. Finally, to activate this very auspicious dragon, the ***land must be totally flat*** !

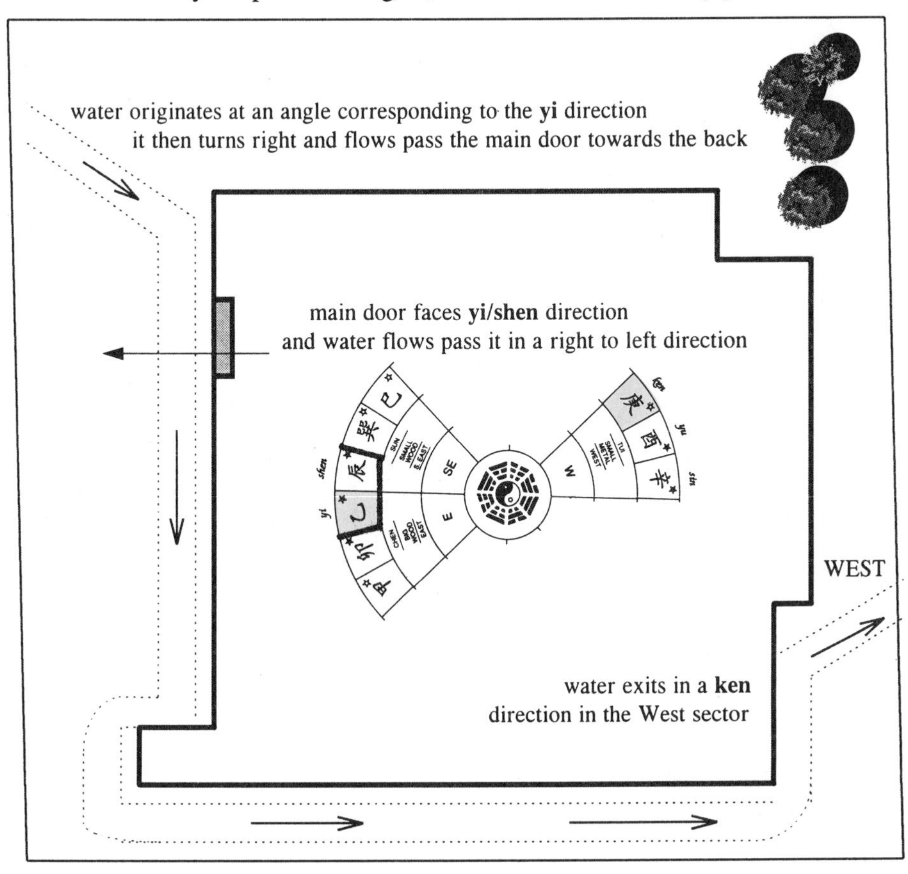

Example 24
A Category Twelve House
The main door direction of this House category is either *shun* or *tze,* both of which are Southeast directions. Houses with this sort of front door orientation have several different auspicious feng shui possibilities, but the best is the ***jade belt direction.*** This has the water flowing pass the main door from ***right to left,*** and exiting the garden via the ***kway or choh*** directions which correspond to an angle bearing between **7.5° to 37.5°** from North. This house which sits on an irregular piece of land has tapped this direction beautifully.

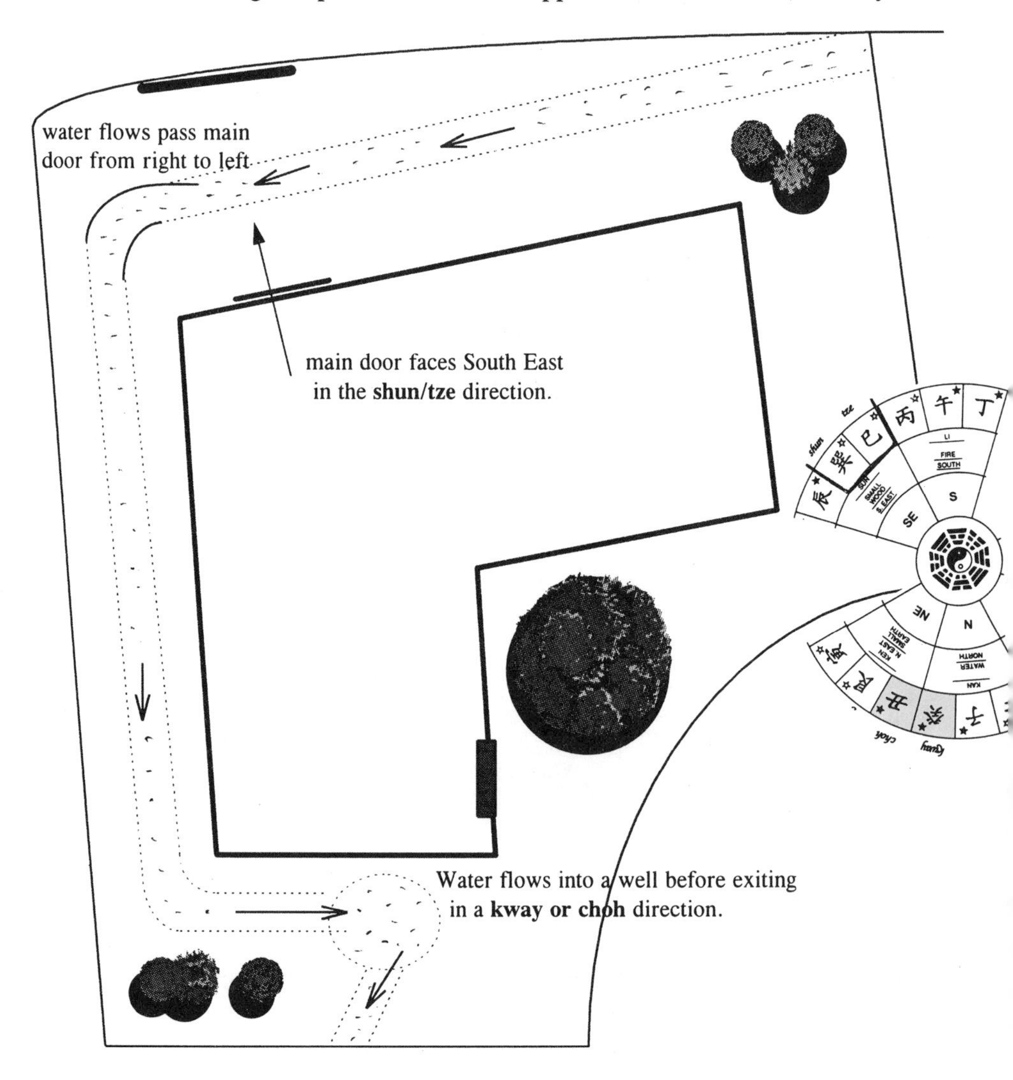

Example 25 

Building a water dragon for a Category Twelve Building

This is a shopping mall which has its main entrance directly facing the SouthEast ie the ***shun*** direction, which makes it a category twelve building. If the drains surrounding the building are oriented to form a water dragon, the shopping mall and all its retailers will enjoy prosperity and wealth luck. The drain water must flow pass the main entrance in a **right to left** direction, and drain water must appear to flow out an angle that corresponds to the ***shun*** direction, but without touching the ***tze*** direction next to it. It must flow for a ***hundred steps***, and then ***loop to the left*** before flowing out. In its outflow the water must slowly trickle out ie the drain must get smaller ... then great prosperity will follow. This water dragon can be built on either flat, undulating or sloping land.

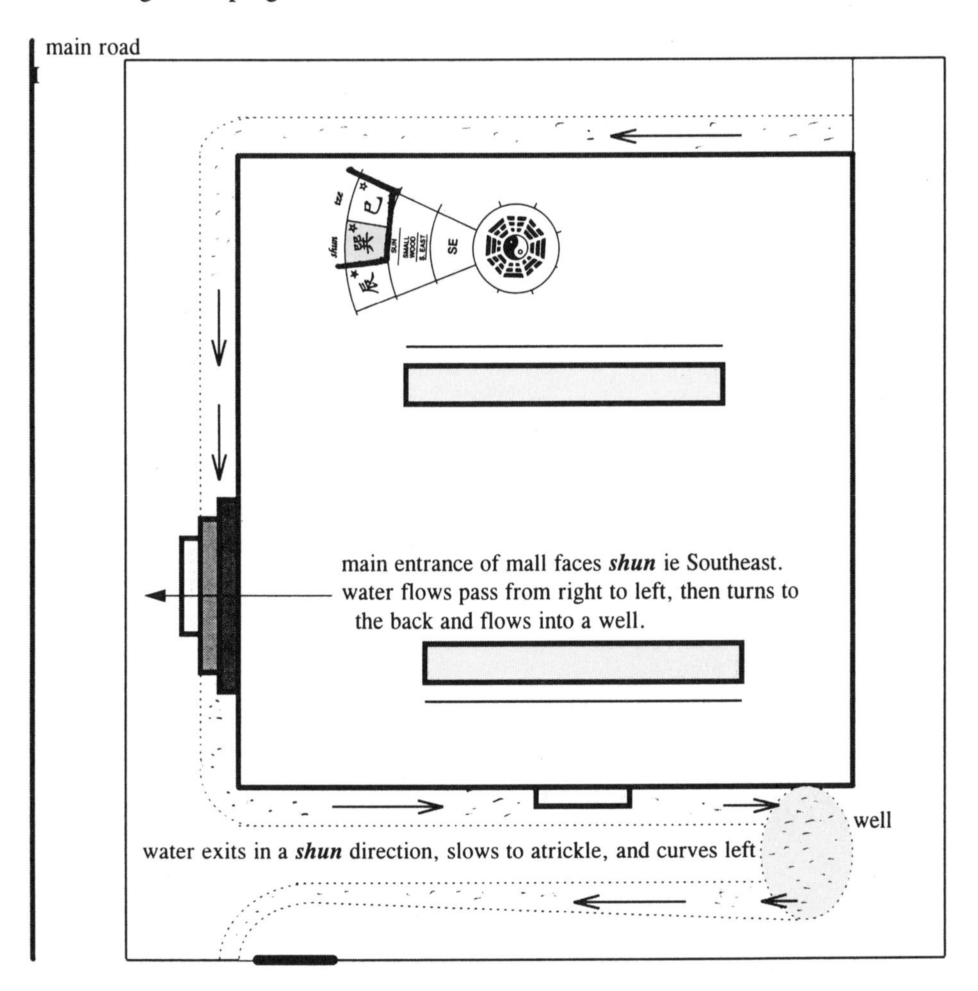

Additional ideas for consideration

Once you have mastered the main concepts of the water dragon formulas, you will find that if you have the necessary space and land, it is also possible to actually construct artificial streams in your garden that flow into a pond to simulate the dragon. This can take the place of drains, and can be made to blend into the overall design of your garden landscape. If you are fortunate enough to have this option, and you do decide to do this, you must then make sure that your drainage via drains must then be either covered, or must go underground. Otherwise the directions of your artificial streams might clash with that of your drains, causing disharmony and inauspicious feng shui. Some ideas and layouts, together with different shapes for ponds are sketched on this and the following page.

Here a stream embraces the house, flows pass the main door, then flows into a pond before exiting. The water flow can be designed according to feng shui water directions by checking the direction of the main door and then consulting the formula in chapter three.

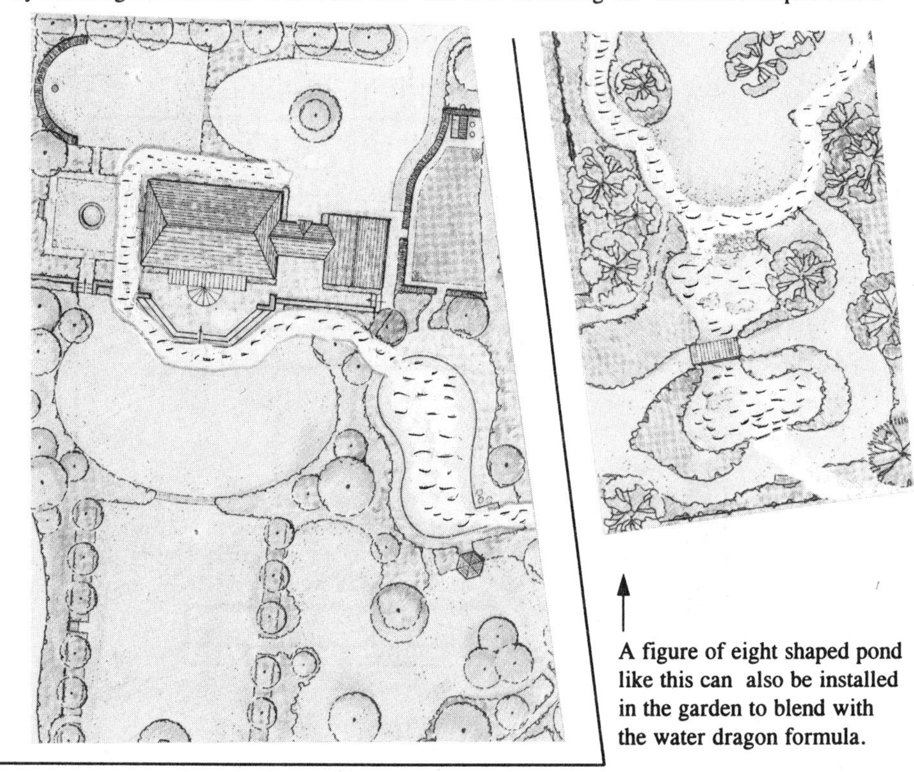

A figure of eight shaped pond like this can also be installed in the garden to blend with the water dragon formula.

A round pond at the far end of the garden, as shown here can be used to collect all the water flows before another stream leaves it in the correct exit direction. The water dragon becomes part of the landscape. Two more ideas are also presented on this page.

A Pa Kua shaped pond lends interesting possibilities for a large Garden. Water can flow in and out from any of the eight sides.

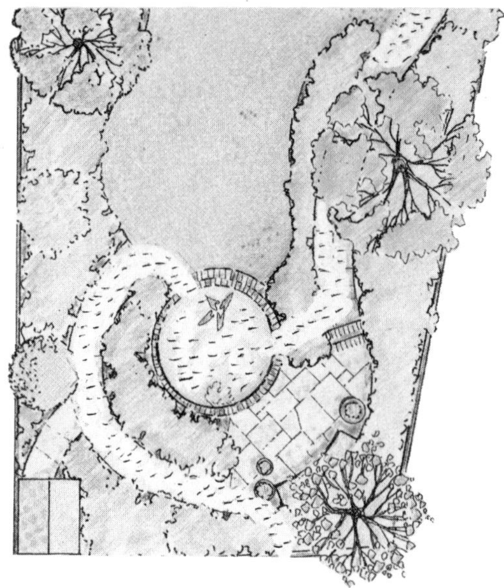

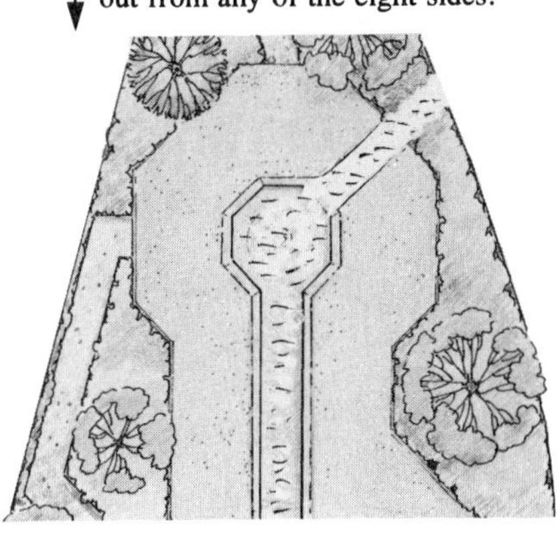

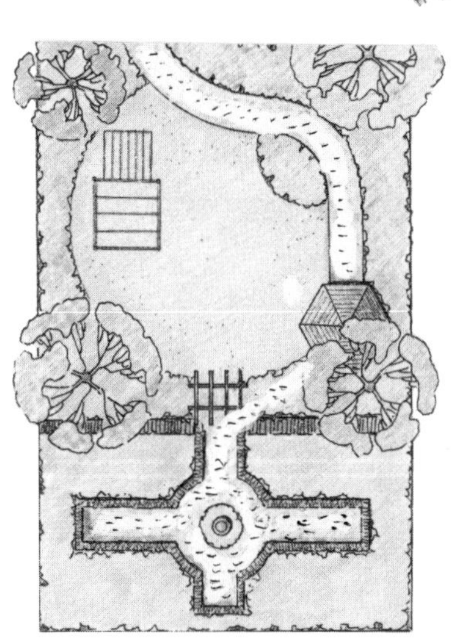

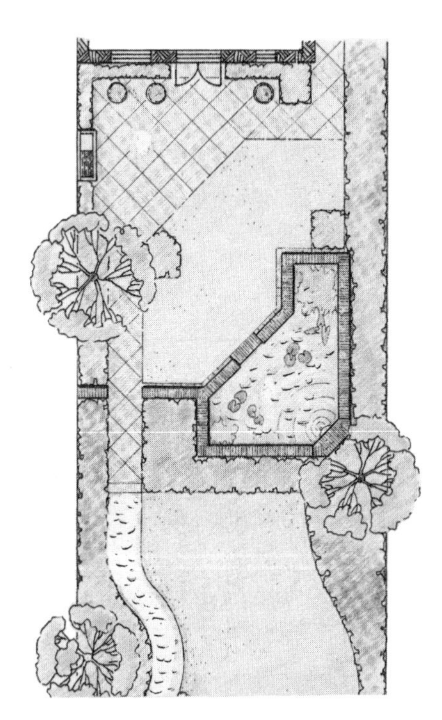

CHAPTER FIVE

TEN MAJOR LANDSCAPE WATER CONFIGURATIONS IN FENG SHUI

The correct way is good fortune
The opposite way is misfortune
If you see it is going to spoil - change it;
If you are careful, you will do it right
If you hurry, you might make a mistake
continuously...

" *Clouds rise to heavens;*
The image of ***waiting***
The superior man eats and drinks
Is restful ... and of good cheer
Waiting with sincerity
Brings solutions - ***it furthers one***
To cross the great water"
from the **I Ching**, on the Trigram Hsu

CHAPTER FIVE

When applying any water formula in Feng Shui, it is useful to understand some of the more detailed aspects of water landscape feng shui. Perhaps one of the most significant branch of this school of feng shui is the ***San Chuan Li Chi*** which, literally means ***Mountain, River Theory Chi***.

This theory offers the *feelings* approach to landscape investigation. When the *feeling* is right or good, the feng shui is supposed to be auspicious. And when the *feeling* is unbalanced, the feng shui is inauspicious.

Most amateur practitioners of feng shui will already be familiar with the green dragon, white tiger landscape configurations, where the left (or East) symbolizes the green dragon and the right (or West) symbolizes the white tiger. And where there is a view of gentle flowing water in front, good feng shui abounds.❋

Feng shui Masters however go much deeper when investigating landscapes. They search for subtle nuances in the shapes and relative size of the landscapes. The size, reach, shape and dimensions of hills, valleys and mountains are always taken into account when analyzing the landscape. Where there is a view of water, the way it flows within sight of a house, the breadth of its flow - in, as well as out - always feature strongly in the Master's assessment of whether the water in view of the house is good or bad.

The ***San Chuan Li Chi*** theory presents *three good feeling water*, and *seven bad feeling water* - and it can be used to complement your knowledge of the Water Dragon Classic. These ten configurations have been included in this book for this purpose, but readers must note that it is **not** a supplementary of the water dragon formula which is part of Compass School Feng Shui. Instead, what is presented in this chapter are supplementary texts to landscape feng shui designed to make your feng shui practice more complete.

❋ For a complete book on landscape feng shui, readers are recommended to look for the author's first book entitled FENG SHUI.
This introductory text contains comprehensive coverage of the subject.

THE THREE GOOD FEELING WATER

First feeling:

Where the water enters into view very broad, then settles rather gently in front of and in full view of the house's main entrance. It then slowly gets narrower, before tapering into a narrow stream flowing outwards.
The mountain on the left of the house (symbolising the dragon) is slightly higher than the mountain on the right (symbolising the tiger).
Behind the house there is another mountain which signifies the gentle turtle hills. This is shown in the sketch below.

Good Feng Shui Water

Second Feeling

Where water comes into view from three different directions, and then collects in front of the building, feng shui is described as extremely auspicious. Water in this case is bringing tremendous wealth luck to the residents, and will stay intact within the families for many generations. This configuration of water is illustrated below.

EXCELLENT FENG SHUI WATER
WATER COMES FROM THREE DIRECTIONS

Third Feeling
Where water wraps around the house like a ***jade belt***. And neither the dragon mountain nor the tiger mountain are too large as to turn pernicious. Behind the house, the turtle mountains form a protective circular range. Residents of a house with this configuration of water will enjoy great wealth, particularly if the water is clean and unpolluted, and it is flowing in a slow meandering fashion. If the direction of flow also corresponds to the Water compass formula, the feng shui is very auspicious indeed.

THE SEVEN BAD SENTIMENT WATER

The first sentiment

Where the water flows very fast in front of the house and turns sharply round, resembling a poison arrow.

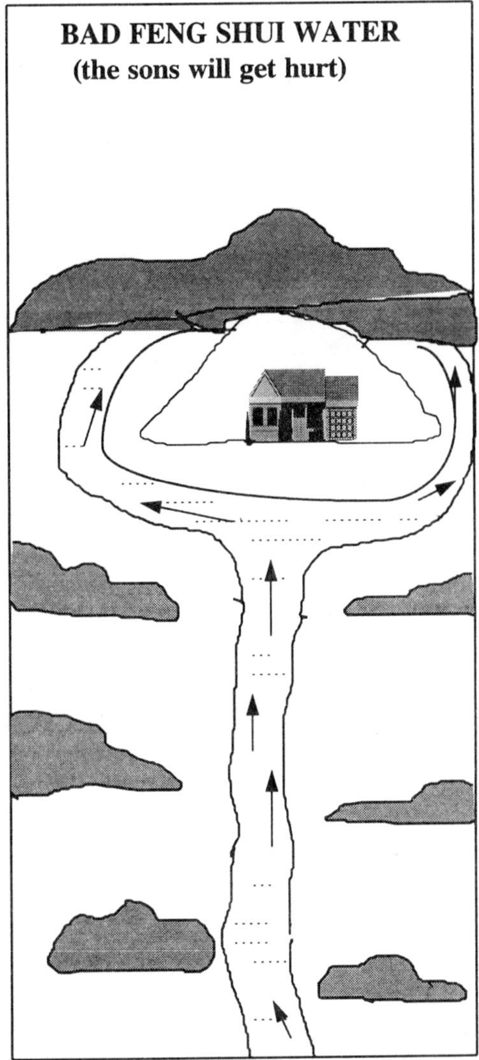

The second sentiment

Where the water flows directly towards the house, and then separates. The sons of the family will be particularly hurt by this configuration of water.

The Third Sentiment

Where the water is much too close to the house, and the house is also situated too low. It would have been different if the house had been sited higher up the mountain. This configuration of water leads to serious loss of money.

BAD FENG SHUI WATER house too low and water too close.

The Fourth Sentiment

Where the water comes from behind, and from two sources, and then flows directly <u>away</u> from the house, in full view of the main door. This configuration of water suggests extreme bad luck causing loss of wealth.

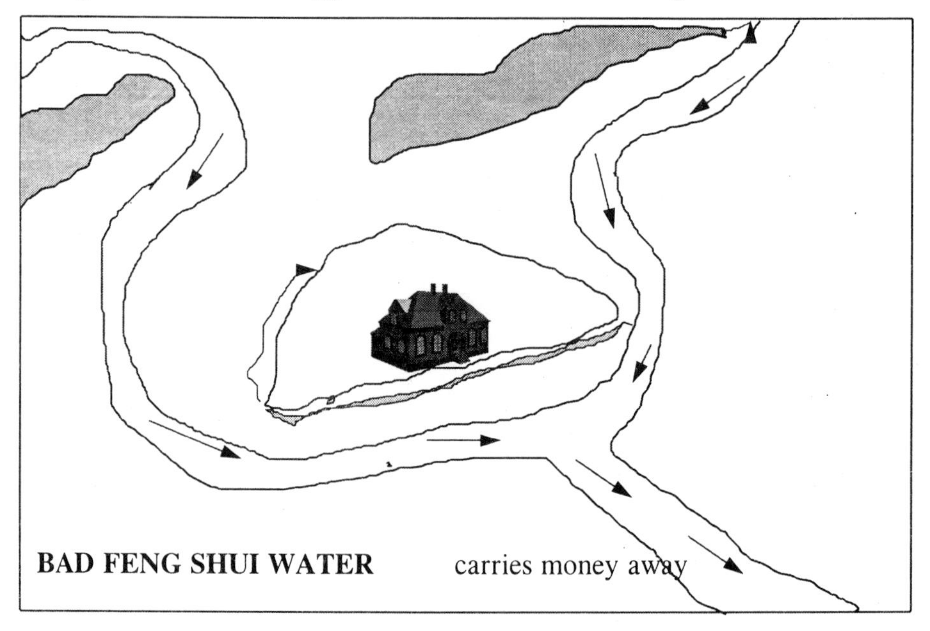

BAD FENG SHUI WATER carries money away

The Fifth Sentiment

Where the water flows in a wide loop in front of the house - resembling a bowl shape. The water is also flowing away from the house. This configuration of water is inauspicious because the river is carrying both wealth and good luck ***away*** from the house. In feng shui, what is required is for the water to bring good fortune towards the house, not away from it.

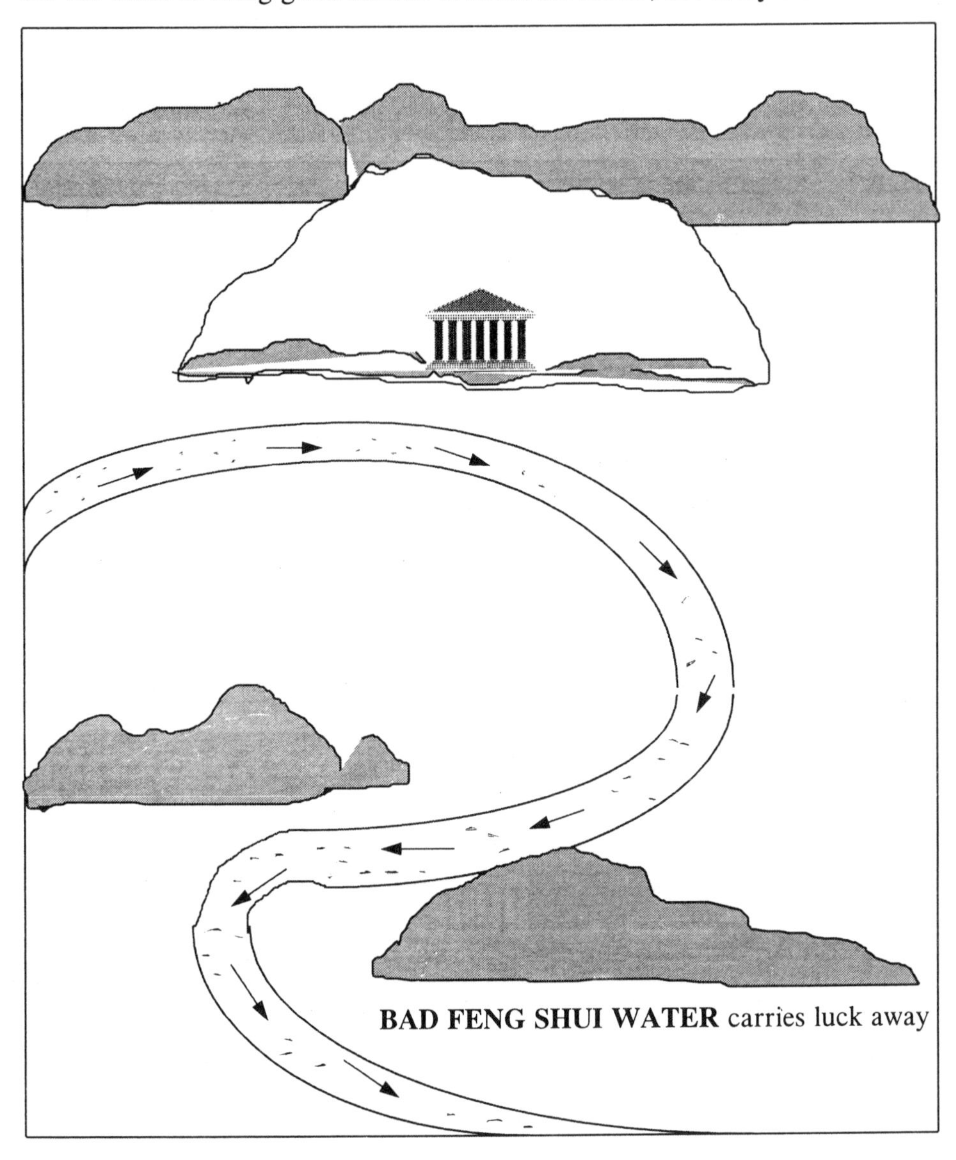

BAD FENG SHUI WATER carries luck away

The Sixth Sentiment

Where the water flowing into view the of the house is **narrow,** and when it flows out of view, it broadens. This symbolises nothing very much coming in, and plenty flowing out. In feng shui terms this is considered inauspicious. Water coming in should be broad, and leaving should be narrow so that it resembles a money bag.

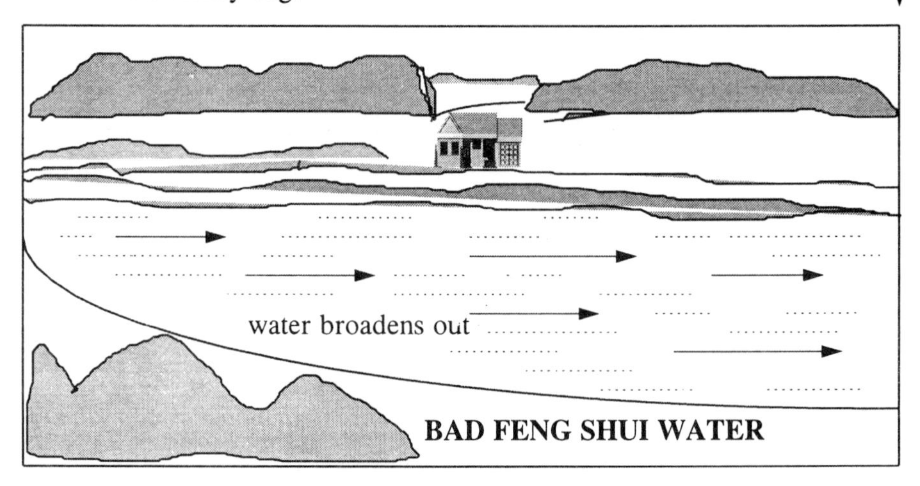

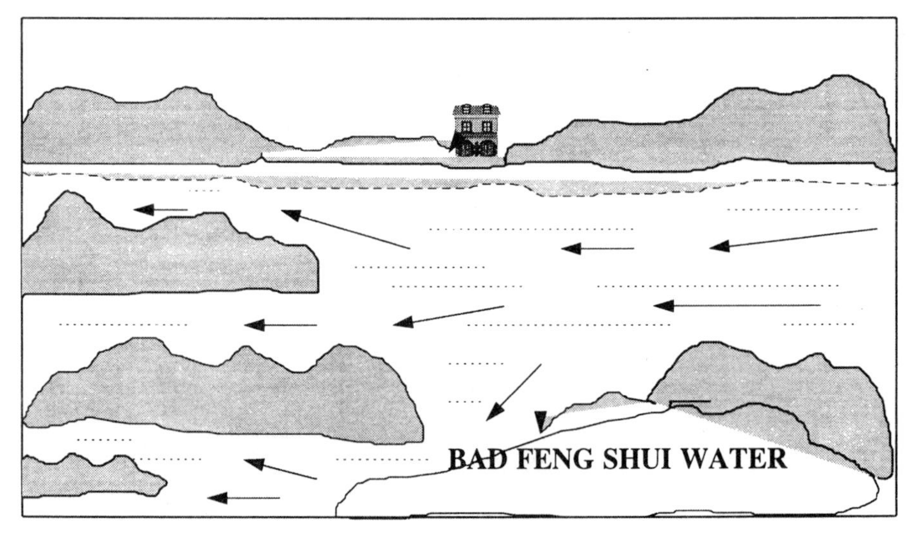

The Seventh Sentiment

Where, although the water flowing in is broad, it spreads out like a broom when it flows outwards thereby causing sentiment to be bad. This configuration of water will cause the children to squander off the family wealth. Children will come to a bad end.

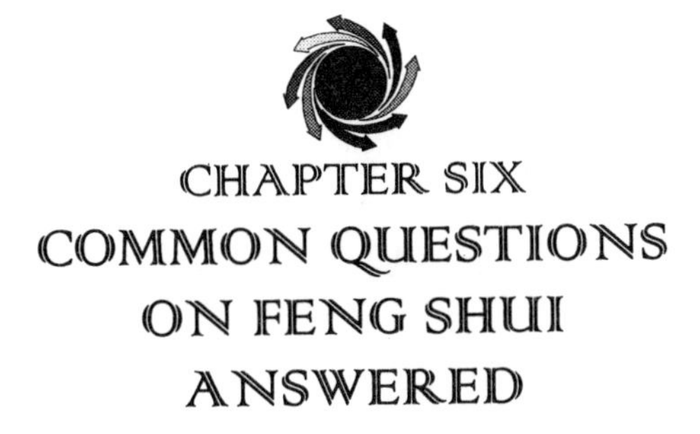

CHAPTER SIX
COMMON QUESTIONS ON FENG SHUI ANSWERED

The wind blows over the earth
the image of contemplation;
Thus the kings of old
visited the regions of the world
Contemplating the people
And gave them food for thought.

" *On the earth is water*
The image of ***holding together***
The superior man cultivates goodwill
With truth and loyalty
Truth, like the full earthen bowl ...
Thus in the end
Good fortune comes from without "
from the **I Ching**, on the Trigram Pi

CHAPTER SIX

Feng shui means *wind* and *water*. In its literal sense, it refers to the topography of the earth, its mountains, valleys and waterways whose shape and size, orientation and levels are created by the continuous interaction of these two powerful forces of nature.

To people of Chinese origin all over the world, feng shui connotes a mystical practice that blends ancient wisdom with cultural superstitions, a broad body of traditional knowledge that lay down guidelines for differentiating between auspicious and inauspicious land sites and that presents instructions for orienting homes and designing room layouts in ways that promise to dramatically enhance the quality of their lives.

How does Feng shui work ?

Feng Shui advocates living in harmony with the earth's environments and its energy lines so that there is created an auspicious balancing with the forces of nature. Feng shui contends that the environment is crowded with invisible but powerful energy lines - some auspicious and others pernicious - and that these energy lines bring either harmony or discord, health or sickness, prosperity or poverty. The practice of feng shui has to do with the *clever harnessing of energy lines that are auspicious* - what the Chines refer to as the ***Dragon's cosmic breath***. Auspicious energy lines travel in a meandering fashion.

Feng shui is also about *avoiding inauspicious energy lines* that represent the *killing breath*. Thus feng shui Masters strenuously warn against sleeping, sitting, working, eating and living in places that are hit of attacked by these invisible damaging forces. Killing breath is caused by the presence of sharp, pointed objects or structures that are inadvertently aimed directly at front doors, or which hit at where one sits or sleeps.

These offending structures can be straight roads, the sharp pointed angles of roof lines, a single tree, a transmission tower, an overhead beam, a protruding corner or any object that appears threatening or hostile. In feng shui terms, these objects are called **poison arrows**, and the foul energy that emanate from them travel in straight lines,. carrying with them ill fortune and other odious effects.

Thus if one's main door, or sitting and sleeping positions lie in the path of such harmful energy forces, the consequences are believed to be extremely negative and sometimes even disastrous, causing grave misfortune to the residents or individuals affected. The sharper and more threatening the poison arrow, the more dire are the repercussions of being hit by these arrows. Misfortune takes the form of illness, missed opportunities, law suits, quarrels, financial losses and other forms of bad luck - all manifestations of disharmony.

Feng shui practice works by combating these poison arrows. Feng shui offers a variety of solutions to avoid, deflect and dissolve the effects of these arrows. Thus knowledge of feng shui enables practitioners to both diagnose and take proper precautions against them.

Is it advisable to consult a feng shui Master ?

While much of the science of feng shui - both landscape and compass - can be learned without too much difficulty; like any other discipline or profession, practical experience does improve performance. It is from this perspective that feng shui Master practitioners are often so useful to consult. In recent years however, inflation has caught up with this profession, and those who make a living out of offering feng shui consultancy - if they are any good - are so popular and in such great demand that their fees have soared in tandem with the demand for their services. Nevertheless, those masters who are genuinely knowledgeable and experienced are worth their weight in gold - their advice, when properly followed does show very positive results.

In Hong Kong, consulting a feng shui Master prior to building or moving house is standard practice, and there are a fair number of reliable and honest feng shui consultants - but they are also expensive - charging their consultancy fees according to square feet of space covered and rank of the person doing the consulting.

Here in Malaysia and Singapore, demand for feng shui consultants is growing by leaps and bounds, and fees are also escalating. In western countries like Australia and the UK where the practice of feng shui has only recently become known - there are any number of *wannabee* feng shui masters, whose knowledge and practice of feng shui understandably lacks the depth of their oriental counterparts.

But is it advisable to consult a feng shui master ? The author believes that this is a very personal decision. Having consulted many feng shui masters in the past, she has found that feng shui masters have their off days, and can sometimes make mistakes in their analysis and calculations. It is thus extremely useful for one to also have some knowledge of the practice before engaging a feng shui master. Together, the reading and recommendations often take on improved credence.

Also, most Masters base their practice on knowledge gleaned from apprenticeships with learned Masters of another age. It is rare (but not impossible) to find a Master of feng shui who is also learned about the intellectual and philosophical underpinnings of feng shui. Thus, rather than blindly accepting all and every recommendation offered, and every diagnosis made, it is infinitely better to educate oneself about it, and attempt to understand feng shui in its entirety, before spending a few thousand dollars consulting a Master, who at best can only have enough time to help you with specific aspects of the practice.

Many feng shui Masters specialize - some are better with landscapes than with compass formulas. Some have expertise in improving relationships, or in tapping feng shui for health purposes, while yet others specialize in water flows for creating prosperity feng shui ... there are many dimensions and aspects to the practice of feng shui.

So unless you have a specific problem requiring expert attention and you can afford feng shui consultancy fees, my advice is: invest some time to read about feng shui - and try to practice it yourself. At least know about how to diagnose and combat bad feng shui. Just taking this defensive approach should vastly improve the quality of your life without you having to spend too much.

How much should I pay to consult a feng shui Master ?

Based on the author's personal exposure to feng shui masters, their fees range from as little as a nominal *ang pow* (or *lai see* in Hong Kong) - a red packet containing perhaps M$300.00 - to as high as several hundred thousand dollars ! There is thus no standard fee. In Malaysia and Singapore feng shui masters charge approximately M$380 - M$600 for a link house and about M$2,000.00 for corporate offices. For larger projects, the fees are often negotiable.

The author herself does **not** undertake feng shui consultancy work. But the feng shui masters she has recommended charge according to the time required for the diagnosis, and is often dependent on the number of premises that have to be investigated as well as the amount of travel time involved.

There is no such thing as the *best* feng shui master. Those who make feng shui consultancy their profession often have their own code of ethics - and when confronted with a problem they are unable to solve often recommend someone else who has the expertise, and is better able to assist.

Does feng shui require massive renovations ?
Not at all ! The clever feng shui practitioner will always be able to find the least expensive way of combating poison arrows, or or activating good feng shui. This is because there are so many dimensions to the practice that it is often *not* possible ***to get everything right.***

Thus a huge dose of common sense should always be factored into the practice. Diagnose the problem you seem to have, and then list out the options before deciding on the course of action that requires the least disruption to the building. Often, just a small and subtle change in the direction where you sleep, where you sit and where your oven mouth faces is sufficient to tap into the auspicious energy flows of the environment.

Feng shui changes do **not** need to be huge and massive for them to work. The energy lines of the environment are very very subtle - think of a television and its aerial - with just a small shift in the antenna the reception can be bright and clear or fuzzy and snowing !
So it is with feng shui - the energy lines can always be manipulated to be auspicious. All you need to get it right are the formulas - study and understand them carefully, and you will be able to practice !

What if I cannot afford to undertake too much renovation ?
Even if you do not wish to make any structural or decorative changes requiring sand and cement, your feng shui can be improved. Use the compass school of feng shui exclusively. Use it to find out your auspicious and inauspicious directions and then make sure that you are sleeping with your head pointed in your *best* direction; and sit with your face facing your *best* direction. And for good measure, make sure also that your oven mouth is facing your *best* direction ! All these suggestions do not require any renovation at all ! But they will make a difference to improving your life.

What should I do when faced with contrary advice ?
If you ask too many people about anything, you are sure to get different answers and different recommendations. It is the same with feng shui. This is because, apart from it being such a complex science, it is also based on principles which require expert analysis and subjective interpretation.

Much of feng shui, for example is based on an understanding of the trigrams of the **I Ching** - and no one who has ever lived would dare to offer definitive interpretations of its texts. Even Confucius who spent an entire lifetime studying the I Ching proclaimed that even if he spent another lifetime studying it some more, he would still not fully comprehend the depth of the I Ching's wisdom. And again, much of feng shui depends on one's interpretation of the interactions of the five elements - earth, water, fire, wood and water - and yet different masters will offer different conclusions of its interactive forces.

Because of this, different feng shui masters will have different interpretations and different solutions to problems. The best approach therefore is to gain some in depth knowledge of feng shui and then, use your own judgment to decide what makes the most sense for you. It is also a good idea for you yourself to monitor the results of certain feng shui inspired changes which you may have put into practice. Not a very scientific way of doing things to be sure ... but for the author it has worked magnificently !

How do I know when I am suffering from bad feng shui ?
When you have just moved office or moved house, and then everything starts going wrong in your life, where before things had gone on quite well - then you might want to start becoming aware of your new surroundings - to investigate whether there are any poison arrows hitting at you - where you sleep, where you sit and so forth. If you have just moved into a new house, and your children start getting sick, one after the other; or if family members start having quarrels for no reason - there could be cause to believe that perhaps something is out of harmony. It could be a question of bad feng shui.

It is also possible that having lived in the same house for many years, suddenly things start going wrong with your life - problems of financial loss, problems at work, problems with the children, with your health - these are indications that perhaps the time dimensions of feng shui are exerting their intangible forces.

Or maybe you have just had some renovations done. Maybe a new house has just been built in your next door plot of land. Or perhaps a new multi storey building has just come up nearby affecting your feng shui. It is also possible that a new road or a new flyover has been built near you - all of these have an effect on your feng shui.

If you are alert to these changes in the environment, you will be sensitive to the subtle changes of the energy lines that surround your home. And if you know what to look for, if you know what to check and investigate, you will be able to neutralize any negative effects caused.

Is feng shui an art or a science ?
This question is debatable. There are those who contend that the subjective elements of feng shui analysis suggest that it is best regarded as an ***art*** - one requiring understanding of mysticism and even having spiritual connotations. The author prefers to regard feng shui as a ***science*** - one that is based on the Chinese view of the Universe as well as its explanation of the forces that shape the Universe. Where the complimentarity of the two forces **yin** and **yang** call for harmonious blendings of opposite forces. And where the hidden meanings of the symbols that encompass the Universe and the human race can be interpreted by studying the formulas implicit in the theories that underpin the practice of all Chinese divinitive sciences - including feng shui.

Besides, much of the descriptions of feng shui's fundamentals - despite their colourful names - seem to be converging with much of Western scientific discoveries of recent times. One example is the **dragon's cosmic breath - the chi**, which can be likened to the energy lines of the earth, invisible lines like radio and other waves which we now know, crowd our atmosphere, and which can even be controlled by Man; Indeed, examples abound that suggest a host of waves pulsating throughout the atmosphere - completely invisible to the human eye yet powerful enough to send signals through mobile phones, fax machines, satellite transmissions and the like ! What would we do without the television these days ? Is there some kind of connection between the ***chi*** that the ancients speak about when they tell us about feng shui, and these same atmospheric lines ? It is entirely likely that within the foreseeable future someone will be able to offer scientifically acceptable explanations. Meanwhile, does it matter whether we regard feng shui as a science or an art - the important thing to note is that if so many millions of people over the centuries believe in its efficacy, and it costs nothing to believe and practice it, there seems to be compelling argument in favour of trying it out !

Is feng shui the same as fortune telling ?
The author thinks not ! Feng Shui is regarded as one of the divinitive sciences, and in this it is often categorized alongside the Book of Oracles - the **I Ching** - which is also known as the Book of Changes. This is based on he hypothesis that the Universe is not static, rather that it is dynamic and evolving all the time. That things change, fortunes change, and that the cycle of change goes on and on.

The Chinese also believe in the trinity of luck **tien, ti, ren** - heaven, earth and man luck ! The ancient sages pronounce that the luck that comes from heaven and which determines our fortune at birth is out of Man's control.

To find out about one's **heaven luck**, the Chinese - and almost all other cultures - have devised methods that offer us readings about our life's *destiny*. Hence in the Chinese systems of fortune telling references are made to the stars (the ***purple star*** system of fortune telling) and to the five elements (the ***paht chee*** system of fortune telling) both of which are based on complex calculations derived from one's date, time and place of birth. These two methods also make references to the Chinese Ghanzi system - the lunar calendar, the ten heavenly stems (the five elements with an *yin* and a *yang* dimension); and the twelve earthly branches (the twelve *animals* of the Chinese Zodiac). References are also made to good days and bad days, to prosperous days and days of potential loss - these and a host of other matters are listed out annually in the **Tong Shu** where special calculations based on the numbers of the *Lo Shu square* advise on these very same good and bad days. We have no control over our Heaven luck. But we **have** control over our **ti luck** and our ***ren*** **luck.**

Ti luck refers generally to the luck we are able to tap from the Earth, which in the Chinese scheme of things is feng shui - the environment in which we live. Live in harmony with the environment, we are advised, and good luck shall be ours ! Equally, ***ren*** luck is the luck we create for ourselves. We determine the kind of life we wish to live. We ourselves determine the kind of people we become

Together ***ti*** and ***ren*** can overcome the lack of ***tien*** luck !
It is because of this close association between the heaven and earth luck, and also because they are both based on the same fundamentals - the stems, branches, elements and so forth - that often, the uninformed confuse feng shui with fortune telling.

Are the formulas given in your books complete ?
In all, the author has written **three books** (including this one) which are based on ***specific formulas of the compass school***. Two other books deal with more general aspects of the practice.

The first formula offered a method for calculating one's four auspicious and inauspicious directions - complete with directions on how to use this formula to create wonderful feng shui. (APPLIED PA KUA LO SU FENG SHUI)

The second formula was based on *fey sin feng shui* or flying star feng shui. This offered a method for calculating the time dimensions of feng shui based on the Lo Shu magic square. With that formula it is possible to work out the lucky and unlucky corners of the house or office during different times of the year. (CHINESE NUMEROLOGY IN FENG SHUI)

This third formula which offers a method for working out auspicious water directions for the house holds out the promise of long term wealth for families. ***It is probably the most valuable of the three formulas, and also probably the only book of its kind in English in the world*** !

All three of these formulas are extremely potent.
They represent the life's work of several acclaimed feng shui masters, and are based on ancient texts which have somehow survived, by being passed on from master to disciple over the centuries.

The formulas contained in the three books that deal with each separately, are as complete as they can be. And in this the author has been most fortunate. Numerous factors helped to ensure that these formulas are going to survive into the next millennium. If readers invest time and effort into reading the formulas and the text , they will find that the formulas given are not only practical and workable, but also easy to understand and put into practice.

Will I be able to do my own feng shui from reading your books ?
Definitely !
These books were written with the specific purpose of introducing this wonderful science to the English speaking world. If you make an effort to understand the subject and its fundamentals - and the books are sufficiently comprehensive for any serious reader to do this - you will have no difficulty in practicing feng shui, AND benefiting hugely from the process.

The author is completely aware of people who are presently using her books to conduct classes in feng shui in places like the UK, Australia, New Zealand and even Switzerland and Germany - and even to open consultancy practices in these far away places - only because the books are not **yet** available in these countries.

So if you are a reader, genuinely keen on investigating your own feng shui, just be diligent in your study of the subject and you will be surprised at how easily you can do it !

What if feng shui just cannot work for me ?
Earlier reference was made to the trinity of luck.

Feng shui must be viewed in this context. Thus there may be periods when you are really going through a trying time - when bad luck seems to dog you - during such times if you have good feng shui, it will assist you to survive bad times, recover from illnesses, protect you from getting too badly damaged. But if your heaven luck decrees you experience some hard times, that is all feng shui can do for you - reduce the severity of the trying days.

Often people who enjoy protective feng shui luck are not even aware of it until years later. Like the author - who survived much during her mid thirties under very trying conditions. Also, please remember that feng shui is not magic. It does not work overnight. When the energy lines are beneficial the effect will be felt over a period of time. Feng shui works for everyone, you just need to understand **how** it works.

Does feng shui require faith and belief for it to work ?
Not at all ! Feng shui is neither a religion nor a spiritual practice. It does not require you to have faith in it, at least not in the way we bring to our belief in God. However, it is helpful to be confident. The author prefers to adopt a positive rather than a negative (or confrontational) approach to the practice. You can quite easily do the same. Feng shui does not require you to subscribe to any spiritual rituals or beliefs. Look on it as a science, and view it as an ancient wisdom that teaches us to live in harmony with the forces of the Universe. Seek out the harmony, and in doing so you will enhance your life, and your life style substantially

"Feng shui is Chinese Geomancy and Lillian Too's books on this centuries old Chinese practice is timely and topical ... her book is convincing and thoroughly researched ... it is a beautiful effort at chronicling the many perspectives of Feng Shui to Malaysians and visitors alike "

YAB Datuk Seri Dr. Ling Liong Sik
Malaysian Minister of Transport and
President of the MCA.

" ... Lillian's research is a most welcome addition to the fast growing body of literature on FENG SHUI written in English "

Dr. Ken Yeang. Ph.D. (Cantab)
Architect & Environmentalist

" Lillian Too's FENG SHUI is outstanding and spellbinding ... the well matched marriage between theory and practice contributes to the comprehensiveness of the book ... a reader's interest is sustained throughout the book, given the clear and precise style of writing, the effective illustrations and the interesting anecdotes ... highly recommended "

Dr. Leong Yin Ching, M.Ed. (Mal). Ph.D. (Lon).
Professor of Education
University of Malaysia.

"Highly readable ... and with interesting anecdotes"

Dr. Tarcissus Chin, CEO
Malaysian Institute of Management.

" ... Lillian Too's book will provide the kind of information you need to keep the endless *chi* flowing into your homes or workplaces, and thwart the poisonous arrows of the *sha chi* which brings misfortune, ill health and bad luck ... one could get hooked on the subject after reading Too's comprehensive book ... it provides an invaluable introduction to a subject that combines philosophy and conceptual principles extracted from ancient classical manuals"

New Straits Times Book review (May 1993)

LILLIAN TOO

**lives in Malaysia where
she heads her own publishing and investment company.
She is the author of several books including
her bestselling Feng Shui series of books.**

An MBA graduate from the Harvard University, Graduate School of Business in Boston USA, she had a varied and successful corporate career in business and government. In the early Eighties, she became Malaysia's first woman to head a publicly listed company; and in August of 1982, she became the first woman in Asia to become Chief Executive Officer of a Bank when appointed Managing Director of GRINDLAYS DAO HENG BANK in Hong Kong.
Lillian was also Executive Chairman of DRAGON SEED LIMITED, which she successfully packaged as a leveraged buy-out, until she sold out of this Hong Kong based company and returned to Malaysia.

" APPLIED FENG SHUI offers practical and detailed information which promises easy application methods for those who seriously want to improve the feng shui of their dwellings and work places ... I wish to commend Lillian Too for this insightful guide "

YAB Datuk Seri Dr. Ling Liong Sik
Malaysian Minister of Transport and
President of the MCA.

" ... Lillian Too's remarkable books on Feng reveal extraordinary new insights into this ancient Chinese practice and kept me utterly fascinated ... I strongly recommend them "

Atok Ilhan, Chief Executive, PHILLIPS GROUP MALAYSIA
President, Malaysian International Chamber of Commerce

" A masterful second book on Feng Shui ... containing amazing compass school secret formulas "

Yet Ling, Editor, Fu Ni - Chinese Women's Magazine

" Highly readable and well illustrated, this book will delight you ... "

Her World magazine (Aug 1993)

" ... the attraction of her two books is that they bridge linguistic, cultural and philosophical gaps ... offers integrated set of guideposts that transcends limitations of culture ... it is Lillian Too's considerable achievement to have transposed and elucidated the linguistically locked knowledge, philosophy and practice of Feng Shui with such clarity, yet not losing its essence. "

Syed Adam Aljefri. MA (Yale). MsC (Lon)
Diplomat, Management Consultant & Writer.

THE FENG SHUI SERIES
by
LILLIAN TOO

The introductory book on Feng Shui.
Readers are invited to enter into
the world of dragons and tigers
and to share the secrets of the
Chinese business tycoons of Asia.

Why do some families prosper more than others.
Why does one restaurant flourish,
And another does not ...
Why do some companies enjoy robust growth,
While others diminish and weaken ...
Why does affluence occur so easily for some people
While ruin and bankruptcy befall others ...

The Chinese believe Feng Shui offer potent explanations.
They believe that positive and negative fortunes arise from
auspicious and inauspicious Feng Shui.
Today, interest in this centuries old Chinese wisdom
and practice is going through a spectacular revival.

In Hong Kong, Singapore and Taipeh, three of the world's most
commercially successful cities, Feng Shui is a principal consideration
when businessmen build their homes or construct their offices.

They believe that getting their Feng Shui right will create
abundance and prosperity for themselves and their descendants.

With such promise,
can anyone afford not to know about Feng Shui ??

" Too's credentials are impeccable. She has had a colourful career in the corporate world being the first woman to hold many senior posts in multi million dollar companies in Malaysia and Hong Kong "
Sarawak Sunday Tribune.

" ... Too is a person who practices what she preaches "
New Straits Times

" The pursuit of excellence is one never ending story for Lillian Too. Having reached the peak of the corporate world years ago, she has now turned her sights onto new things ... like writing "
Corporate World

" Lillian Too's talk ... was as breathtaking as the person herself ... "
Malaysian Industry

" She is introduced as a lady of many seasons, one with many accomplishments, constantly pursuing new frontiers and always meeting up with success ... Lillian Too in the flesh removes all doubts as the veracity of her introduction. For once Too gets on the rostrum, time's winged chariot does literally fly by. Her audience sits enthralled as she leads them through the seminar with insightful tips and entertaining anecdotes "
Certified Management Digest.

" Everything around her ... is reflective of her warm, vibrant personality ... and though she considers herself retired, to the readers of her best-selling books throughout Malaysia, she's only just begun"
Business Times

THE FENG SHUI SERIES
by
LILLIAN TOO

The second book on Feng Shui.

Which reveals the secrets of the powerful
PA-KUA LO-SHU formula,
a potent branch of the Compass School.
The formula pinpoints each person's
four auspicious and
four inauspicious directions.

AND

explains how these can be
applied to one's homes and offices.

The highlight of this second book
is to share
a very powerful Compass School formula
that uses Compass directions

to align individual chi flows
with that of one's surroundings

and in the process
tap into the luck of the Earth
and achieve abundant prosperity
and great wealth ...

" In an arena largely dominated by men,
Too stood out like a rose among the thorns ... but
this rose knew what she was doing, and
did it better than most of her male counterparts.
An ex colleague described Too as
extremely knowledgeable, a real tough cookie
who knows and gets what she wants "
The Sun - Business page.

" All good things come to those who wait ...
after climbing the corporate career ladder for two decades,
it is only now, retired and nearing her fifties
that Lillian Too is getting the kind of attention
most people only dream of.
She is the author of six books ... with
more on the back burner "
The Star newspaper

" Lillian Too's talk ... was as breathtaking
as the person herself ... "
Malaysian Industry

" Whether or not you agree with her principles
and beliefs, Lillian Too is not to be taken lightly.
Well known for her books on the ancient
Chinese practice of feng shui and numerology ...
she has become one of Malaysia's best selling authors."
Success magazine ... on the launch of her latest
book EXPLORE THE FRONTIERS OF YOUR MIND.

" Anyone suffering from a crisis of confidence
could do well to spend some time
in the company of the very spirited Lillian Too ..."
The Leader

" This is a how-to book packed with practical advice.
Follow it faithfully ... with a bit of luck
you should be on your way to making your first million "
Straits Times book review
of her book MAKING YOUR FIRST MILLION

THE FENG SHUI SERIES
by
LILLIAN TOO

The third book on Feng Shui.

Puts the spotlight on
PRACTICAL APPLICATIONS OF FENG SHUI

An easy to follow, well illustrated manual for those who wish to seriously utilize Feng Shui to enhance their luck and their fortunes.

PRACTICAL APPLICATIONS OF FENG SHUI

ADDRESSES COMMON PROBLEMS FACED BY NOVICE PRACTITIONERS AND PROVIDE ANSWERS TO A BROAD RANGE OF INTERPRETATIVE QUESTIONS

a valuable easy reference manual loaded with examples and illustrated to answer your every question on the practice of Feng Shui

THE FENG SHUI SERIES

by

LILLIAN TOO

The fourth book on Feng Shui.

Introduces the

Time Dimension

to the Practice of Feng Shui

AND

explains the intangible forces
of the
Flying Star
School of Feng Shui

CHINESE NUMEROLOGY IN FENG SHUI

explains the significance
of changing forces
during different time periods.
The formula highlights the influence of
NUMBERS
thereby adding vital nuances
to the practice of Feng Shui

AVAILABLE AT ALL LEADING BOOKSTORES
AND

THROUGH INTERNET

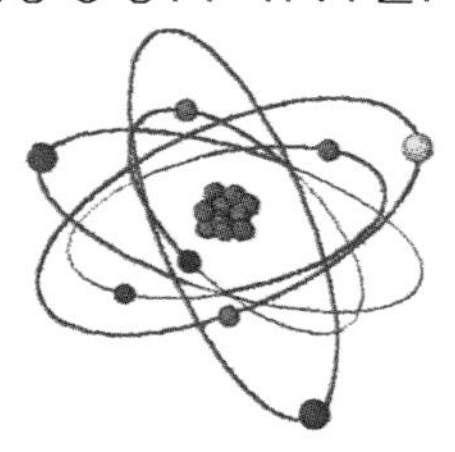

VISIT LILLIAN TOO IN
CYBERSPACE

The World Wide Web URL address is:
www.asiaconnect.com.my/lillian-too

E-mail address is:
ltoo@asiaconnect.com.my